AMAZON WOMAN

AMAZON WOMAN

FACING FEARS, CHASING DREAMS, AND A QUEST TO KAYAK THE WORLD'S LARGEST RIVER FROM SOURCE TO SEA

DARCY GAECHTER

PEGASUS BOOKS
NEW YORK   LONDON

AMAZON WOMAN

Pegasus Books Ltd.
148 W. 37th Street, 13th Floor
New York, NY 10018

First Pegasus Books cloth edition March 2020

Interior design by Maria Fernandez

Library of Congress Cataloging-in-Publication Data is available.

ISBN: 978-1-64313-314-0

10 9 8 7 6 5 4 3 2 1

Printed in the United States of America
Distributed by W. W. Norton & Company

To my parents—Ann and Bill Gaechter. To my sister, Lacey, and to Don. Thanks for always believing in me no matter how crazy my ideas or plans are.

CONTENTS

A NOTE ON RIVERS

In this book, I call the Amazon River the world's "largest" river rather than the world's "longest" river. This is because there is strong debate among geographers about which river is longer—the Amazon or the Nile—and I didn't want to produce a book that gets passed by because of potentially inaccurate information in the title. Measurements vary widely depending on which route is measured (river runners or map tracers can choose from literally hundreds of channels to make their way down these leviathan rivers), and which part one exits from each river's massive delta. Many geographers believe that the Nile is longer, though not all agree, and there is much ambiguity around the subject. At the time of this writing, the History Channel had published an article claiming the Amazon was longer, while *Guinness World Records* tells us the Nile is longer.[*] A Google search will turn up all kinds of conflicting articles from reputable sources such as *National Geographic* (voting for the Amazon)[**]

---

[*] Nate Barksdale, "What Is the Longest River in the World?" History Channel.com, updated August 22, 2018, https://www.history.com/news/what-is-the-longest-river-in-the-world and "Longest River," GuinnessWorldRecords.com, https://www.guinnessworldrecords .com/world-records/longest-river/, both accessed October 17, 2019.

[**] John Roach, "Amazon Longer than Nile River, Scientists Say," NationalGeographic.com, June 18, 2007, https://www.nationalgeographic.com/science/2007/06/amazon-longer -than-nile-river/, accessed October 17, 2019.

to the United States Geological Survey (voting for the Nile).[*] I like to believe the Amazon is longer, but I don't have definitive proof. The entire scientific world does, however, agree that the Amazon is the world's *largest* river by volume, holding up to 20 percent of the earth's fresh water, so I chose that wording.

[*]   "Rivers of the World: World's Longest Rivers," US Geological Survey, updated 1990, https://www.usgs.gov/special-topic/water-science-school/science/rivers-world-worlds -longest-rivers?qt-science_center_objects=0#qt-science_center_objects, accessed October 17, 2019.

GLOSSARY OF KAYAKING TERMS

Eddy: A calm spot in the river where water flows around an obstacle, such as a rock, and then reverses course to fill in the space behind it. The water in an eddy is moving upriver, but is usually relatively calm and offers a haven from the downriver moving current. Eddies are used for resting, getting out of the current, getting out of the river, and scouting. Eddies are typically the only way to stop when you are on a river.

Hydraulic/Hole: A feature in the river caused by water pouring over the top of a submerged object such as a boulder or a ledge (as opposed to around but not over the top of a rock, which would create an eddy). The water on the surface of the river reverses back on itself and flows violently back upriver. Only deep under the surface can you find water that is still flowing down the river. Holes can keep a kayaker trapped in their back-wash. If you don't have the skills to escape this backwash—to work your way out the edges of the hole—you will have to swim free of your kayak and let the river push you to the bottom of the river where there is downriver traveling current so you can escape. Kayakers are taught to curl up into a ball if they are swimming free of their kayak and are still caught in a hydraulic (instead of trying to swim toward the surface). "Balling up" will allow the river to push you down toward the bottom where you have a better chance of escaping the backwash of a hole.

Wave: A wave in the river is much like a non-breaking ocean wave. It is formed when there is an increase in gradient, when the riverbed constricts, or when the current flows over deeply submerged rocks. While waves in the ocean are moving features that eventually dissipate, river waves are stationary. The water in a river moves downstream, but the wave stays in the same spot, creating an obstacle that a kayaker can paddle around or paddle through.

Breaking wave: A wave in a river where the top is breaking and creating whitewater and backwash. This can sometimes be strong enough to surf a kayaker.

Sieve/Siphon: A place in the river where the water flows underneath a pile of rocks or logs (think of a large-scale spaghetti strainer that water can fit through but a kayaker cannot). These are very dangerous for kayakers and are to be avoided at all costs.

River right: Directions on the river are always given as though you are traveling (and facing) down the river. River right will always be the right side of the river for a downriver-traveling person.

River left: River left will always be the left side of the river for a downriver-traveling person.

Upstream: The opposite direction that the current is flowing.

Downstream: The same direction that the current is flowing.

Ferry: A maneuver used to cross a current with little or no downstream travel.

Peel out: To leave an eddy you have to paddle into the current—which can sometimes be a violent transition—and you "peel out" into the river and head downstream.

Roll: The process to right an upside-down kayak. This maneuver is tricky to learn and involves concurrent movements of the knees, hips, torso, head, and paddle.

Combat roll: The ability to roll in whitewater once you've capsized by accident. Most people learn to roll in a swimming pool or in an eddy. Translating these skills from calm water to the middle of the rapid is quite difficult and usually takes a lot of mental and physical training.

Portage: To walk around a rapid.

Boof: To launch your kayak up and over an obstacle; kind of like jumping on skis. Boofing is a good skill to have to get over holes—if you can jump your kayak over a hydraulic, there is a smaller chance of getting stuck in its backwash.

Seal launch: To drop into the river (in your kayak) from a height above the water. This is most commonly used while portaging when you cannot climb back down to water level. If you can find a ledge that is not too high, you can set your boat on that ledge, get in your kayak, and free-fall into the river.

Brace: A kayaking stroke used to keep from tipping over.

CFS: Cubic feet per second. A standard measure of river volume in the United States.

CMS: Cubic meters per second. A standard measure of river volume in most of the rest of the world.

Cockpit: The opening in the deck of a kayak where the paddler enters the boat.

Spray skirt: A neoprene skirt that kayakers wear around their waist and then seal over the cockpit of their kayak to keep water out.

Swim: When a kayaker is unable to perform a combat roll, they must swim free of their kayak in order to reach the surface to get air. The term "swim" in general means to get out of your kayak while you are in the river. In order to swim, the kayaker must first pull off the neoprene spray skirt that is keeping them in the kayak. It's not a good thing to do, as swimming in the river is much more dangerous than kayaking down the river. Swimming might also be necessary when a kayaker is stuck in a hole they can't get out of, or if they are pinned to rocks on the bottom of the river and can't free their kayak.

River difficulty: People running whitewater typically use a scale of Class one (I) through Class six (VI) to describe the difficulty of a river or rapid, and the skills necessary to safely navigate it. The rating also takes into consideration the consequences of mistakes. A plus (+) or a minus (-) after a rating means slightly harder or easier than the designated class. Class III+ means a river is a little harder than Class III, but not hard enough to warrant a Class IV rating.

Class I: This means moving water, but it can hardly be called whitewater. No real hazards or obstacles to avoid and self-rescue is easy.

Class II: There will be small waves, and perhaps rocks to avoid but all obstacles are obvious and easy to miss. Paddlers with few technical skills can navigate Class II whitewater. The consequences of a swim are minimal and self-rescue is easy.

Class III: Intermediate paddlers can usually handle Class III. More maneuvering is necessary, and there will be rocks and holes to avoid, but penalties for screwing up are still minimal. You can make multiple mistakes and/or you can swim free of your kayak, and you are still likely to come out of the river with little more than bumps and bruises. Scouting may be necessary for beginner paddlers, but not for most intermediate or advanced paddlers.

Class IV: Kayakers with more experience and a solid set of skills come to enjoy the challenges and complexities of Class IV whitewater. There may be multiple moves to make in a single rapid—dodging rocks, moving around or through hydraulics, and paddling through big waves. Paddlers need a solid set of skills to execute these moves. Technical kayaking skills are necessary, and paddlers should have good boat control, know how to use the edges of their kayak, and be able to brace and have a combat roll. The stakes are higher in Class IV, but mistakes are still usually survivable.

Class V: Class V is different. It is more committing, more dangerous, and much more consequential. Class V rapids are long, complex, and demanding. Kayakers must have a high level of skill, physical fitness, and mental fortitude. A paddler can get away with *small* mistakes in Class V. You can bobble, brace, or tip over as long as you recover quickly; but a series of small mistakes, or a single big mistake, is going to have serious, potentially fatal, consequences.

Class VI: Class VI rapids are usually considered to be unrunnable, and most kayakers must walk their boats around these sections. But as kayakers continue to push the limits of what is possible, Class VI rapids do occasionally get run.

INTRODUCTION

July 24, 2013

Dear Mom, Dad, and Lacey,

If you are reading this, it's because something went wrong and I am not coming home from the Amazon.

I realize that anything I say here probably won't lessen your grief, but please know that I very much loved my life! I thank you all for supporting my "unusual" lifestyle choices and for never pressuring me to do all the things that families often pressure their daughters/sisters to do. (Parents, I haven't forgotten that you forced me to go to college, but I forgive you for that.)

I'm sad it ended this early, but there are a lot worse ways I could have gone.

What I am most worried about as I type this, is the three of you. Don't forget about me, of course, but please remember that you still have a lot of life left to live. So live it.

Know that I was happy while I was on this earth, and take whatever solace you can out of knowing that I won't have to suffer when I am old.

I love you all very much. Thank you for everything you gave me.

Now put down this letter, and go out and do something you enjoy. Do it for me, because that is what I want you all to do.

Love, d.

✑

While my friends were busying themselves with the tasks of adulthood—buying homes, starting families, saving for their retirements—I was sinking deeper into a hopeless obsession with running progressively more life-threatening whitewater in increasingly more remote places on our planet. What few ties I had left with mainstream American society were slipping from my hands and I couldn't find a reason to tighten my grip.

I was living in a strange sort of purgatory where I no longer fit in with the young kayakers I was sharing daily life with, or with my own age group. In my mid-thirties, I was considered old in the whitewater world and it was weird (in a way that also provoked awe and admiration) to the twentysomethings that I was still kayaking the world's hardest rivers with them. To my peers in age, I was also an anomaly. From their more fixed positions, they couldn't keep track of me. I was not centered. I had no kids. I had no house. International kayaking guide was my career and, I'd learned time and time again, most people don't consider that a real job.

I loved my job and my life. I had, until recently, found it fulfilling. But there was an underlying guilt, or fear, about it all that had begun surfacing more often. After being asked so many times when I was going to change my life and settle down, I started to wonder what was wrong with me for not desiring this change that the rest of the world felt so certain was inevitable. Had my addiction to adrenaline taken over my brain to the point of delaying or permanently derailing my maturation into true adulthood? Or was I just being brainwashed by society into thinking that I was the problem for not fitting the mold? I'd always been taught to follow my own path, that being different was okay. But now it seemed I'd been too different for too long.

The more people questioned my life choices, the more I began to worry. The more I worried, the more I retreated to the rivers to hide. I didn't have time to contemplate any of this when I was kayaking down a Class V river—the hardest runnable classification of whitewater. In the midst of hard rapids, I had to give one hundred percent of my focus to survival. More and more, I found this the preferable state of mind. I began to withdraw so much that it got to the point where I couldn't tell if my lack of real life connections was driving me to rivers or if my relationship with rivers was stopping me from engaging in any human community. It had become what felt like an inescapable cycle.

In my late twenties and early thirties, I felt confident and happy that I had followed my passion to a life of kayaking and travel. I watched others muddle their way through life taking one job after another that they hated—there was no passion behind their decision-making. They wanted a house, a nice car, a big television, and a family, so they put up with unfulfilling jobs to have money for these other things. I wondered at them. How could they trade happiness for material things? I underestimated the powerful fact that my parents encouraged me to chase my dreams and live the life I wanted to live. Only later did I realize that maybe others weren't so lucky.

A decade ago, I didn't understand any of this and I was proud of myself for having it all figured out. I had only a tiny fraction of the money most American adults my age did, but that didn't matter. I had enough to eat and I was free. No corporation owned me, I wasn't a slave to a 401(k), a mortgage, or a health insurance plan.

I had pushed back against the American ideal that one's net worth is intrinsically tied to one's self worth. Still, this dogma haunted the recesses of my mind and a faint voice told me that if this is the true metric, I'm not worth a damn. It was becoming painfully apparent that my freedom had a cost and no amount of emotional support from my family could make up for how my life decisions had affected my financial stability. As the years ticked by and friends' conversations turned toward their diverse and strategic investments, my savings remained minimal and my stress level about this grew exponentially.

As I stood on a figurative precipice staring into the abyss of my future, I decided I would try to kayak the Amazon River from source to sea. Free as I had been, I worried that I might soon become a slave to my own poverty— in terms of a lack of money, lack of connection, and lack of skills for the next step in life. I realized I'd spent so much time kayaking that I hadn't developed many talents for a second career. I'd earned a master's degree in environmental history, but what could I do with that? There would be a day when I was too old to be a kayak guide, or got injured, or just decided that I was tired of being homeless. I was beginning to understand that being unattached might not be all it's cracked up to be in later life, and that terrified me.

And so, on July 20, 2013, I found myself on a plane heading to South America to kayak the world's largest river. Maybe getting on that plane was an easy way to escape grappling with my fate; but whatever my reasons, I was happy to be flying away. I was with David Midgley, an eccentric computer programmer from London, and Don Beveridge, my boyfriend of ten years. Don and I had recently sold our adventure travel company, and then I'd gotten both of us fired after a string of disagreements with the new owner. Our income, our identities, and our happiness were all tied to that business much more than we had ever realized, and Don was not pleased with me.

Thanks to our newly imposed life situation—namely, starting over from nothing—I viewed paddling the Amazon as our transitioning point. It would serve as the perfect capstone project to our adventuresome life, the final crazy exploit that would set us free to embark on the next chapter of our lives. Don, however, thought of the Amazon as the final insult to the already low point in his life—not only did he just lose his career, his home, and his identity as a whitewater kayak guide, but now I was also making him paddle months of flatwater. Don hates flatwater.

The plan was to kayak the Amazon River from its source in the Peruvian Andes all the way to the Atlantic Ocean in Brazil. It would be a journey of more than 4,000 miles. Nine other people had done some sort of source-to-sea descent of the Amazon, compared to twelve people who have walked on the moon. None of those people had kayaked the entire river, and none of them were women.

I would be the first.

When I signed on, I expected one month of kayaking on some of the most challenging whitewater in the world, through the depths of one of the most formidable and inescapable canyons on earth. I was okay with this. I'd spent the previous sixteen years of my life intensely focused on whitewater kayaking adventures, so this sort of thing was normal for me. The whitewater would be followed by the longest and flattest paddle of my life. I estimated that the roughly 3,900 miles of flatwater would take us three to four months to paddle. We'd be camping; there would be bugs; we'd be hot, tired, hungry, and bored. But who can't deal with that stuff? Suffering is a given on any expedition, and we'd be doing it all for the sake of adventure, in the interest of being first at something in a world where most of the firsts have already been taken.

I also harbored faint hopes that this big adventure would be my last hurrah; that it would validate my worth as an expedition kayaker and set me free from my wandering life. Afterward, I might finally settle down and get around to all the things I was supposed to have done years ago.

It was, after all, inappropriate for a thirty-five-year-old woman to still be traipsing around the world on kayaking adventures—wasn't it? I'd shirked my duties long enough as a responsible member of American society. While my natural reaction is to shy away from people and hide in the wilderness as often as possible, something told me that I needed to start contributing in some meaningful way. Was I finally bowing to the outside pressure I'd successfully fended off for more than a decade? Or was I growing up—albeit much later than I should have? I had no clue. Either way, the Amazon project seemed like a worthwhile endeavor.

This was until we got to Peru where I bought a copy of *El Comercio* from a street vendor just outside of Lima's international airport and read that eight Peruvians had been murdered by the indigenous Asháninka people in what they call the Red Zone—a remote and unpoliced area of the upper Amazon River that has become synonymous with danger and violence. The Asháninka feared the outsiders were there to set up an illegal logging operation. We would be paddling through Peru's Red Zone in just over a month. The human factor we'd have to contend with suddenly seemed much more dangerous and unpredictable than the whitewater.

In Lima, we were in contact with Ruth Buendía, president of the Central Asháninka del Río Ene (C.A.R.E.), in the hopes of securing permission letters from the Asháninka people whose lands we would travel through and who we hoped would refrain from killing us as they had done to the eight Peruvians and the two Polish kayakers a couple of years earlier. C.A.R.E. represents seventeen Asháninka communities along the Rio Ene—the start of the flatwater and the Red Zone—and their cooperation with our expedition would be crucial to our survival. Ruth, whose father had been murdered by Shining Path terrorists in this region twenty years ago, issued us these permission letters along with plenty of dire warnings.

The Asháninka represented only one of our mounting problems. We met with the head engineer of a huge hydroelectric project being built in the deepest canyon in the Amazon's headwaters. He advised us not to paddle through his construction zone. It was simply too dangerous due to the dynamite work. "I am too busy," he told us, "to deal with any fatalities."

Guillermo Castro Escudero, who was once a river runner and has boyhood ties to people high up in the Peruvian navy, was next in the succession of people we met who were certain that our undertaking was a bad idea. He was adamant that we arrange a navy escort to protect us from the Asháninka, the Shining Path rebels, the narco-traffickers, the illegal loggers, and the river pirates. He kept saying, "Remember Sir Blake, remember the Polish couple, remember Davey," naming off all the people who had been killed, or nearly killed, on the Amazon in recent years.

People opposing my choices was nothing new. I've spent my entire life hearing all about why I can't, or shouldn't, do things. This is because I love doing things that aren't normal for women to do. It felt different this time, though. I'd never tried to do something as big as this, or as dangerous. For the first time in my life, I thought that the people laying out all the reasons I was going to fail might actually be right.

My motivations for wanting to do this trip quickly came under scrutiny. With violent death looking like a probable outcome, I started to wonder why I'd gotten on that plane without thinking things through a little better.

It was one o'clock in the morning, and we were supposed to start our drive to the source of the Amazon River in five hours. I was exhausted from the previous days of running around Lima taking care of last-minute preparations; logistics for an expedition this long are truly mind-boggling. More troubling than my fatigue were all these images of how we were likely to die on this expedition, each subsequent danger certain to kill us provided we survived the ones before. If river pirates didn't rob and murder us, then narco-traffickers or Shining Path insurgents would. If we somehow avoided being crushed by dynamited rock in the dam construction zone, then the scared and insular Asháninka people would kill us. Or we might stumble upon an illegal logging camp and get murdered by rogue loggers afraid of being reported. And if we escaped all those fates, we were sure to meet our end in the fierce winds, tides, and monstrous waves of the lower river.

This wasn't what I had imagined five months ago when I casually said, "Sure, what the hell, I'd like to kayak the Amazon from source to sea."

I wanted nothing more than to just collapse into bed. I was drained from dealing with the monumental orchestration of the expedition. The last four days had been filled from sunrise to nearly midnight dealing with tasks as trivial as running out to the hardware store to buy two-by-fours to build a makeshift roof rack on the rental van, to bigger challenges like tracking the progress of our sea kayaks that were on a container ship leaving Mexico, and trying to figure out if they'd make it to Peru by the time we hit the flatwater. I forced myself to sit down at the hostel's lone computer and, in a pathetic attempt to assuage my guilt for going forward despite the myriad dangers, I wrote my goodbye note.

I emailed the letter to my friend Larry with strict instructions to deliver it to my family if I died.* Then I crawled into bed, hoping to get a little rest—but mostly I lay there wondering if I would succeed in becoming the first woman to kayak the entire Amazon River, or if, as so many people had predicted, I would die trying.

It was my thirty-fifth birthday.

---

*   *Hey Larry,*

        Sorry to ask this of you . . . but if I happen to die on this trip, can you give this letter to my parents? You can read it too if I don't make it back.

        Let's just hope it doesn't come to that! But I thought I should write something for my family because I know my mom will not do too well if this is the outcome.

        And, rest assured, I will do everything in my power to come back. But you just never know when there are people with guns involved . . . Thanks LV.

        We are heading toward the put-in tomorrow and will supposedly start paddling Saturday. Love you man!

AMAZON WOMAN

Chapter I

LOSING MIDGE IN THE DAM SITE

"It was written I should be loyal to the nightmare of my choice."
—Joseph Conrad

AUGUST 16, 2013
DAY 20 OF THE EXPEDITION

I was having a hard time forcing myself to care whether or not Midge made it out of the construction zone alive. What I wanted to do was ditch him and thus, I believed, vastly improve my own chances of staying alive. The adrenaline surging through my body told me to get moving—but I was caught between my own instinct to survive and my feelings of responsibility to Midge. We were a team after all. He was completely beaten down after so many days of difficult whitewater, not to mention the energy-sapping stress of the last three hours. I understood. Still, my patience was drained, and I wasn't in the mood for compassion.

It was our twentieth consecutive day of kayaking. We were paddling at the bottom of the deepest and most committing canyon I had ever been in. We were all tired, but Midge especially so. The stress of just barely making it through one rapid after another, pushing his whitewater skills to their absolute limit, was taking its toll. Maintaining high levels of adrenaline requires a lot of energy, and with our limited food intake, we didn't have energy to spare.

Our introduction to the Cerro del Aguila dam construction site a few hours earlier had been a cascading rapid where most of the water flowed underneath school bus–sized boulders—pieces of the cliff dynamited from high above. When water flows under and through piles of boulders, instead of over them, it creates what kayakers call a sieve, or siphon (think of a giant spaghetti strainer that lets water through, but not kayakers). These features can be deadly for paddlers because of the risk of getting trapped under a boulder. On both sides of this unrunnable rapid, tall cliff walls rose straight out of the river. It was more frightening than anything I had ever seen on a river.

Paddling upriver a short distance in the pool above the rapid, we found a small egress in the cliff. It was still a nearly vertical rock face, and Don had to climb up the cliff and secure a rope at the top. I climbed up after Don and we used the rope to haul the three heavy kayaks seventy feet up the embankment. There we found a narrow bench where we could perch, put the boats down, and assess the situation.

Walking along the bench to its downstream end, Don found a steep gully leading back down to the river below the rapid. Looking further downstream, we saw more colossal rapids that defied the natural riverbed; these, too, had obviously been created by dynamite. Downstream, though, the river left cliff wall was slightly less sheer and the rubble from the construction work had created precarious piles of debris. The left shore was a scree and slag pile that, while visibly unstable, did offer a place to walk if necessary.

We hadn't yet spotted a single worker, but we'd witnessed some troubling results of their efforts. The sheer cliff walls and inaccessible river bottom restricted construction activity to between five hundred and two thousand feet above our heads. Blasting activity had sent everything from fine sand to house-sized boulders tumbling down the cliff walls. Some of the debris now cluttered the riverbed, while here and there it had caught on natural benches in the cliff face, resting so precariously that we felt even a sneeze from down below might set it in motion again.

It took us another thirty minutes of careful work to lower each kayak down to the water with our ropes, but finally all three of us sat at the river's edge with our boats and paddles. Getting around the first rapid had taken us over an hour. We spent the next two hours running what rapids we could and devising creative ways to walk around those we couldn't. Paddling up to one horizon line, we discovered the most awesomely powerful—and unrunnable—rapid any of us had ever seen. It was a maelstrom of powerful hydraulics all leading into one monstrous, fifteen-foot-tall cascade into a river-wide ledge hole (think low head dam) with such strong backwash that it was pulling water back into itself from thirty feet downstream. We felt certain that no kayaker would ever get out of that hole alive.

There was a way to walk around the rapid (a portage route) on river left, but it required a delicate dash across a loose debris pile. Clambering around on what little shore there was seemed dangerous, yet infinitely safer than kayaking down the rapid. We decided we would go one at a time, but that we needed to move as quickly as possible across the scree slope and get into the pool at the bottom of the rapid—we feared that lingering too long on the unstable slope would cause a landslide, sweeping us into the rapid we were trying to walk around.

We were all exhausted, but I knew we could not stop moving under any circumstance. We had only negotiated two and a half hours of dynamite stoppage with the Cerro del Aguila hydroelectric dam project manager. Three hours had already passed, and we had no idea how much further we still had to go. I was certain they would resume their blasting work any minute. Time is money, so why wouldn't they? Even if they didn't start working again, we were standing at the base of a thousand-foot-tall rock and sand avalanche that had not yet found its angle of repose. It was active and shifting and we needed to get out of there before it moved in a significant way.

Just as I picked up my kayak to start the portage, I heard Midge's plea: "I'm knackered, can we please have a snack break?"

"No!" I shouted, surprised at the anger I heard in my voice. Calming down a little, I added, "Midge, can't you make it just a little bit farther? We've got to get out of here before they start blasting again."

"Don't be ridiculous, Darcy," he retorted. "There is no way they will start blasting again with us still down here."

"They can't even see us to know where we are, Midge! Maybe they think we're already through! Plus, our allotted dynamite-free time frame has come and gone."

I felt certain that, despite the construction boss's claims that it was "mandatory they have no fatalities," three kayaking tourists were insignificant compared to their $910-million dam project.

Midge kept repeating his belief that there was no way the workers would start blasting with us still in the canyon. He couldn't seem to bring himself to imagine the possibility of our group getting blown to pieces. I sensed he felt too important to die in such an impersonal manner. Or maybe he was simply too tired and scared to allow himself to consider this outcome.

The reality was that it didn't matter whether or not the blasting recommenced—there were so many other ways we could die in the construction zone. A big rainstorm might destabilize the slopes. One of us might take a fatal slip or blunder into an unrunnable rapid. But Midge was too stubborn and too tired to consider this. It was easier for him to just believe he would be okay. Plus, he was hungry. It's hard to argue against the fact that calories are useful in these sorts of situations, but his timing was impeccably bad.

The heart of the problem was that I was convinced all three of us were going to die in this canyon. I was scared—strong feelings of imminent death definitely had me on edge. Making matters worse, it seemed to me that Midge refused to acknowledge the real danger we faced. Scenes from those cheesy horror films flooded my mind where the audience knows damn well that everyone is about to get murdered, but one foolish kid keeps repeating, "everything is going to be okay," while the group keeps walking right toward whatever it is that is going to kill them. It took every ounce of self-restraint I could muster to refrain from screaming that Midge was a complete idiot if he really believed the workers would hold off from blasting for as long as it took his delusional ass to get through the construction zone, even if, as he said, blowing up three tourists would create a public relations problem for the company.

We had more pressing issues to deal with than my anger, so I took a few deep breaths and tried to calm down. I looked downriver. We had no choice but to keep moving and, to my amazement, Midge finally agreed to eat something quickly while Don and I portaged and to hold off on his break until we made it out of the canyon.

We portaged the massive rapid as quickly as we could and got back into our kayaks, trying to stay clear of the potential landslide area. As we paddled downstream, we noticed something peculiar in the river. The object seemed contorted and it disturbed the water in a strange way. It was clearly not a rock, or any other natural object. Paddling closer, we realized that it was a dump truck lying on its side in the middle of a rapid. We gazed upward, but could see no road. The truck must have fallen more than a thousand feet. As we paddled frantically to avoid being swept by the strong current into the underbelly of the truck, we tried not to think about what had happened to the driver when his vehicle plunged off the cliff. So much for the mandatory no-fatality policy.

We no longer felt like kayakers out having fun. The setting of our adventure had begun to feel more like a war zone, and I had turned all my focus toward survival. Just after the dump truck, I could see a steep horizon line with water spraying up in all directions, signaling that we had yet another massive rapid in front of us. Fortuitously, one of the huge boulders that had been relocated from the top of the cliff into the river below was creating a large eddy—a calm spot in the river behind the rock—at the top of the rapid where we could stop. In rivers, especially fast-moving difficult rivers, eddies offer kayakers the only opportunity to stop in what otherwise feels like an out-of-control torrent.

Don, Midge, and I huddled into the eddy and peered downstream. The rapid was so big and steep that we couldn't see the bottom of it, and there was now constant rock fall on the right bank that was also obscuring our view. We knew they weren't blasting, because we heard no explosions but something up above, probably a backhoe or other heavy equipment, was shoving rocks and debris off the cliff and straight into the river about halfway down the rapid.

I sank to my thighs in dust and gravel as I clawed my way up to the top of the boulder hoping to get a better vantage point. The view was demoralizing; the rapid was runnable, but the very first move was a nearly river-wide hydraulic violently reversing back on itself with only a kayak-width tongue between its right edge and the cliff wall. The lead-in was chaotic, and most of the current pulled strongly toward the hydraulic (also known as a hole in kayaker lingo). A kayaker not actively fighting the force of the current would be swept into the massive hole.

The awful hole was only the first obstacle in a very long rapid full of hazards. Plus, the only safe line forced us to paddle directly under the river right wall beneath the rock fall. Some of the falling rocks were small enough to appear survivable, but every now and then a boulder came crashing down that was easily big enough to crush a kayaker. The last thing we needed was for another dump truck to come tumbling off the cliff as we paddled past.

I could see one eddy a few hundred yards down from the entrance of the rapid, but I could not make out what was beyond it around the corner. Based on what we had experienced so far, we needed to assume that more unrunnable rapids lay ahead. As tired as Midge was, I didn't think he would be able to make the powerful move around the hole. I also suspected that if he fell into the hydraulic, got trapped in its backwash, and was forced to swim out of his kayak, Midge would have a terrible, potentially unsurvivable, ordeal ahead of him.

Starting to look for portage options, I shouted down to Don, "Come up here and have a look with me."

Midge didn't like looking at rapids so he stayed in his boat and rested, trusting in Don and me to make the right decision for him. He had the feeling that if a rapid was too hard or too complicated for me or Don to be able to describe the line to him, that he would just prefer to walk around it. Of course sometimes walking wasn't an option.

Now there was a group of ten or fifteen workers standing on the right bank about sixty feet above us, the first humans we'd seen since entering their work zone. They were impatiently waving us on. We had already taken more than an hour longer than we had anticipated, and the workers were obviously anxious to get back to it. Seeing me looking up at the left bank for a portage option, they started whistling to get my attention. They were indicating that we could come up the right bank to where they were standing—but it was a vertical cliff, and Don and I could see no way to climb it.

When we pointed to the left bank, they emphatically shook their heads in unison—"No!"—and began drawing their fingers across their necks in the universal sign for death.

After a couple of minutes, Don stated calmly, "We can make that move, Darcy."

"I know *we* can," I replied, "But I don't think Midge will make it. He's too tired."

Our kayaks were heavily loaded with eight days' worth of camping gear, food, clothes, and emergency equipment, making them extra sluggish and hard to move around in fast-moving water. The move we would have to pull off to make it through this rapid required crossing the full width of the river in a steep section where the current's pull would be strong. It would either take intense mental composure to channel ten years' worth of whitewater kayaking training to use the perfect technique for such a crossing or amazing brute strength to fight that current when Midge's tired brain couldn't call upon the stash of tools stored away for such a maneuver. I had lost faith that Midge was ready for either of these scenarios.

I tried to think of another solution to our problem. "I know the workers don't like it, but there's a chance we could portage on the left. It looks sketchy, but if we can get across that scree field there, one of us could climb up to that flat bench and then rope the boats up."

"Suicide for all of us, Darcy." Don insisted. "If, and I really mean *if*, we make it to your bench, then where will we go? At least if we run this rapid, two-thirds of us are sure to make it and chances are that Midge will be okay, too."

The rapid didn't look great, but it was beginning to seem like the safest of our dismal options. We figured that if Midge could summon the strength and the skill to make that first move, he would probably be okay. After the hole, we just needed to move into the middle of the river to avoid the rock fall. From there on, the rapid appeared to be big but doable for Midge.

It was just a matter of making that first move.

Another problem was that the eddy we could see at the bottom of the rapid was at the base of another cliff that also did not look climbable. We were taking a huge gamble that we would be able go farther downstream after making that eddy. Using our very limited geology skills, we made our best guess that, even if the next rapid turned out to be unrunnable, the character of the cliff wall looked as if it would offer us a place to climb out of the river just out of view. We said that, at any rate, to make ourselves feel better. I'm not sure if either of us believed it.

Don looked again at the rapid and at the portage routes and said, "We need to run this. There is no other option."

It was a risk for all of us, but we couldn't stand there forever. We had to go.

Don, the strongest paddler of the group, would go first so that he could catch the eddy at the bottom of the rapid, with the hopes of getting a look around the corner to know what we would be dealing with in the case of a rescue. If there was an easy rapid or a big pool around the corner, a rescue would be simple. If it was another rapid like this one, or worse, rescue would be difficult to impossible.

I would follow Midge through the rapid, and if a rescue became necessary, Don and I would do our best to get Midge into that eddy. But we knew we had to consider the option of letting him go if it meant dragging all three of us into an unnavigable rapid down below. It was a conversation I was not comfortable with, and one we did not share with Midge. Being whitewater professionals for nearly two decades, we had saved hundreds of boaters as they swam from their kayaks or made other mistakes in the river. Now, in a moment of painful reckoning, we realized we were facing a situation in which we might not be able to help. Things had gotten that dire in the last three and a half hours. We were still working as a team, but there was an underlying knowledge that each of us was, in a very real sense, in it for ourselves.

Don and I climbed back down from the boulder and got into our kayaks. We explained to Midge that we had to run the rapid. We told him that we were going to leave our eddy, which was on the left side of the river, and paddle with all the strength that remained in our bodies to the right side of the river where the safe tongue of water bypassed the hole.

"Hit the right cliff wall with your boat," Don told him. "After you're safely past the first hole, paddle hard left to get away from the right wall so you don't get crushed by that rock fall. Then, once you pass the rock fall, bust your ass into a small eddy on river right."

"Right, left, right. Got it?" I added as Midge was absorbing his instructions.

Midge nodded in understanding.

Don prepared to launch as I told Midge to watch precisely where he went. Don took a few deep breaths to prepare himself, but just as he was about to pull out of the eddy, Midge said, "Hold on, Don, is your GoPro on?"

"Midge!" Don said with clear exasperation. "Are you sure your head is in this? You need to concentrate on your survival here, not my video camera."

Don peeled out of the eddy and made it to the right side of the river, nodding his head emphatically when he had made it to the tongue, which would ensure his safe passage past the hole.

Nervous, and wanting to focus on my own line rather than worrying solely about Midge, I concentrated on what I needed to do. I took my paddle into my hands and was comforted by the overly familiar feeling. Years of practice put my brain and body on autopilot. Sitting at the top of another massive rapid, the pressure playing its role in my brain, I focused my energy to the job of making the necessary moves to get down this section of river alive.

I asked Midge if he was ready, and then offered one more reminder: "Midge, put your boat on that right wall." I nodded at Midge and he peeled out of the eddy. I followed him closely and I fought the current as I crossed from river left to river right trying to maintain control, similar to how a skier might try to ski across the slope out of an avalanche they'd triggered. As I'd expected, the current was forceful and kept trying to pull me back to the left. Utilizing boat angle against the current and taking powerful, efficient paddle strokes, I made it to the right side of the river.

My battle with the current wasn't easy and I watched helplessly as Midge yielded to the powerful river in front of me. He was above the hole and nowhere near the right wall. He did make a heroic last minute effort to get farther right, but it was not enough, and he dropped into the deep vortex of the hydraulic, disappearing instantly.

Chapter 2

THE TEAM

"I hate to hear you talk about all women as if they were fine ladies instead of rational creatures. None of us want to be in calm waters all our lives."

—Jane Austen

D on, Midge, and I were an unlikely threesome for a river adventure. If a group of strangers glanced at us and passed a snap judgement, probably Don would be the only one they would pick out as an adventurer, and maybe they would even look past him because of his age. Looking at me, they'd undoubtedly write me off as a scrawny little lady best suited for sedentary work. And after one look at Midge, it'd be pretty apparent that his devotion is to computers and city life, not athletic endeavors. Digging deeper, however, these strangers would find that all of Don's and my actions thus far in life suited us perfectly for five months of deprivation while duking it out with various forces—natural, unnatural, evil, kind, fierce, known, and unknown—in order to move from point A to point B on the world's largest river. They would also find that absolutely nothing about Midge's life suited him for such an undertaking except for perhaps a crazy streak and fierce stubbornness to go with it.

As we were about to leave for our trip down the Amazon River, someone asked what made me think I could do a trip like that. They had made their initial judgement of me and were having a hard time getting beyond it.

Didn't I doubt myself?

Wasn't I worried I would fail?

Wasn't it a lot of pressure to try to be the first woman to do this?

I answered honestly that it had never occurred to me that I *couldn't* complete a trip as big as kayaking the Amazon. Physically paddling down the river was always something that I knew I could do. (I might have been wrong, but I *knew* I could do it.)

But others didn't see it this way. I'm small, I'm a woman, and I'm a vegan; all of which are seen as forms of weakness to some people. Little female plant-eaters can't do things like kayaking the Amazon, or so I'd been told.

Being a small woman—I'm 5'4" and weigh 120 pounds—has never stopped me from doing what I want to do, or at least trying to do all the things I want to do. Still, it was hard to not let the opinions of others affect me when I was constantly told:

"You are too little."

"You are not strong enough."

"You are a girl."

Maggy Hurchalla said of her sister Janet Reno, the first woman attorney general of the United States, "She didn't really break barriers. She just didn't notice they were there." I would like to say that this is true for me, too, but it's not. I started my life not noticing the barriers of my gender and my size, but it didn't take long for the world to make sure that I became acutely aware of them. I am, however, resolute in my desire to break them.

I decided sometime in my early childhood that I would never allow myself to be vulnerable enough to need help. I have no memory of what precipitated this, but afterward my youth was filled with strange expressions of my desire to prove my independence and strength, like the time I talked myself into the weeklong Geneva Glen, Colorado, sleepover camp for six- to twelve-year-olds when I was only five. Then I shouted out "Single!" in the lift line when I was six because I was embarrassed to be seen skiing with my mom. (Only babies have to ski with their mommies, I thought.) Or the time I rode my skateboard down a steep hill when I was eight years old because my dad told me I shouldn't.

"It's your first day on a skateboard and you don't have enough experience," he'd said.

It was perfectly reasonable advice that I interpreted as a challenge to my worthiness. I defied my dad's advice and crashed spectacularly, giving myself road rash all over the front of my body and shredding my coveted Camp Geneva Glen T-shirt.

The more I touted myself as tough and aloof, the more others expected this of me, and my armored stoicism became a self-fulfilling prophecy.

By the time I arrived as a freshman at Aspen High School, I was 5'0" and weighed an impressive eighty-two pounds. I was pathetically small. But that was not my image of myself. I was an athlete, I was strong, I was smart, and I was invincible. I played volleyball, basketball, and soccer, and I ran track. I may have been little, but I made up for that with determination, speed, and a strange ability to jump high.

Not everyone saw the potential I saw in myself, and this was problematic. The sports writer for the local newspaper nicknamed me "Diminutive Darcy." At first, I was just happy that I'd made the newspaper—"Aspen forged back on the shoulders of diminutive Darcy Gaechter"—but then I started wondering about the word *diminutive*. I was fourteen and had to look it up. The family dictionary told me that diminutive meant "extremely or unusually small; of very small size or value; an insignificant thing." I was beginning to understand how the rest of world saw me.

In high school, some of my volleyball coaches wouldn't let me play in the front row where I could spike the ball over the net. I was short, but I had a twenty-seven-inch vertical jump and was good at reading the positions of the other team's players. When I got a chance, I could spike the ball as well as the tall girls. Still, some of the coaches overlooked me.

I got mad.

I sat on the bench watching the game but seeing nothing besides my own lost chances. I couldn't hide my anger, and my scrunched-up, scowling face would belie my insistence that "I'm fine." My world was tiny and I had a lot to learn.

As a teenager, I was convinced there was no reason to live past the age of thirty and I saw no reason to ever leave Aspen, Colorado. A huge fight ensued when I entered my senior year of high school and my parents began forcing me to write college applications.

I wasn't going to college. I wanted to move the half mile up the road from Aspen High School to Aspen Highlands Ski Area and become a ski patroller, just like my dad had been. What did I need a college education for?

My parents won, but I showed them, by choosing far away Skidmore College in upstate New York. My volleyball coach at Skidmore, Hilda Arrechea, put some trust in me and let me hit the ball. She wasn't disappointed. I broke nearly every record for Division III women's volleyball in New York State for number of kills (when you spike the ball so well that it hits the floor on the other team's side, uncontested). I won Player of the Year, Most Valuable Player, and many other awards. Once I'd proven my point, I thanked Hilda by transferring to Montana State University after my sophomore volleyball season. I didn't fit in with the money-driven students at Skidmore. Plus, the school was too far away from ski areas, and the ones that were within range sucked compared to Aspen Highlands. I picked Montana State for the sole reason that it was sixteen miles away from Bridger Bowl Ski Area.

At Montana State, I met Adam, who asked me to skip fall semester of 1998 and go kayaking in Nepal. The fact that I barely knew Adam and was terrible at kayaking didn't, at the time, strike me as reasons not to fly across the world to kayak hard rivers with a stranger.

I said yes, though I was certain my parents would never allow me to go. They were paying for college and I didn't think they were the type of parents to let their twenty-year-old daughter skip school to go kayak in Nepal with a strange boy. To my utter amazement, they said yes. My mom's words were, "That sounds like an incredible opportunity."

My dad agreed, to which I could think of nothing else to say besides, "What? Are you really my parents? Have you lost your minds?"

I was just starting to understand what kind of people my parents were. They weren't the boring jerks who always made me stick to my curfew and never let me do anything fun. They were adventuresome themselves and saw the value in this trip for me. They were serious and I went. It was the first time I had left North America.

Immediately after getting out of my taxi in downtown Kathmandu, I saw three men kill and then slaughter a goat right in the middle of the dirtiest street I'd ever laid eyes on. My $1.75 per night hotel room in Kathmandu was so disgusting that I put my sleeping bag on the bed so I wouldn't have to touch the grease-stained sheets that used to be white but were now tinted yellowish-brown and smelled like they hadn't been washed in months. The bus seats were too small for even me to get comfortable in during the many fifteen-plus-hour rides we had to take. Worst of all, I stuck my hand in human poo while climbing up a steep embankment after I had swum out of my kayak on a river that was too hard for me. Despite all of this, something clicked.

From that trip forward, I've built my life around opportunities to travel and kayak, and these journeys have brought me to some unexpected and incredible destinations. It would lead me to Don and give me the opportunity to meet incredible people from areas as diverse as the Himalayas to the rainforests of South America. Kayaking led me to become a business owner, with all the skills that requires, which have nothing to do with the water, whether it is web design or guerilla marketing. And eventually, it would all lead me to Midge and the Amazon River.

But during those initial halcyon years, I immersed myself in my raft-guiding job during the summers. Things have improved somewhat in the last twenty years, and now most rafting companies have a large number of female employees, but back then raft-guiding was, as many people liked to explain to me, "a man's world." Many guests were afraid to get in a raft with what they saw as a little, weak girl, and I constantly felt the need to prove that I was just as competent as my male counterparts. At the start of one rafting trip, a guest loudly proclaimed, "I will not let my family get in the raft with that little girl as our guide, it's not safe!" In this statement, he succeeded in embarrassing me and everyone else on the trip.

He got in the raft with the male guide and I got the other group. The male guide flipped his raft, this little girl didn't. It was glorious retribution when I paddled my raft over and pulled the offending guest—who was panicked and gasping for air—out of the river.

Yet even while gaining satisfaction through my actions, I couldn't help but listen a little bit to the noise of the world. As often as I was listening to direct commentary on my inherent inferiority, I was hearing things like "he throws like a girl" or "I cried like a little girl" and "stop being such a pussy." All this had an impact on my subconscious. Whatever the intention behind that constant chorus of judgment, it's hard to not let the hum of the world affect you.

Succumbing to a lifetime of these subtle hints, whispers, and undisguised comments would have been the natural thing to do and, to a certain extent, I did. Even after I was successfully kayaking some of the hardest Class V rivers around the world, there was still a little part of me that wondered if I was truly good enough. I was afraid to go kayaking with the "really good" kayakers in case I made a mistake. I worried they might discover that I wasn't as good as them. Maybe the dam keeper on the notoriously difficult Milner section of the Snake River was right, running out of her booth to me as I was putting in the river to say, "You are so little, are you sure you can take on those big rapids down there?" As annoying as it was, I often took on these strangers' doubts as my own. I could logically convince myself that rivers don't lie—if I made it down a really hard river, it was because I was talented enough to do it. But there was also a little emotional voice whispering, "Maybe you just keep getting lucky."

What I tried hard to focus on was the pissed-off voice in my head that shouted, "You are absolutely wrong!" to my detractors. I mentally filed them away as morons and set about to prove every one of them wrong.

When the doubters started questioning my decision to try to kayak the Amazon, it was me who looked at them like *they* were crazy: "Of course I can kayak the Amazon; what kind of idiot would think otherwise?"

✑

David Midgley (Midge) is the youngest of eight children. By the time his parents got around to having him, their oldest children were starting families of their own and everyone's attention was focused in directions besides his. He grew up mostly unnoticed despite his valiant attempts to get attention. These included: dressing in ridiculous Goth outfits, getting severely beaten up in these outfits, joining a punk rock band, dropping out of school, and showing brilliance in computer programming.

Computers suited him best, and he shut out the world while he sharpened his skills, eventually writing software and algorithms to automate the buying, optimization, and monitoring of advertising campaigns. Midge comes from a family of weavers, but his computer programs earned him a lot of money and respect within the programmer world. Now he lives a comfortable, some would argue wealthy, life in London, and receives the admiration of his peers.

But Midge saw his life slipping away from him as he sat behind a computer writing code. Just after turning thirty, he decided that he needed to do one big thing in his life. Midge was looking for a meaningful place in this vast, anonymous world and he thought for years about what it might be.

Climbing Everest was his first thought, but he discovered that far too many people had done it. In Midge's perception of tackling the mountain, the only qualifications necessary were the ability to walk, to suffer, and to part with about $65,000 to pay for a guide. He concluded Everest was too pedestrian for him. Sailing around the world had also been overdone, he thought, and Midge wasn't that interested in polar explorations. He racked his brain for "the coolest thing I could do in the most remote part of the world." The Amazon River entered his consciousness and, after doing some research, he discovered that only five people had done a human-powered source-to-sea expedition down the world's largest river.* Piotr Chmielinski and Joe Kane did the first complete descent of the Amazon River in 1985. They used a combination of rafting, kayaking, and hiking to get them down the river. In 1999, Colin Angus, Scott Borthwick, and Ben Kozel descended the Amazon in a raft.

Five individuals out of seven billion people on this earth (it was only 6.44 billion in 2004, but you get the point). That caught Midge's attention. Midge also noted that everyone who had descended the Amazon to date had used some combination of walking, rafting, and kayaking. No one had kayaked the entire river and no Brit had ever done it. When Midge learned

---

* Only five people had traveled, via the river, from the Amazon's source to the sea when Midge came up with his own plan to kayak the entire river. Eight people had done it by the time we started our expedition. To see a full list of Amazon expeditions, including people who did not do the whitewater, who used motorized travel for the flatwater, or who walked the entire route visit this link: http://www.adventurestats.com/tables /RiverAmazon.shtml.

that more people had walked on the moon than had gone from source to sea on the Amazon River, he made his decision.

Have I mentioned that Midge didn't know how to kayak?

In fact, he'd never even sat in a kayak.

When Midge came up with the idea that he would kayak the Amazon from source to sea, he had also never camped out a day in his life, had never been to South America, and had exactly zero requisite skills to undertake an expedition down the world's largest river. He was a nerdy computer programmer who lived in London, ate fancy food, and partied too much, and who was far more concerned with the quality of his hair wax than his ability to whitewater kayak.

I'm not sure I will ever know what gave Midge the audacity to think he could kayak the Amazon, besides the detail that he came up with the idea in a bar in Scotland. He had been drunk enough to think he could pull it off, and, in his sobriety, was stubborn enough to make his ridiculous idea into a reality. Also, one of his big brothers told him he was full of shit and that he would never do it.

Midge has an uncanny amount of determination, and I have no doubt it was the thing he relied upon the most throughout the entire Amazon ordeal. Much of what he did over the next ten years was a result of his singular focus on the Amazon objective. Jungle survival courses, adrenaline sports like skydiving—this was part of his quest to find something scarier in the world than kayaking—fitness regimens like running marathons, and making enough money to pay for the expedition all began to occupy a significant space in Midge's life. Of course, learning to kayak was the obvious first step. One of the first things Midge learned about kayaking was that you needed a way to transport your kayak to the river. He realized he'd need a driver's license if he was going to be a serious kayaker. So, at the age of thirty-two, he had to go out and pass a driving test.

✐

Don Beveridge was born on Beale Air Force Base in Yuba County, California. Moving was a staple of Don's life; first as the son of an air force man, and then as the son of a preacher—same dad, different careers. After living on the air force base, then in Berkeley, and then Sacramento, the family settled for what would be their longest stint—nine years—in Moscow, Idaho.

Don loved everything about his life in Idaho. He had neighborhood friends, school friends, and church friends. He could ride his bike freely around town and he could climb the rock walls of the post office building when he got bored. His family took regular ski trips to Schweitzer Mountain Resort and camping trips in the summer. He had a loyal dog—Kelly—who would follow him to the comic book store and wait outside while he shopped. He even had a grade school sweetheart. It's hard to imagine a more perfect small-town childhood.

His utopian youth was cut short when he was abruptly yanked away from his small, comfortable community just as he was about to begin high school. He didn't even get to say goodbye to his friends. Instead of embarking on this journey into adolescence in a small town with friends he'd grown up with, Don was forced to start high school alone, in the suburbs of Portland, Oregon, with over two thousand students he didn't know and didn't have much in common with. Having no other options, he adapted, but he didn't like it.

Don finally had enough when, as he was about to start his senior year at Sunset High in Beaverton, Oregon, his parents decided to uproot themselves again. This time they were going to Arlington, Virginia, and Don didn't go with them. After battling three years of loneliness as an outsider, he finally felt he was beginning to fit in. He had friends, he had a girlfriend, and he was determined not to let his parents ruin this for him, again. He stayed behind and endured a senior year fraught with the problems inherent in being seventeen years old and living without a family, without a car, and generally untethered.

Moving disrupted Don's life in ways that are still evident today. Lacking strong attachments to either people or places, Don feels most comfortable with a transient life.

Don's older brothers, Bill and Paul, introduced him to the sport of kayaking during his junior year at St. Lawrence University in upstate New York. Bill spent his winter break at St. Lawrence teaching Don how to roll in the university pool, and Paul took him on his first river trip down the Potomac River outside Washington, D.C. Don was instantly hooked. The potential freedom and adventure that kayaking offered had a powerful hold on him.

After graduating from college, Don moved to Colorado where he talked his way into a raft-guiding job. He fabricated solid guiding experience out of a few family outings on the Class II/III Lower Youghiogheny River in Pennsylvania. For Don, this was enough. His natural athleticism and ability to learn quickly helped him rise to the top of the rookie class early that summer. His quick wit and easy way of talking to people were perfect attributes for a young raft guide. Living in a tent on the banks of the Arkansas River gave Don ample time to hone his kayaking skills after work.

Don spent his summers on the Arkansas River in Colorado for the next fifteen years. During the winters, he chased rivers around the world, concentrating his efforts on Central and South America. As Don's skills and strengths grew as a whitewater professional, so did the admiration he received from others. It was obvious to all who watched him in action that he had found his calling.

Don is on a different level than most kayakers. There are recreational kayakers who dabble in the sport, there are good kayakers (I think I fall into this category), and then there is Don. The same laws of gravity and fluid dynamics don't seem to apply to people to like Don. He's dedicated his life to the sport and his time and effort have paid off. Watching him kayak, it's quickly apparent that he floats across the water in a seemingly effortless dance while others clumsily (in comparison) struggle just to make it down in one piece.

Don is an excellent and patient teacher. Though he'd happily run Class V whitewater every day for the rest of his life, he's perfectly content running something easier if he's leading a friend down the river or teaching a client how to refine their paddle strokes.

Don also has amazing longevity for a Class V kayaker. Class V paddling is usually a phase that twenty- to thirty-year-olds go through as they make the transition into adulthood. Don found himself pushing back against his aging kayaker friends who started questioning their dedication to running hard whitewater and who were discovering more important things in life. Don watched as one friend after another gave up extreme kayaking, turning to tamer sports. Don keeps himself in shape and tuned up to the mental rigors of paddling Class V because he is not yet ready to part with his passion. He is proving himself immune to the kayaker's version of an existential crisis.

Loath as he is to admit it, Don was well suited for this expedition in part because he seems to be driven solely by the sport of kayaking. He shuffles through the rest of life lacking a certain purpose and energy. Sometimes I imagine him never doing anything again; but when it's time to go kayaking, a transformation happens. He springs to life, gets impressively motivated, and his energy is uncontainable.

The first time I went hiking with Don was a disaster. He trudged along ridiculously slowly and complained the entire time. For the duration of the two-hour hike, all I heard was how his knee hurt, how his feet hurt, and the constant question, "What is the point of just plain hiking anyways? I get it if we are skiing or kayaking, but we're just doing this to turn around at the top and come back down."

Two weeks later we started a river trip with a tricky put-in. We had to carry our kayaks thirteen miles up and over 12,000-foot-tall Bishop Pass to reach the Middle Fork of the Kings River in California's high sierra. The hike would take one day, and the river would take us six days to paddle. Our kayaks were loaded with seven days' worth of food and camping gear and weighed about eighty-five pounds apiece. A typical whitewater kayak is eight to nine feet long and makes an ungainly backpack. Don was nauseatingly spry and giddy. He kept stopping to ask if I was okay—making furtive references to my extremely slow pace. A blank, uncomprehending look overtook his face when I told him, "I'm fine, it's just slow going when you are carrying seventy percent of your body weight on your back."

He shrugged and trotted—hiked—up the trail.

He is smart, too, but doesn't like to show this side of himself. I think he worries that if people discover he is smart, they will demand he do something besides kayaking. After a few beers, though, this side of him pushes its way out, emerging in the form of him holding his own in a scientific conversation that he should know nothing about.

He can be kind of grumpy, but he loves to help people. Midge and I would both need a lot of help on our journey down the Amazon and neither of us ever had any doubt that Don would have our backs.

And though he loves to complain, Don can suffer through just about anything.

Chapter 3

BUT WHY DO IT?

*"Fate is like a strange, unpopular restaurant filled with odd
little waiters who bring you things you never asked for and
don't always like."*

—Lemony Snicket

2004
NINE YEARS BEFORE THE EXPEDITION

It must have been some strange cosmic coincidence that led Midge into
my life. I don't really believe in fate, but it did take a lot of specific choices
in both of our lives to force our polar-opposite paths to cross.

Once Midge decided that the Amazon would be his big adventure, he
started taking whitewater kayaking courses in the United Kingdom and
joined the Regents Canoe Club in London to help get him out on the rivers.
Eventually he built enough skills to be able to survive some intermediate
whitewater. That is when he started to branch out to look for new rivers,
different coaches, and more exotic destinations.

A moldy poster in a kayak shop in Scotland is what first made Midge
aware that there was good kayaking in Ecuador and that there was a company there to guide him. Don Beveridge, Larry Vermeeren, and I were
the owners of Small World Adventures. We ran weeklong kayaking trips
in Ecuador and offered everything from instruction for total beginners to

guiding and skills development for expert kayakers. An instructor from that Scottish kayak shop had been kayaking with us in Ecuador and brought a poster home to display on the wall.

Midge had to transform himself from a flabby, unathletic computer programmer into a hardcore whitewater kayaker if he hoped to survive the whitewater portion of the Amazon. Heading to Ecuador was, in his mind, the next logical step in his progression. Ecuador is, after all, in the Amazon River basin. My graduate school obligations had me holed up at the University of British Columbia in Vancouver, and I did not kayak with Midge his first trip to Ecuador. Had I been there, I might have been indelibly put off by him. I was running the office at the time and remember saying something to Don and Larry along the lines of, "Some crazy British guy wants to come to Ecuador for two weeks. He says he can paddle Class III+ and IV-, and has a somewhat reliable combat roll."

Midge had a lot to learn, beginning with the fundamental impassivity of the river. The river is eternally confusing, bringing us great joy and great hardship, often in the same day. Its power is insurmountable and, to many, inconceivable; but it is an indifferent power. The river is unmoved if you stylishly drop over a fifty-foot waterfall. It is equally unsympathetic to the fact that you are having a bad day and have tipped over and are dragging your head across its rocky bottom at ten miles per hour. Sometimes it seems that no matter what you do, the river counteracts your every move and you flail, turning upside down, gasping for air, wondering why you even like this sport.

For most extreme kayakers, however, kayaking is not just a sport. It's a way of life. A way of living that has no easy way out, as many of us realize as we grapple to reconcile our aging bodies with the almost superhuman demands of Class V expedition kayaking. Midge was beginning the process of morphing from a computer geek into an extreme kayaker and he had no idea what he was in for.

It takes a special kind of person to think kayaking is fun, and an extremely dedicated person to build the skills and mental fortitude to be able to run the most difficult whitewater—Class V whitewater. You have to be okay with being trapped inside a small plastic boat, all while being swept downstream by the equivalent of an avalanche while maintaining as much control as possible.

It typically takes years of training, dedication, experience, and mental resilience to become what we call a Class V expedition paddler. This means that you can negotiate whitewater that looks like suicide to everyone else. You can kayak for hours on end and still have the stamina (both mental and physical) to safely pass through chaotic and dangerous rapids, and you can scramble along banks and employ climbing skills to scale cliffs when you need to get a view of the river before descending farther. It means you are comfortable existing at the bottom of a boxed-in, claustrophobic river canyons for days on end.

Midge had typical abilities for your average beginner-intermediate kayaker when he got to Ecuador, but he had a strange mentality to accompany his skills. "Portage" was a not word in his kayaking lexicon, and he would stubbornly paddle every rapid he encountered, consequences be damned. While it is somewhat okay to be foolish and unskilled on Class I, II, and even III whitewater, these things will get you in a lot of trouble as you push into the Class IV and V realm.

A rapid called *Curvas Peligrosas* (Dangerous Curves) in Ecuador became instrumental in Midge's whitewater education and drastically altered the way he thought about kayaking. Curvas Peligrosas is a Class IV rapid on the Quijos River in Ecuador. This stretch of whitewater gets its name from the tight *S*-turns that make up the rapid. The lead-in is comprised of a wide-open riverbed and gravel piles. As the river enters its curves, it also enters a bedrock canyon changing not only the feel of the river, but also how the water reacts. Instead of flowing predictably downriver over small river rocks, the water in the canyon churns, flowing upstream, downstream, and side to side in a completely unpredictable manner. This causes conflicting currents to collide, resulting in whirlpools where the water, or a kayaker unfortunate enough to be near one, gets sucked downward, spiraling underneath the surface toward the bottom of the river.

Larry told Midge that he should pick up his kayak and walk around Curvas Peligrosas. Midge refused. Portaging was not an option. How could he ever expect to kayak the raging whitewater of the Amazon's headwaters if he couldn't even manage a Class IV rapid in Ecuador?

Midge shoved off from shore following Don, and got flipped over by the chaotic currents at the top of the rapid. Being upside down, deprived of oxygen, and trapped in a plastic kayak is not a good position to be in at the top of a challenging rapid. Moments later, to Don and Larry's relief, Midge was able to perform a combat roll and was upright again. When he rolled up, he was on the left side of the river and needed to get to the right side of the river. He missed his move in the middle of the rapid and ended up stuck in a giant hydraulic where most of the water was violently reversing back on itself, no longer moving down the river.

After fifteen seconds of intense thrashing—imagine being trapped inside a giant, hyperspeed front-loading washing machine—it became apparent to Midge that he was not getting out of this hole in his kayak. Because the kayak floats on the surface, where all the backwash is moving upstream, it can be difficult to maneuver your way out of a hole while still in your boat. While experienced kayakers can often achieve this, Midge certainly didn't have the skills to do it at the time. He was completely out of control, getting tossed around like a rag doll. He did summon the composure to pull off his neoprene spray skirt that was keeping him securely in his kayak. Without his spray skirt he was able to swim free of his boat. Once out of his buoyant kayak, he was quickly pushed to the bottom of the river, and then downstream, out of the backwash of the hole.

His troubles were just beginning.

Midge relaxed once he was free from the grasp of the hole, thinking he was out of danger. Despite Don and Larry's screams for him to "SWIM TO THE RIGHT," he did no such thing and was quickly swept straight into the clutches of a cave where the water exiting the rapid pounded up against the cliff wall. Once there, it was all Midge could do to get the occasional breath of air before being sucked deep below the surface again and again only to get battered underwater.

Midge had no idea what was happening, and he didn't know how to stop it. He was new to kayaking and was naïve to the myriad dangers of the river. As it pulled him deeper below the surface of the water, Midge no doubt wondered what malicious force he was dealing with. You can only really know the power of the river once you've experienced a swim in a violent rapid. The currents pull each limb in a different direction and no matter how hard you pull back on your arm or your leg you can't do anything against the strength of the river. You feel like a starfish careening uncontrollably toward oblivion. Water forces its way into your ears, nose, and mouth, and you finally know what it feels like to have zero control—no control over your body and no ability to reach the surface for that breath of air that you desperately need.

Don and Larry knew time was running out for Midge. He was having far more downtime (time spent underneath the water) than anyone can withstand; and while he was busy drowning, Don and Larry decided that Don would paddle across the river to look for a place on the river left cliff wall where he might climb out of his boat and get a rescue rope to Midge.

Meanwhile, despite great personal risk, Larry deliberately paddled into the cave to try to relieve some of Midge's hypoxia by giving him the buoyant platform of his kayak. He knew Midge did not have time to wait for Don and he decided he had to do something. Larry's kayak did give Midge a brief reprieve from his oxygen-starved world, but it was all too fleeting. It was too turbulent in there for Larry to remain stable for very long. In less than a minute, Larry was upside down in his kayak with a scared, drowning Englishman trying desperately to climb on top of him. Amazingly, Larry rolled up a few times, but he was getting exhausted, too. Each second came and went with increasing urgency.

It was starting to look like Don was Midge's (and now Larry's) last chance of survival and the pressure was mounting. Adding one more person to that cave would not help the situation. Ferrying across the river just upstream of the cave took focus and perfect execution. Unlike Midge, however, Don understood the forces of the river and harnessed its power to help him. Using a wave just upstream of Midge's cave, Don surfed over to the safety of the opposite bank. In a typical river paradox, the same water that was killing Midge was helping Don.

Don made it to the left side of the river, but trying to find a foothold on the cliff wall that was close enough but not too close to the cave proved tricky. As he was about to give up and think of plan B, Don found a three-inch protrusion in the rock wall just big enough to get a solid toe hold, and a couple feet above it was a hand hold. He delicately climbed out of his kayak in the roiling eddy. He clipped his boat to a line on his life jacket so he would not lose it, and got his rescue throw rope ready. He got momentary eye contact with Larry and realized in that instant just how dire things were. Don fought the adrenaline coursing through his veins and channeled enough patience to wait until he saw Midge resurface and then he flung the rope, holding onto one end. With Larry's help, Midge got a hold of the other end the rope and Don pulled him to the relative safety of his turbulent eddy and rock outcropping.

Fifteen feet of rope was left trailing behind Midge as Don pulled him out of the cave. The churning water wrapped the tail of the rope around Larry's paddle, making the already problematic task of staying upright in the cave impossible. As Don was securing Midge's hold on the back of his kayak so he would not lose him again, he looked up and saw the rope fixing itself around Larry's paddle, no longer allowing him to take strokes. Pushing off the wall and paddling with his hands to the best of his ability, Larry held on as long as he could; but the river eventually got the better of him, flipping him over one final time.

Larry's only option was to swim out of his kayak. Knowing that swimming would make him lose the flotation of his kayak and therefore would allow the river to pull him under along the wall as it had done to Midge, he pulled his spray skirt anyway. Already tired from fighting in the cave with Midge, Larry didn't have much time. Gasping, exhausted, and fearing the worst, he resurfaced after close to ten seconds of downtime—an eternity in a situation like this. What he saw as his face broke the surface of the water was Don poised and ready with his end of the rope ready to haul Larry to safety.

Thanks to Don and Larry's skills, composure, quick-thinking, and courage, everyone made it out of the river that day; but it certainly would not take much imagination to see a different outcome. It was a life-changing lesson for Midge. Not only did he realize his own limitations and what the consequences of overreaching those boundaries were for himself; more importantly, he saw what the consequences could be for other people. It was one thing to be reckless with his own life, but realizing how close Larry came to dying that day added important perspective to the choices he made on future river trips. Witnessing Don and Larry's actions that day on the Quijos also gave Midge a new respect for river professionals and what expert knowledge can do for any situation.

Every longtime kayaker has had a close call on the river or at least an experience that felt dire to them. For many, this one bad experience is enough to hang up the paddle forever and move on to a saner and more controllable sport. For those who stick around, compartmentalizing these brushes with death is the only way to keep going.

Midge had to learn his lessons from that day but then push the rest of the memory to the back of his mind. It's easy to obsess about all the what-ifs and close calls you've experienced on the river, but you can't think this way and still be a kayaker. Instead, most of us get on the river each day, not ignoring the dangers, but not letting them control our minds, either. Keeping a cool head is the most important skill in kayaking, though by far the most difficult to master. Many kayakers can't overcome this mental aspect of the sport and they end up spending their days on the river in a constant state of fear, or they quit the sport. It's a testament to Midge's mental fortitude that he was able to control his mind.

For the next eight years, Midge came to Ecuador for at least two weeks each season, sometimes for as long as two months. With each passing week, we realized more and more just how serious he was about kayaking the Amazon. We even started to believe that he might accomplish his goal.

∽

2012
ONE YEAR BEFORE THE EXPEDITION

People say things happen for a reason. I believe this, too, but it's rare that the reason is because some British guy was drunk in a bar in Scotland and came up with a crazy idea—especially when I didn't even know the guy at the time. I decided I would try to become the first woman to kayak the Amazon River from source to sea because David Midgley (drunk guy from bar in Scotland) asked me to.

It was that simple.

During one happy hour after kayaking in the fall of 2012, Midge skipped over all socializing—including his usual mocking of my American accent by greeting me with an "Oh my God, today was totally awesome!"—and got right down to business.

"Did Don talk to you about you guys coming with me for the whitewater sections of the Amazon?"

"He did." I hesitated. "And he also talked to me about a lot more."

Joining Midge for the whitewater was an easy "Yes!" I had been kayaking for sixteen years and was good at it. I had done a lot of expedition paddling, and I was far more comfortable and competent on the river than I was behind a desk or in the middle of a city. Being offered a fully funded (by Midge) chance to kayak a remote river in the Peruvian Andes was an incredible opportunity. More importantly, Don, Midge, and I had proven that we could spend large amounts of time with each other, a special skill in its own right.

Just before bed one night, Don asked me, "Are you really going to be okay with saying goodbye to Midge after the whitewater and walking away from a chance to become the first woman to kayak the entire Amazon?"

My answer, embarrassingly, was, "I honestly hadn't considered it, but you're right, I might not be okay with it. Doing the entire river sounds like an interesting idea."

It was as casual as if I'd said yes to a cup of coffee. At the time, it felt that simple.

Don suggested I think on it. "Don't make any rash decisions," he cautioned.

After Don put the idea into my head, I realized this would be no mere cup of coffee, it would be an adventure on a larger scale than I'd ever seen before. This was different than just being a stubborn kid determined to do everything that people thought I couldn't do just to prove them wrong. This would be a four- to six-month commitment. It would mean doing something that no woman had ever done, and, if we were able to kayak the entire river, it meant doing something that no person had ever done.

The expedition was almost too big in scope to comprehend. I couldn't even begin to realistically think about what it would be like to kayak over four thousand miles across South America on the world's largest river, so I decided not to dwell on the details.

After a couple of days, I told Don that I was sure I wanted to do the entire Amazon.

"Are you absolutely sure?" he asked in exasperation. "Seriously? You want to do this?" Then, "Why?"

I didn't thoroughly examine my reasons for wanting to kayak the Amazon, perhaps out of fear of what my answers might reveal. Just the simple fact that I liked adventures was sufficient for me. I already had the skills for the whitewater, and in some deluded haze, probably accentuated by alcohol, I concluded that kayaking the flatwater would be a good idea, too.

I knew there would be plenty of problems associated with saying yes to this expedition. I'd have to leave behind a lot of important things: my family, my friends, real food that doesn't come freeze-dried in a bag, my truck, my phone, my computer, restaurants, bars, grocery stores, my pillow, clean clothes, showers, and all the other comforts I could possibly imagine. I would give these up and head to the jungle to sleep in a stuffy nylon tent where sweating and sleeping take up equal time each night. I'd eat the same dehydrated meals every day for breakfast and for dinner (I'd skip lunch), and I'd be doing all of this in a mosquito- and gnat-infested hell.

And why did I want to do this to myself?

I'm sure Don didn't appreciate it when, instead of answering the why question, I just reminded him, "Technically, it was your idea."

The truth was that I wasn't prepared to answer this difficult question. I still can't clearly explain why I wanted to go. Maybe because I was getting older and thought a big adventure was just the thing to keep me young? I think the idea of this expedition just meshed well with all my lifestyle choices up to this point and lately I'd been drawn to the unknown. I really hadn't done much so far in my life that would constitute a mainstream existence, so escaping people and "American norms" for half a year had a lot of appeal. I was already tired of people constantly asking me the regular slurry of annoying questions, which were just getting worse the older I got:

When would I settle down? People apparently didn't like the fact that Don and I lived in a van traveling around North America when we weren't guiding kayakers in Ecuador.

When did I plan on having kids? I had two friends corner me at a party after they had recently given birth to each of their first kids. I sat politely, but incredulously, and listened to one tell me, "Your life will be meaning-less if you don't have children," while the other told me, "It hurts my soul to think of you never having your own kids."

When would I stop playing around all the time and get a real job? Because running a kayaking business apparently doesn't count as "real."

And didn't I want some security for the future?

I thought it would be nice to get away from all of that for a while.

In an unexplainable contradiction, I also harbored a faint hope that kayaking the Amazon could set me free from my adventuresome life and allow me to do all those things that everyone else wanted me to do.

Plus, throwing myself into a river so enormous that its reach and volume are impossible to accurately imagine seemed like the perfect way to gain perspective on my own existence.

So, the question wasn't why should I kayak the Amazon, but rather, why not?

No doubt, Don regrets to his core ever suggesting we join Midge for the entire Amazon, and he still maintains that I forced him to do the trip.

Back at happy hour with Midge, I continued, "We are one hundred per-cent in for the whitewater. And we'd also like to join you for the flatwater."

Midge was ecstatic. "I never in a million years imagined you guys would also want to paddle the flatwater! This is great. But why?"

"I don't have a good answer to that question, it just seems like an oppor-tunity I probably shouldn't pass up."

Don had joined us by then and the three of us sealed our commitment to descend the Amazon River as a team with a shot of tequila along the Quijos River in Ecuador—the same place where Francisco de Orellana, the first European to travel down the Amazon—started his own journey in the 16th century.

Chapter 4

THE SOURCE

"All rivers, even the most dazzling, those that catch the sun in their course, all rivers go down to the ocean and drown. And life awaits man as the sea awaits the river."

—Simone Schwarz-Bart

JULY 25, 2013
THREE DAYS PRIOR TO LAUNCHING THE EXPEDITION

D riving habits in South America are different from those we are used to in the States. The horn is used at all times, and can mean a variety of things: it's okay to pass, it's not okay to pass, you can go, I am going, get out of my way, I am letting you in.

The "oh-shit handles" were getting heavy use in our Toyota van as Amazon River veteran West Hansen tried to learn the rules of road before we were killed. West Hansen is a longtime flatwater canoe and kayak racer hailing from Austin, Texas. He spent years immersed in the sport of flatwater racing. West has entered the 260-mile Texas Water Safari race an amazing twenty-four times. He'd hallucinated countless times during these races—it turns out forty-plus hours of being awake and paddling is the limit for normal human brain function. After reading about a race on the Amazon River near Iquitos, Peru—the Great Amazon River Raft Race—he turned some of his boundless energy toward South

America. After participating in the Amazon Raft Race, he fell in love with the Amazon River. Long accustomed to suffering on flatwater rivers, West hatched, and completed, his own expedition down the Amazon River in 2012. West kayaked the whitewater sections that his skills allowed and rafted the rest. Then he got into a flatwater racing kayak once the whitewater was over and he was truly in his element.

West kept an up-to-date blog during his own Amazon expedition, and Midge had been following along to glean as much information as he possibly could. Midge eventually decided to reach out to West for some logistical help in the early planning stages of our own expedition, and West was more than generous with his time. Knowing where to start dealing with logistics for a trip this big and this expensive is nearly impossible, and talking with someone who had already been through it was immensely helpful.

Team Skype calls were always frantic, chaotic affairs with me scribbling down West's coordinates of dangerous places where his team was held at gunpoint, and taking down names and phone numbers of locals who might be willing to do food drops for us. Meanwhile Midge pressed him on the costs of importing the sea kayaks, while Don wanted to know how many miles per day his team averaged in the flatwater. Eventually, West volunteered to come to Peru to help us in the early stages of our trip. West was interested in revisiting the headwaters, since the exact starting point of the Amazon was yet to be officially settled.

Lizet Alaniz, West's wife, is a health and human services project manager, and she was eager to take a little vacation herself. She'd never seen the headwaters of the river her husband descended the year before and she thought this would be a good opportunity to do so. The two of them stayed with us for the first ten days. They provided us with transportation, met up with us at night when possible, offered moral support, and, most importantly, helped us locate the source of the Amazon.

West's frantic desire to escape Lima's many traffic jams had him stomping on the gas and then the brakes with equal vigor as he zigged and zagged us through the narrow and crowded colonial streets. A noisy assortment of overly full buses, private automobiles, and motorcycles shuttling entire five-member families (sometimes with dogs or chickens) across town was congesting the streets like it did at most hours of the day. This mass of vehicles belched out a collective cloud of diesel exhaust obscuring our vision even more than the smoke from the "street meat" vendors who lined the sidewalks. After about two hours, a few missed turns, and several hundred swear words, we escaped the confines of Peru's capital city and were bouncing through the countryside on our way up the Andes.

Our first night outside of Lima the five of us stayed in the quaint little city of Tarma. Sporting the nickname "Pearl of the Andes," the town sits in a beautiful valley where farmers grow flowers for export. The bright red, yellow, and orange colors blanketing the steep-hilled flower farms contrasted sharply with the more natural brown and barren foothills of the Andes. The town's architecture is typical of the Peruvian Andes, with a style that is half European and half molded by the harsh and steep mountain environment. Cinder block houses cling precariously to the steep valley walls, and each clay-tiled roof sports two ceramic bulls and the cross. This combination of Incan and Catholic mythology is placed on the roof to bring good fortune to the house and the families who live there.

At 10,016 feet in elevation, we thought Tarma would be a good place to stop and acclimatize before climbing to higher altitudes. Tarma is also a relatively large town where we could pick up everything we'd forgotten in Lima before the more sparsely populated route leading to the source. Don and Midge bought all the Sublimes (pronounced su-BLEE-mehs) they could find. Sublimes are Peru's version of the Snickers bar, and after less than a week in the country, the boys were already addicts. We were also lacking bottles of Pisco, Peru's famous grape brandy. West recommended that we carry a few bottles to present to the locals whose permission we would need to travel through their livestock gates and to camp on their land. I had mixed feelings about bribing people with booze, but West was adamant that this is "what they wanted." I decided not to argue with him—we'd be riding in the same vehicle the next day, after all.

We didn't sleep that night thanks to the Festival de Apóstol Santiago, which was taking place in Tarma's main square, beneath our hotel window. A mix of loud Andean music and cheerful shouting filled the night air. The chaotic noise outside mirrored the frenzied thoughts in my brain as I lay in my bed, wishing I was carefree and out partying with the revelers rather than worrying about how to find our expedition's starting point, not to mention what would happen once we did. When our 6:00 A.M. departure time approached, none of us had trouble rousing ourselves, since we had never managed to fall asleep in the first place. Bleary-eyed, we piled back into the van and set off on the ridiculous task of locating a single starting point for the world's largest river.

River-running is typically a straightforward undertaking. You know your starting point and your ending point and you just follow the course of the river between these two locations. The Amazon would prove tricky on numerous occasions, with its thousands of different channels to choose from and tides to deal with, but even before we could get going, we had to face the fact that we didn't exactly know the location of the famous river's beginning.

Nobody did.

The question of the Amazon's true source has persisted for hundreds of years and remains somewhat unsettled today. That's because trying to pinpoint a singular birthplace for a river that has more than 1,100 major tributaries and drains an area three-quarters the size of the United States is a preposterous undertaking. Not to mention the debates about whether the Nile or the Amazon is the world's longest river.[*]

The arguments about the birthplace of the world's largest, and possibly longest, river are a never-ending quagmire of questions about length, volume, surface versus subsurface water, and natural versus unnatural riverbeds. At the time of this writing, there is still no definitive answer about the source of the Amazon, the principal problem being that scientists do not even agree on a single definition of the word *source*.

The most widely (though not universally) accepted definition of a river's source is "the most distant upstream point in the drainage along the natural course of the river or its tributaries from which a drop of rain will make its way to the river's mouth."[**] But it's not that simple. The three biggest

---

[*] For a brief discussion of the world's longest river, see "A Note on Rivers" on page ix.

[**] J. Contos and N. Tripcevich, "Correct Placement of the Most Distant Source of the Amazon River in the Mantaro River Drainage," *AREA* 2014 46, no. 1 (March 2014): 27–39.

sticking points are how source status is affected when the water goes underground for a time, if the flow is insufficient during dry periods, and whether a man-made structure—such as a dam that diverts the flow of a river—should negate a source designation.

Since the 18th century, geographers and adventurers alike have been arguing about the source of the Amazon, giving the designation to five different rivers in Peru and one in Ecuador over the centuries. The Napo (in Ecuador), Urubamba, Marañón, Ucayali, Apurímac, and now Mantaro have all held the distinguished title at some point throughout the debate. During the 1950s, the arguments settled down and the Apurímac River became the accepted source. Piotr Chmielinski and Joe Kane, who did the first full descent of the Amazon in 1985, started on the Apurímac River. This source was reconfirmed by a 2011 study published in the *Hydrological Sciences Journal.*[*]

This sixty-year consensus was upended when an interested kayaker started looking more closely. We started hearing rumors that the Amazon River *might* have a new source just over a year before our departure. In February 2012, Rocky Contos, a kayaker and neuroscientist, was studying topographic maps in his California home as he prepared for a trip to Peru. He was drawn to the Mantaro River for its whitewater potential after he noticed that it cut an impressive chasm through one of the more rugged sections of the Andes. As he started looking more closely, he was struck by the length of two massive bends in the river where the Mantaro nearly doubles back on itself. After tracing the river's course with Adobe Illustrator line vectors, Rocky had a new candidate for the source of the Amazon.

In subsequent measurements, Rocky determined that the Mantaro was inarguably longer. Rocky found that the Mantaro River is 46.5 to 57 miles longer than the Apurímac River. (The discrepancy is because Rocky got slightly different lengths with each of the measurement tools he used.)[**]

---

[*]   B. Jansky, Z. Engel, J. Kocum, L. Sefrna, and J. Cesak, "The Amazon River Headstream Area in the Cordillera Chila, Peru: Hydrographical, Hydrological, and Glaciological Conditions," *Hydrological Sciences Journal* 56, 138–151.

[**] J. Contos and N. Tripcevich, "Correct Placement of the Most Distant Source of the Amazon River in the Mantaro River Drainage," vol. 1 (February 2011): 27–39.

Rocky and James Duesenberry finished the first descent of the Mantaro River on June 4, 2012.

This was huge news that rocked both the kayaking and geographical worlds. How could the source of the world's largest river have been wrong in the age of GPS and Google Earth? It made sense when they got things wrong in the 19th century, but everyone who was paying attention wondered how geographers could have missed this. Rocky's guess is that the "Península de Tayacaja—a great twisting bend that [the] Río Mantaro courses around in its lower half—has the effect of making the total river length appear shorter than the Apurímac on casual inspection."[*]

As Rocky was proving that the Mantaro was longer than the Apurímac, geographers were still arguing about what constitutes a river's source and which waterways should and should not qualify for the designation. As Jeff Moag reported in *Canoe & Kayak* magazine, "The Mantaro is the longer river, but that doesn't settle the question. Geography can be as much a political subject as a scientific one."[**] The contentious points were the three major dams along the Mantaro's 450-mile course, in contrast with the Apurímac's still free-flowing waters.

Contos and others argue that man-made structures are temporary and should not count against a river's eligibility for source status. Meanwhile, proponents of the Apurímac maintaining its source status argue that the source should be defined as "the most distant point of a river's longest tributary that flows continuously."[***] Some experts even propose that the Apurímac and Mantaro should share the designation. In this scenario, the Mantaro acts as the source during the rainy season when there is substantial flow through its natural riverbed, while the Apurímac takes over the job during the dry season, when the Mantaro's dams are diverting too much of the flow.

Don, Midge, and I decided that we would descend the Mantaro River. The three of us felt that Rocky had supplied sufficient evidence that the Mantaro was longer, even though his scientific paper would not be officially

---

[*]   Ibid., 37.
[**]   J. Moag, "True Source," *Canoe & Kayak*, www.canoekayak.com/true-source-part-2, accessed February 28, 2016.
[***] Ibid.

accepted until November 2013. We got the good news that the Royal Geographical Society's *AREA* journal had accepted Rocky's findings while we were making our way down the flatwater near the city of Manaus. Phew! We were all relieved to find out that we didn't have to head back to Peru to start all over again.

Now we just needed to do our best to locate the highest-elevation flowing water that fed the feeder streams of the Mantaro. West had successfully found the source lake one year earlier, but his memory was fuzzy. We spent the better part of the afternoon driving around Peru's *altiplano*—Spanish for "high plain"—dodging sheep and llamas. We were looking for Lago Acucocha, the highest lake we could drive to, and the place where we would start our search for the source.

Although sparsely populated, this grassy plateau is home to farmers and ranchers of the Quechua people. We drove through one gate after another, most of them displaying fox and coyote carcasses on the fence line as a warning to other would-be predators. We bounced past tiny high-elevation lakes that were full of pink flamingos, Andean geese, and flocks of crimson-faced black birds called common gallinules. As the sun dipped below the horizon, we drove right into the heart of the rugged Peruvian Andes. Jagged granite spires reached high into the sky, framing the altiplano with their formidable towers.

Our hopes of getting the kayaks wet faded as the hours ticked by. After repeated backtracking to correct wrong turns, we finally arrived at our destination. There was less than an hour of daylight left, so we decided to wait until the next day to begin our expedition. Our disappointment quickly faded as we set up camp in one of the most beautiful places any of us had ever seen. Lago Acucocha is a large clear lake surrounded by granite mountains that seem to jut straight out of the water. The water's brilliant blue added welcome color to the otherwise imposing gray landscape. The one part of the lake that was not enclosed by rock was its outlet—soon to be our own initiation into this vast journey. I looked in the outlet's direction, the only place where the view wasn't blocked by mountains, at the high plains and down into the valley below. I was only seeing the tiniest fraction of this river we were to descend and tried to consider the enormity of what we were about to attempt.

Don and I, the group's two Spanish speakers, and Midge, the expedition leader, headed over to the little house near the lake to explain what we were doing, ask permission to camp, and present the owners with a bottle of Pisco. We talked with Marilena, who owns the land with her husband, Matteo. She was gracious and worried we would be cold. We assured this slightly stooped woman of probably sixty years, clad head to toe in wool skirts, jackets, and a hat, that we had plenty of high-tech cold-weather gear. She looked at us through cataract-clouded eyes, the result of spending her life outside in the sun, and talked admiringly about her animals and her land. We were struck by how kind and content this woman seemed despite having none of the amenities that Americans have come to believe are necessary for happiness.

We cooked dinner with water from the Amazon River's source, then lay back watching shooting stars traverse the high-altitude night sky. The stars shone brighter on that dark patch of earth than anywhere I'd previously seen. We had cell service, which is surprisingly common in remote parts of South America, so I called my parents to let them know we were on the verge of starting our journey.

That night our water bottles froze solid inside our tents. Lago Acucocha sits at nearly 15,000 feet above sea level, and even when the sun is out, it is constantly cold. I slept in my sleeping bag liner, inside my sleeping bag, inside my bivy sack, inside my tent wearing every single piece of clothing I had brought, including dry pants, and still had a cold night. Marilena had been right to worry.

In the morning, probably guessing that we were unprepared despite our assurances to the contrary, Marilena brought us hot coffee and home-baked bread. Imagining how annoyed we'd be if strangers were camped out in our own backyards, we were deeply impressed by this act of generosity. I have no doubt that everything is in short supply in their household. Her willingness to share what little they had was a display of true compassion and was in stark contrast to the anxious thoughts of the Asháninka that had consumed me for the past forty-eight hours.

On July 28, 2013, the sun crested the mountains and thawed us out along with the frost encrusting the landscape. We ate the first of many dehydrated breakfasts and started preparing for the true start of the expedition. At 10:20 A.M. we pushed our kayaks into Lago Acucocha and started kayaking toward its far shore. As we paddled in the brilliant sunshine and frigid air, we savored our beautiful surroundings. The water was so clear you could easily see twenty feet down. A condor flew by and quickly disappeared. An hour and a half later, we reached the far side of the lake where we stashed our kayaks and started hiking. Even at 14,830 feet, we needed to climb higher to locate the source of the Amazon.

We plodded up the mountainside through the wind, cold, and thin air, searching for the highest place where surface water flowed. Don said he felt like he'd been given a tiny plastic straw to breathe through, but we had to plod upward. We spread out, at times crawling, individually examining every tiny trickle that ran through the tundra-like grass. The absurdity of our situation was not lost on us. Gasping for air and feeling the oxygen-deprived burn of our muscles, we pressed on, knowing that from this moment forward, our lives had a singular focus—kayaking the entirety of the Amazon. And to do that, we had to begin at the beginning.

We pinpointed the spot we could agree upon as the start of our expedition after a few hours of hiking. It was a sinkhole with enough water at the bottom to create some sort of perceptible flow. We checked in with our SPOT devices—GPS satellite messaging systems*—high-fived, snapped some photos, and began the hike back down to our kayaks with the satisfaction of having achieved our first goal.

Our paddle back across the lake was fraught with strong winds and waves whipping at our cold hands and faces. It took over two hours to paddle back and, when we arrived, Midge broke out a flask of expensive Lagavulin Scotch to celebrate the beginning of the expedition. The boys, suffering headaches and nausea from the altitude, could only manage the tiniest of sips, leaving me to happily down the rest. Though I've often blamed my high-elevation childhood for my stunted growth, I suppose there are some perks to being raised at 8,000 feet.

I lay awake anticipating our simple yet daunting task as we settled back into our inadequate sleeping equipment that night. It was refreshing to have

---

* SPOT is a satellite GPS messenger that allows users to notify friends and family of their GPS position and status, mark waypoints, track progress on Google Maps, and notify rescue officials in an emergency.

a clear goal for the next five months. Don's and my lives had drastically changed just before the expedition began. Thanks to my inability to get along with the man who bought our adventure kayaking business, Don and I were without a home, without jobs, and without a purpose. It didn't do wonders for our relationship, either. Consequently, a lot hinged on the Amazon trip.

Would this trip be the fresh start in life I was craving? The words from the naysayers and my own doubts about my chosen path in life swirled in my brain. My love of running Class V whitewater collided with the hypothetical fear of dying alone in a government-run assisted living home, impoverished to boot. But hell, if I could become the first woman to kayak the Amazon, surely I'd be able to tackle whatever the future could throw at me.

Chapter 5

DON VERSUS MIDGE—ROUND ONE

"Good luck dodging turds."
—Bill Gaechter

JULY 29, 2013
DAY 2 OF THE EXPEDITION

Vehicle problems delayed our morning start on day two of the expedition—our first day of truly paddling down the river. We couldn't very well abandon our support team with a broken down rental van, so I jogged to the nearest town to look for help. I found the owner of the one vehicle in town. He was extremely friendly and eager to help and roused a couple of friends. Three of us pushed the car around the field a few times before the owner could roll-start it. My participation in this spectacle caused all the schoolkids to leave their classroom and come outside to laugh at me. Then the guys grabbed jumper cables and gas to spray on the carburetor, and we drove up to where our van was broken down. We got the van running again and off its precarious perch near the bank of the lake, thanks wholly to the goodwill of these strangers.

After getting the van running again, we put our kayaks into the waters of Lago Acucocha exactly where we had taken them out the day before. Midge was obsessed, to the point of being maniacal, with making sure we kayaked every inch of the river. No, I take that back, every millimeter of the river—an inch is too large a measurement. Plus, it's American. Each day after kayaking, Midge marked the point on his GPS ensuring that the next day we would start not one single degree off the previous day's ending coordinates. Meanwhile, Don and I took meticulous mental notes—just in case the GPS failed—about exactly which blade of grass we had crushed with our kayaks upon exiting and which pebble we had to be just upstream of while launching.

We paddled just three hundred feet to the outlet of the lake where there was an irrigation head gate. We ceremoniously got out of our kayaks once again, made the short portage around the gate, and got back into what was now a tiny stream barely wider than our kayaks. We made our way down this stream alternately careening uncontrollably into small boulders and pushing our way over shallows. Each of our actions drew cheers from the small group of kids who had amassed and were running along the banks chasing us.

Our stream—the humble beginnings of the mighty Amazon River—was funneled into an irrigation ditch just downstream of the lake. At first it was a grassy ditch, then a concrete one. Paddling through the ditch was quite pleasant, strange as it was. There was just enough water to float our kayaks. It was like being enclosed safely in a bowling lane with the kid bumpers inflated in the gutters to ensure that the ball (or the kayaker) couldn't get out of the lane (or ditch). This enclosure allowed us to float along, enjoy the scenery, and only occasionally pay attention to the periodic barbed wire fence or low bridge spanning the canal. Then, all too abruptly, our ditch ended and spilled out into a wonderful, but more or less unpaddle-able wetland. This was great for bird watching—we pushed our boats painstakingly slowly past Chilean flamingos, Junin grebes, and Puna ibis—but not at all good for kayaking. We failed to reach our meetup point with West and Lizet before it got dark.

West, having done this trip one year prior, had a list of mileages he had done, maps with potential road access points to the river, and ideas on where we should try to meet up each night. The idea was that Don, Midge, and I could paddle empty boats and, without being weighted down with all our food and equipment, could make better time. West and Lizet would drive the van, which carried all our gear, to the appointed meetup spots. Along the way, they did some sightseeing and West took photos and video and further documented the river for his own purposes.

After the initial ten days, the road access points would become few and far between. At this point, West and Lizet would fly home, leaving us to our own devices. But not before West introduced us to the contacts he'd made during his 2012 expedition. He introduced us to a man named Lucho in Huancayo who owned a pickup truck and was willing to drive ridiculously long distances—sometimes as long as sixteen hours—to do food drops for us (for the right price, of course). Once our river left the road, we'd have a series of three- to eight-day stretches in remote parts of the Mantaro canyon. Here, we'd have to carry everything we needed until we reached the next resupply point, where we'd wait for Lucho.

Because of our three-hour delay with the van not starting, we anticipated that we might fail to meet our designated meetup point with West and Lizet later that day, so we packed a bare minimum of camping gear into our kayaks. West warned us that there could be a fair amount of carrying the kayaks this day so we didn't want to weigh ourselves down too much.

We regretted not bringing more as it got dark and our GPS told us we were still a long way from where West and Lizet sat in the warm comfort of the minivan. We each had a bivy sack and sleeping bag, no camp clothes, no stove, and no real food, just a couple of emergency energy bars. We were still well over 14,000 feet in elevation and it was freezing cold. Ice was already beginning to coat our paddling gear and we had a good laugh at the irony of being so cold over a delicious dinner of one Clif Bar each.

We bedded down among the rocks and grass, and settled in for the frigid night ahead. I spent the night shivering in my wet paddling gear, tucked completely inside my sleeping bag. I alternated between near-suffocation with my head inside the bag for warmth versus the chillier, but more oxygen-filled option of having my head outside. Despite temperatures again dipping low enough to freeze the non-flowing water around us, we all made it through the ten hours of darkness with good attitudes mostly intact. We awoke at dawn to a discouragingly thick fog that refused to burn off. The sun had been a savior the past two mornings, but the fog was resilient this day.

Slowly we climbed out of our bivy sacks. We were already fully dressed for the river, as we had no other clothes to change into, but we had one problem—our canvas and neoprene river shoes and socks, which we had taken off before bed, were frozen solid. Impossible to put on in their icebound, unmalleable state, we spent the next ten minutes each engaged in personal combat with our shoes. I pulled mine into my sleeping bag and tried to cuddle them into pliability, with no luck. I just did not have enough body heat left. I stomped on them trying to break the ice off, but this technique failed me, too. I could not bring myself to resort to the desperate measures Midge and Don were taking so eventually I just forced them onto my feet drawing blood in both my numb fingers and toes during the process.

Don peed on his shoes in the hopes that the warm liquid would loosen them up but even this was not enough. Don and Midge ended up immersing their shoes in the almost frozen river, thawing them enough to pull back on. I had imagined suffering through all sorts of hardships on this trip, but frozen shoes were not a problem I had considered.

We got moving once the heroic act of putting on our shoes was completed. The river here was too wide and shallow to float a kayak, so we walked along it or in it—until our feet were too numb to take it anymore—and dragged our kayaks through the riverbed. West hiked up from his camping spot to walk with us and try to boost our morale by telling us the van wasn't terribly far away. Around 10:00 A.M., two hours into our slog, the sun finally broke through the fog. The warmth felt great, but it was not enough, we were all chilled to the bone. By 11:00 A.M., we reached the van, stripped off all our wet clothing, pulled on dry, warm gear, and ate our first meal in nearly twenty-four hours. One benefit to suffering is that it lends incredible significance to the simple things in life—being warm, dry, and fed.

We spent the next four days walking the Amazon with intermittent bouts of paddling. We dutifully dragged our kayaks either in the river or just alongside it as not to detour from the river bed.* We made the rest of our meetup points without problem. On the fifth day, we reached the Upamayo Dam on the edge of Lago Junin and found them releasing two thousand cubic feet per second (cfs)—we had more than enough water to float our boats and we were kayakers again. Everyone was happy, for now.

---

* Midge walked in the river the entire way believing it was the truest course he could take. Don and I both walked along the shore at times, but we never cut corners or strayed far from the bank of the river.

We were a compact group of three. We had a variety of sources of outside support, but on the river, it was just Don, Midge, and me. We had proven our ability to withstand long periods of time in each other's company. Over many trips to Ecuador, including two recent trips where Midge stayed on for a month at a time, and a two-week paddling trip to California where Midge did his first two overnight kayaking trips, we had lived and kayaked in close proximity to one another. Really, we had managed to do quite well in the art of still enjoying one another's company after prolonged, intense exposure. Despite our group's cohesion, I knew that things wouldn't always go well on an expedition this long. I just didn't expect things to get bad so quickly.

∽

AUGUST 3, 2013
DAY 7 OF THE EXPEDITION

We'd had a successful day on the river, logging plenty of miles, and had completed a sketchy, and apparently illegal, portage around our second dam of the trip—the Malpaso Dam. We forced ourselves and our kayaks through a tiny hole that someone else had cut in the concertina wire.

West and Lizet would be heading home soon, and we were enjoying socializing with them while we could. From a cheerful camp that evening, I called a woman named Deborah McLauchlan, our "fixer," on the satellite phone to check on the progress of the sea kayak delivery to Puerto Ene (the beginning of the flatwater). Without any telephone pleasantries—satellite phones are expensive, after all—Deborah opened with this news: "There's been a problem. Another vehicle got hijacked by narco-traffickers near Quinua."

How could anything bad happen near a town called Quinua? I wondered at the cute name of the town.

Deborah continued, ever practical. "I suggest you hire my friend Omar to ride the bus with your kayaks to Puerto Ene. The bus is much less likely to get hijacked. The robbers won't believe there is anything of value on there."

Midge hired Deborah to be what he called "the fixer" for the expedition. Aside from a twelve-year stint in London, Deborah has spent the majority of her life in Lima, Peru. As a media production professional, she had contacts throughout Peru and agreed to help us with many of the logistical hurdles of the expedition. This wasn't her usual line of work, but Midge was willing to pay good money, and Deborah was excited about working on a different kind of production. One of her jobs was to help us import the sea kayaks into Peru—dealing with customs and imports in a country where you don't understand all the laws can be a daunting process, and having Deborah take care of this was a huge burden off our minds. Then, Deborah was tasked with getting the sea kayaks delivered to Puerto Ene.

Deborah also helped us in communications with dam engineers, with our support boats farther down the river, and with securing our permission letters from the various indigenous groups whose land we traveled through. She was an invaluable asset to the expedition, there is no doubt about that, but she often had strange ideas that seemed more tailored to her and her friends' benefit than to the good of the expedition. We spent a lot of time arguing back and forth over our plans and hers.

I hung up the phone, and a discussion ensued on our beach camp about how best to move the three sea kayaks three hundred miles on a notoriously dangerous route from Lima, over the Andes, and down to the remote, steamy jungle town of Puerto Ene. Not that any of us were experts in moving seventeen-foot sea kayaks along sketchy dirt roads, but we all had plenty of ideas, and Deborah's suggestion was not top among them. As some polite consideration of the bus idea was happening among Don, Midge, and me, West suddenly shouted, "Fuck the bus! I will drive the sea kayaks there myself."

We stopped our discussion. I could see the look of "Oh honey, you can't be serious" on Lizet's face, but she didn't verbalize this. What West was proposing would be about the most conspicuous way possible to move the kayaks through this reportedly dangerous road—a white guy behind the wheel of a minivan with three brightly colored and very long sea kayaks strapped to the roof.

"What about the drug traffickers, the murders, the robberies, and everything else that Deborah is worried about?" I asked.

"I can deal with them, don't worry. Plus, I'll bring Cesar along, he can help me."

Cesar Pena was someone Midge hired to accompany us through Peru's Red Zone. Cesar had been West Hansen's Red Zone liaison the year before, most likely making him Peru's only Red Zone "tour guide." Tourism does not exist in the Red Zone. In fact, every tourist-related document issued by Peru's government pertaining to the Red Zone is some form of a warning not to go there, citing myriad dangers stemming mostly from Peru's civil war of the 1980s and 1990s. Cesar's unique experience made him the natural choice for our expedition as well. In West's mind, he was also perfectly suited for the cross-country trip with the sea kayaks. But Cesar wasn't with us and had no idea that West was volunteering him for this job.

The plan, once we got to where the flatwater started, was to hire a motorized canoe to carry our gear and Cesar through the Red Zone, where two of the last six tourists who traveled this area were murdered and one other was shot, but survived. Having both Cesar, who lived along the Amazon River in Iquitos, Peru—which gave him local knowledge and cachet—and eventually an Asháninka boat driver, were things that we hoped would help our chances of surviving this dangerous area. One problem was that we still hadn't found a way to transport Cesar from his home in Iquitos to the confluence of the Mantaro and Apurímac rivers. This confluence area is far removed from good roads and most modes of transport in Peru and is not easy to reach. The most logical way Cesar had come up with so far to get to Puerto Ene was to travel upriver by boat, but this would probably take a couple of weeks and would require many short hops with Cesar having to switch boats at least fifteen times. West's proposal was solving two problems at once.

Cesar would fly from Iquitos to Lima, a direct and cheap flight. West would drive Lizet back to Lima to catch her scheduled flight home. West would change his flight and extend his stay in Peru another ten days. Then West, Cesar, and the sea kayaks would make the epic road trip to the jungle. It all seemed perfectly reasonable except that it was a needlessly complicated solution to our problem. Subtract all the changing of schedules and flying and driving all around Peru, and just let Deborah do her thing with Omar and the bus and we have another perfectly fine solution with a lot fewer headaches for a lot fewer people.

Don is a meticulous decision-maker. He weighs every single option thoroughly before settling on one. Whether this stems from his hatred of making decisions or his obsessive attention to detail is still up for debate. He is regularly annoyed by the quick decision-makers of the world (me). Don expressed his opposition to West's plan: it would be expensive (new plane ticket for West to extend his stay, a plane ticket for Cesar to Lima), it would use up a seemingly unconscionable amount of West's and Cesar's time, and put them in an unnecessary risky position. And it would piss off Deborah. Every time we didn't follow her plan, no matter if it was sensible or unrealistic, she got offended and never tried to hide her disgust. Plus, she was convinced the kayaks couldn't possibly be transported on the roof of a small minivan. She claimed the road was so narrow and winding that kayaks would most certainly hit the cliff walls on one of the tight turns. She had never driven the road, either.

Don made some good arguments against West's plan, but after repeating them two or three times in slightly different ways, Midge lost patience and cut Don off mid-sentence. Physically turning his back on Don to accentuate the point, Midge plainly stated, "Good plan, West. Let's make it happen."

What Don didn't verbalize at the time was that Midge had been growing increasingly anxious for West's time with us to come to an end. We were all incredibly grateful for everything that West and Lizet had done for us, but we were ready to simplify things, be done trying to reach meetup points with land support, and for it to be just our team of three focused on nothing but downriver progress. Don was having a hard time reconciling what Midge was saying to us in private versus what he was saying to West now.

Midge's decision wasn't the problem. In a way, it was refreshing to see him take charge and decide on a plan. The problem was his rudeness. It would have been easy for him to sit for another thirty seconds to let Don finish. We didn't have anywhere to go, it was getting dark and we couldn't go kayaking until the morning. Or he could have acknowledged the validity of Don's points and then stated his decision in a nicer, more diplomatic fashion. Midge was tired, hungry, and cold, and apparently wanted to attend to these needs as quickly as possible—getting this decision out of the way would allow him to focus on getting comfortable.

Midge is also a self-proclaimed "emotional dummy," lacking in all "emotional intelligence" and, from his point of view, completely blameless for these things because he'd diagnosed himself as falling somewhere on the Asperger's spectrum; which in this case struck me as a convenient excuse for being a jerk.

Don got up and went to our tent. I wanted to give him a little time to cool off and to realize it wasn't that big of a deal, it was just Midge being grumpy and rude, so I stayed outside with Midge, West, and Lizet.

Don was not overly thrilled about the expedition from the beginning. Even though it had been his idea to accompany Midge, I don't think he was ever fully sold on the plan. It was just an example of him considering all possibilities, one of which was me being disappointed if we left Midge after the whitewater. When the original plan was for Don and me to only kayak the whitewater with Midge, the possibility of doing the entire river had not even crossed my mind. Being one of the annoying, hasty decision-makers, I was fine with the first plan, until Don mentioned the possibility of the full river. Then, I just as quickly decided that doing the whole Amazon sounded good. From Don's perspective, he was stuck on this river precisely because of my flippant decision-making.

Don wondered why he was kayaking the Amazon. I was doing it to become the first woman to kayak the Amazon and to try to make peace with the recurring nagging questions within myself. Midge was doing it to lend some meaning to his life. Don was seemingly doing it to fill an empty time slot, or, as he claims, because I forced him. Let's not forget that this empty time slot was my fault.

✑

Don, Larry Vermeeren, and I sold our business, Small World Adventures, in the spring of 2012. The company wasn't for sale, but a client named Guy who was looking to drastically change his life as a hardware engineer for Apple offered to buy it. He was looking to escape conventional life and get back to his passion, which was kayaking. Being opportunistic—in an incredulous, wow!, someone-actually-wants-to-buy-this-business kind of way—we sold to him with the idea of working for him for the foreseeable future. We all still enjoyed our careers and weren't necessarily looking to change, but this was a convenient out for when that day came.

In the spring of 2013 we had just completed year one of a two-year contract, and part of the work was to mentor the new owner. During the last weeks of the season, I asked Guy what he thought about Don and me paddling the Amazon with Midge and breaching our duties to him—we would miss the first two months of the kayaking season, and I would shirk my office duties during the summer. His reaction was supportive and positive. Stating what an amazing opportunity the trip was, he gave us his blessing to leave, saying it would be a good jump start on his taking over the office and getting more involved in the guiding aspect of the business.

The 2012–2013 season had been a trying one. It was the busiest season for Small World Adventures on record, we were short-staffed, and we were trying to train Guy as the new owner. Adding to an already stressful situation, Guy had very different approaches to business, life, and communication than I did, and he and I were butting heads at every turn. While I focused on giving our clients the kayaking vacation of a lifetime, as we promised on our website, Guy tried to wrap his ultra-intelligent engineer's brain around the fast-paced decision-making and logistical gymnastics necessary for a whitewater kayaking business operating in the volatile South American rainforests. One overnight deluge could flood the rivers and derail the itinerary just as easily as indigenous people blocking the roads in protest against a government that wanted to drill for oil in their ancestral lands.

We were on different wavelengths and we were incapable of having an honest, open conversation. We drifted through the season not trusting each other, not learning from each other, and barely communicating on any level. The tension was so palpable that it bubbled right under the surface, constantly threatening to overflow.

I wrote Guy a five-page email sharing with him my feelings and opinions about how things were going and what I thought about his plans for moving forward with the business when I got back to the United States that March. It wasn't the nicest email I'd ever written, but it was honest. When I called him on the appointed hour to discuss my email, the conversation went like this:

"Darcy, I've been thinking about it, and I think you and Don should go to the Amazon and not come back."

Long pause while I processed this sentence. Surely, I thought, he's not suggesting that he hopes we die on the trip—the email wasn't *that* mean. So he must mean that he doesn't want us to come back to Small World Adventures?

Finally I managed to get out, "So, you are firing us?"

Another long pause. "Yes. Yes, I guess I am."

Then he said he saw someone he knew, said he had to go, and hung up on me.

I was dumbstruck. I had sought Don and Larry's permission before I sent the email because I was slightly worried something like this might happen. But deep down I didn't believe he would do it. But he had.

I broke the news to Don. My email had gotten me, and by extension Don, fired.

We were completely lost. Don had been with Small World Adventures since 1995, and I'd been there since 2001. It was our livelihood and consumed most of our lives. It was our identity. Our hotel room in Ecuador was the closest thing to a home either of us had ever had during our adult lives. Everything we knew and were comfortable with was gone.

I had forced myself to think of this Amazon trip as a nice chunk of time during which Don and I could gather our thoughts and come up with a plan for the next stage of our lives. Don wasn't yet ready for this. He was still mad about getting fired and right now he was mad about being on this expedition with Midge disrespecting him.

≈

Midge eventually turned to me and said, "Uh oh, do you think I pissed him off?"

"Yes, I do."

"Should I go apologize?"

Then Midge proceeded with his Asperger's explanation, reminding me that he was ill-equipped when it came to interpersonal relationships.

"Remember," he said, "I'm lacking the ability to understand social cues."

I continued to listen to his excuses as he explained to me that he couldn't be held accountable for being a jackass because he couldn't help himself, or rather, didn't know any better.

I dreaded getting stuck in the middle on this expedition. Midge, analytical as he was, had spent a lot of time studying various expeditions throughout history. He'd found that three team members was the ideal number for success on a long expedition. Teams of just two people, or more than three people, tended to fail because of internal fighting and the breaking apart of the expedition. I knew Midge had taken a risk inviting a couple to come along with him, and I had vowed to myself when I signed on not to side with Don just because he was my boyfriend. If Don deserved to be sided with, then yes, I would be on his side. But if Midge deserved to be sided with, I would do my best to be objective and see that. I didn't anticipate already becoming the middle woman on day seven, but there I was. Trying to be as diplomatic yet as reserved and distant as possible, I said, "Why don't you just let him chill out for a few minutes, then you can apologize."

"Good plan."

We sat in silence for thirty seconds and then Midge followed up. "But what do I apologize for?"

I left him and crawled into the tent where Don greeted me with, "I'm quitting the expedition."

"What? You can't be serious, it's day seven."

"I can't deal with him being such an asshole and treating me this way."

"Well, I can understand that, but it wasn't *that* bad. He was just tired and was being a jerk. I know it's not okay, but surely it's something we can get past?"

The interaction, while rude on Midge's part, hadn't seemed like that big a deal to me. But it had obviously seared some deep part of Don's brain and set off a strong emotional reaction.

Still not grasping what was going on with Don, I added, "Don, we've come so far, you can't quit now."

Yeah, I said that.

After only seven days and a hard-earned, painfully slow thirty miles, it felt like I'd devoted myself to the expedition. Even though we'd accomplished laughably little of what we'd set out to do, I realized that I had become emotionally invested in this crazy idea.

"Plus, now this expedition is really starting to mean something to me," I added.

Suddenly, becoming the first woman to kayak the Amazon had taken ahold of me. It began so suddenly and unintentionally, but now that we had started the journey, it was consuming me. Paddling through the Red

Zone was still a major problem in my mind, but I was strangely beginning to feel that it was now worth the risk—or at least I was deceiving myself into believing that it wasn't really all that dangerous. After all, every single person we had met so far had been incredibly nice. How could there be murderous people lurking just a few hundred miles away? Although we were only a week into the trip, I knew that I had to do everything I could to finish.

But Don, my boyfriend of ten years and my best friend, wanted to go home—not that home meant anything specific to Don at this point. I wanted to finish and didn't want a little spat between Don and Midge to stop me. I figured if I was going to fail, it was going to be because I was murdered at the hands of narco-traffickers or eaten alive by a school of hungry piranhas. I didn't think it would be because the boys were fighting.

A little while later Midge walked by our tent and, in an amazingly condescending voice offered, "Don, I'm very sorry. I did not mean to make you angry."

It didn't help.

"That is exactly what I'm talking about, Darcy. He won't listen to me, he doesn't respect me, and even his apology is totally disingenuous. On top of all that, just earlier today he was telling me how excited he was for West to leave the expedition, now he's got him staying another ten days."

I couldn't argue with these points, but I tried to be as positive as possible.

"Of course Midge respects you. You are his whitewater kayaking hero, and he knows there is no way he can do this trip without you."

"Yeah, but why should I risk my life getting him through the whitewater all the while knowing that when it comes to anything non-whitewater-related, he's not going to care what I have to say? Knowing that he won't let me be part of the decision-making? What's in it for me? You can become the first woman to kayak the Amazon, it's Midge's life dream to kayak the Amazon, but I don't even know why I'm here."

I understood all the points Don was making, and I honestly didn't have good rebuttals. If he didn't want to be there, why should he stay? Except that I didn't want him to leave.

"I can't force you stay, Don, and I don't want you to be miserable for the next five months, but if you leave, what am I going to do? I really don't want to quit. And I really don't want you to go back without me."

It seemed to Don that I was choosing to stay on the river with Midge over going back to the United States with him, although this wasn't true. The reality was simply me choosing to not quit on day seven.

After talking it through, Don agreed to stay, but offered this caveat: "I'm now doing this exclusively for you, to get *you* to the ocean. I don't care if Midge makes it to the Atlantic or not."

I went to bed hoping that Don could find a way to happily spend the next five months kayaking down the Amazon with Midge. As far as Midge's survival was concerned, this needed to happen. We were about to enter the most difficult whitewater of the trip, and Midge was about to rely on Don and me more than he had ever had to rely on another person in his entire life.

☙

AUGUST 4, 2013
DAY 8 OF THE EXPEDITION

We woke up and kayaked through the town of La Oroya, a town depressing enough to match our mood. We spent the better part of the day trying not to let the water touch our faces—more specifically trying not to let it touch our lips. We strained our necks turning forcefully away from the splashes, and we paddled ineffectively as we attempted to block our faces with our hands, arms, and even paddle blades. We flailed about like this as if our lives depended on it. We discussed the idea that it really could be life or death if we swallowed the wrong water molecule. Or at least it could mean the difference between health and violent gastrointestinal problems.

Part of our concerns stemmed from the PVC piping that originated in people's bathrooms and ended in midair over the river. Human effluent would come cascading through the pipes and plop ingloriously into the river below. It's an efficient way to move the poop from the toilet to the river without bothering with expensive or complicated sewage treatment systems, but we did not appreciate the ingenuity.

Cinder block apartment slums lined both sides of the river, and nothing about them was ornamental. We saw just the bare necessities of a frame, roof, and walls to keep the building standing more or less straight and to keep out the elements. They were three stories high, each story with its own pipe. The apartments butted right up against the river, but unlike the riverfront properties we were used to, there were no windows facing the water, just pipes. The terrifying openings confronted us from both sides. Only the middle of the river was out of the landing zone.

Aside from flying poop, there were also heavy metals in the river. We paddled past what instantly struck Don as a Soviet-era Russian chairlift. The conveyor carried the heavy metals and their less useful counterparts, the rocks they were found in, across the river, up a steep mountain to some unseen destination. The contraption looked like an old, single-person chairlift and was antiquated, bleak, drab, and gray.

The transporter serviced the La Oroya smelter. Doe Run Peru processed copper, zinc, and lead without concern for the environmental and human damage they were causing. The town of La Oroya made the Blacksmith Institute's list of the world's top ten most polluted places, ranking as a "Killer Community."[*] The Blacksmith Institute found that 99 percent of the children under six years old in La Oroya had blood lead levels three times higher than what is accepted by the World Health Organization.[**]

The people of La Oroya carry on as normal Peruvians despite this silent killer in their town. In the breaks between the ghetto apartments, we kayaked past backyard barbecues where entire pigs were roasting over pit fires on the shore of the river. We watched kids pick up plastic trash from the streets and make a game of who could throw it farthest into the Mantaro. We saw a woman cleaning a chicken and throwing all the guts into the river. We watched in disgust, our first world sensibilities assaulted, when a dump truck pulled up to the river's edge and dumped an entire load of trash into the water.

The stench from the crap, the guts, the trash, and the mine were too much to handle. We put our nose plugs on—designed to keep water out in

---

[*]   "The Top 10 Worst Polluted Places," Blacksmith Institute Online, 2007, http://www
       .blacksmithinstitute.org/the-2007-top-ten-of-worst-polluted-places.html, accessed
       January 18, 2015.
[**]   Bryan Walsh, "The World's Most Polluted Places," *Time* online, 2007, http://content.time
       .com/time/specials/2007/article/0,28804,1661031_1661028_1661020,00.html, accessed
       January 18, 2015.

rough rapids—so we at least didn't have to smell the place any longer. Some water droplets made it through our defenses and landed on our faces. They dried in the wind and our faces felt crusty. Just as I was imagining what exactly the crust on my face was made of, we passed intact human feces floating in the river. I later wrote about this to my family from an Internet café in Huancayo, and my dad jumped at the opportunity for a joke. He would sign off each subsequent email with one of his new catchphrases:

"Good luck dodging turds."

"Thanks for the blow by blow, poop by poop, description."

Later, we kayaked past an ironic sign painted onto the river rocks by the owner of the smelter that read, DON'T CONTAMINATE THE RIO MANTARO.

People often talk about the pollution in the Amazon down in the main river, which pales in comparison to the pollution we witnessed on the Mantaro River. The principal reason that the pollution lessened as we traveled down the river is dilution. There is simply so much water down there that the crap, the trash, the mining debris, and everything else gets lost in what people call the "river sea," becoming tiny particles engulfed in a massive body of water. Higher up, though, these particles dominate the river. It is more appropriate to imagine flowing sewage, trash, and mine tailings than it is to imagine molecules of two hydrogens and one oxygen.

I had no choice but to deal with the crap on my face as best I could. It was just one of many unpleasantries that I had to endure on this expedition. If I had given myself the option to stop, La Oroya would have been cause to do so. But I had deleted quitting as an option in my mind. I wondered what was going through Don's head. Just last night he desperately wanted to quit the expedition, and the next day he was forced to endure La Oroya. I imagined his hatred for Midge was at an all-time high and that his dismay at being my boyfriend was up there as well. He mostly kept to himself and paddled on with some stubborn resolve that surely was fueled by anger.

We did not allow ourselves to eat when we got to camp. We each did three shots of what claimed to be tequila, but that tasted more like rubbing alcohol. We imagined this toxic beverage would kill whatever human shit, pig gut, lead-leaden river molecules we had ingested. It seemed to work. No one got sick, and it was a group activity that perhaps helped us to rebuild our bond.

Chapter 6

LIES AND HALF-TRUTHS

"It's hard to fail, but it is worse never to have tried to succeed."
—Theodore Roosevelt

W hen running hard whitewater, teamwork is imperative, especially for those members of the group whose skills may be on the edge of just good enough for the whitewater being run. That was Midge. He was the weak link in our paddling group and he knew it. That is why he invited Don and me along in the first place.

Midge started being strangely nice to Don after their fight. I'm not sure if it was his subconscious realization of how desperately he needed Don if he hoped to survive the whitewater, or if he eventually ended up feeling badly for the way he treated Don. Either way, it was a smart move. Three days after their fight, we dropped into our first difficult whitewater canyon of the trip and there was, as I had hoped, an incredible transformation in Don. He was no longer the angry man who hated Midge to the core and who wanted to quit the expedition. He was a badass kayaker helping a lesser kayaker in need.

Kayaking is what makes Don tick and, now that we were paddling difficult whitewater, he was happily leading rapids, coaxing Midge through the most challenging parts, offering him encouraging words or tips on how to best make it through this rapid or that, and telling me to slow down because Midge was getting tired.

West drove Lizet back to Lima to catch her flight home and to pick up Cesar, who had flown from Iquitos to join West on his crazy kayak delivery mission. Don, Midge, and I navigated a difficult big-water section of river upstream of the Tablachaca Dam. Then we paddled across the reservoir and spent a forced two days in relative luxury at the dam workers' camp while waiting for them to start releasing enough water to allow us to paddle the section between the dam and the next significant tributary—the Rio Huarpa. The plan was to meet up with West and Cesar a couple days' paddle downstream of the dam. From there, they could drive along the river with us for one or two more days before the road would leave the river for good.

They sold Lay's Original Potato Chips at the dam camp, which had become my number one most anticipated luxury on this expedition. The grease and the calories from fat were a welcome, even desperately craved addition to the monotony of my dehydrated lentils, black beans, and garbanzos. I'd buy a bag, or three, pulverize the chips inside the bag and then dump the crumby mess into my rehydrated meals. It was like a little slice of my newly formed and very perverse idea of heaven.

Around 8:00 A.M. on our second morning at the camp, a worker came knocking at our door telling us to get going and load all our gear into his truck. He was going to drive us to the base of the dam which would, he said, start releasing water around 10:00 A.M. and he didn't want us to miss this opportunity. We excitedly piled boats and camping gear into his truck and got ready to paddle. We bobbed around in our kayaks in the small pool at the base of the dam for three hours watching the looming concrete wall behind us for any signs of water starting to flow over it. At 1:00 P.M. the dam keeper called us on the satellite phone saying, "We'll start the release in three hours. Maybe."

There was some water—maybe 100 cfs—coming down one of the spillways and there was enough water in the river below to float our boats. It wasn't exactly what you'd call paddling, but we decided to try it. We pushed, paddled, swore, and hiked our way down the riverbed until about

4:00 P.M. We found a place to stop and I got out the satellite phone to call the dam keeper back and ask him about the release.

"It's happening in one more hour," he enthusiastically told me.

I'm such a sucker for believing people so I happily passed on this news to Don and Midge. We were getting tired, hungry, and thirsty and wanted to rest and eat while we waited. We only had one problem. The water quality of La Oroya was fresh in our minds. Granted, much of that water got trapped behind the Tablachaca Dam, but some of it was leaking around, and that would be the water we'd have to use to drink and cook our meals. Plus, garbage lined the river bank and an odd smell emanated from the water we now found ourselves in. We debated the dilemma of going hungry and getting dehydrated versus trusting in our water purification processes.

I'm not sure if we so much made a rational decision or if our hunger and thirst won out. Don got out his gravity filter and filled the bag with the dirty river water. The gravity filter uses, well, gravity, to force water through a filter, theoretically only allowing water molecules to pass through while stopping heavy metals, chemicals, and other water impurities (read: poo). Still, we decided to play it safe and, after the water passed through the gravity filter, we also put it in our water bottles and then nuked it with our UV filter. The Ultra Violet light, we hoped, would kill anything that had snuck past the gravity filter. Then we drank, still slightly in fear. The rest we boiled with our JetBoil stove and put into our dehydrated meals.

Some curious local kids hiked down the steep river valley to investigate us. They brought along slingshots and let us play with them. I'm not sure if they left more impressed by the crazy river running feat we were trying to accomplish or by how pathetically bad we were at shooting the slingshots. Even the four-year-old shook his head at me in disgust.

We sat and waited until dark, at which point I called the dam keeper once more.

"Tomorrow," he told me, "you'll get your water."

We got our water, and we also got to a point where West, Cesar, and our support van could no longer meet us at the end of each day. We were about to drop into the deepest canyon of the Mantaro and we wouldn't see a public road again for many days. We wouldn't see Cesar again for ten or eleven days. Through West's friend in Huancayo, we'd arranged a food drop at a dam worker's camp in the early part of the canyon and then again at the last road access in the whitewater section which was about three days above the flatwater where we hoped to meet Cesar and our sea kayaks. This would allow us to cut our longest self-supported stint down to eight days.

The logistics on this trip were nearly as mind-numbing as the idea of paddling over 4,000 miles. Lucho from Huancayo would first drive to the Tablachaca water reentry camp— Campo Armiño—to drop off our food. Later, he would drive eight hours one way with our prepacked box full of dehydrated meals to meet us at what the local's called the Chiqua Bridge in the middle of nowhere along the Mantaro River. Meanwhile, West and Cesar would drive our sea kayaks multiple days through the sinuous canyon country of Peru eventually dropping the kayaks and Cesar off in the steaming jungle. While all this was happening, the three of us would do our best to survive the whitewater in the deep canyons of the Mantaro River.

Saying goodbye to West, Cesar, and our van helped us act more like a team than any of us would have guessed. Once it was just the three of us again, we relied on each other for survival, for help, and for entertainment. It seemed everyone had forgotten that Midge was an asshole, that Don wanted to quit the expedition, and that I selfishly wanted him to stay.

But leaving our van behind brought up another set of worries. We now had to carry everything we needed in our kayaks—food, tent, stove, gas, clothes, passport, money, satellite phone, headlamp, toothbrush, sleeping bag, sleeping pad, permission letters, first aid kit, extra paddles, rescue gear, gunshot wound treatment kits, everything. Fitting all this gear and food into a little whitewater kayak is no small feat and requires an impressive coordination of efficient spatial conception, tight packaging, and brute force in the form of stomping and stuffing the gear into two tiny compartments in the back of the kayak. Not to mention that you lose an incredible amount of maneuverability when you load your boat down. It is a delicate balance between bringing enough gear to survive and deal with unexpected situations, but not overpacking to the point where your kayak becomes so unmanageable that you can no longer deal with the most challenging whitewater.

An hour before we left West and Cesar, Deborah delivered the news via satellite phone that the Peruvian military had killed two high-ranking Shining

Path rebels just seven miles from where we were camped. The Shining Path is the revolutionary group at the center of Peru's bloody civil war. This had happened last night while we slept on the banks of the river. It was good news, I suppose. It meant that this particular threat had been eliminated. This did, however, alert us to the fact that the Shining Path did still exist in Peru. We had hoped that everything we read about the current activity level of the Shining Path was exaggerated, but this incident reminded us that it was something we needed to take seriously.

⁑

Abimael Guzmán founded the Shining Path, or *Sendero Luminoso*, late in 1969, but the movement didn't come to public attention until the early 1980s, when Peru's military allowed the country to hold its first elections in over a decade. The Shining Path's first act of war was burning ballot boxes on the eve of the 1980 presidential election. Guzmán was a philosophy professor at a university in Ayacucho, and he looked more the part of intellectual philosopher than cold-blooded murderer with his round face, thick glasses, and graying beard. He was a Maoist intellectual with a vision for a peasant uprising, dictatorship of the poor, and a world revolution.

Guzmán traveled to China frequently to study the theories of Mao Zedong, and he believed that the historical struggles of the masses around the world had culminated in that moment in Peru when the Shining Path could spur such a revolution. He uttered enthralling and violent battle cries such as, "We need to put the noose around the neck of imperialism and the reactionaries . . . and garrote them by the throat."* His message was seductive to Peru's many poor and marginalized people.

Peru's central government was adept at ignoring its remote villages, and the Shining Path was equally cunning in their ability to fill this void. With no government oversight, help, or even any enforcement of the country's laws, many Peruvian farmers were living so far removed—physically and

---

* Steve J. Stern, *Shining and Other Paths: War and Society in Peru, 1980–1995* (Durham, N.C. and London: Duke University Press, 1998), 461. Translated from the Guzmán speech given on April 19, 1980, to call the start of the armed struggle.

ideologically—from Lima that they hardly considered themselves Peruvian. Many were descendants of indigenous people, making their alienation from the state that much more profound. The Shining Path stepped in and offered leadership, support, and the rule of law.

Many of the poor people in the highlands did side with the Shining Path in the early stages of the movement. Shining Path leaders offered the people more land, more animals, and a redistribution of wealth in exchange for participation in the movement. Everyone wanted these things. However, it quickly became apparent that there was a disconnect between what the Shining Path leaders said and what they did. The people were not enacting, nor even seeing any positive change. Rather, they were being forced to house and feed the rebels. After a couple of years of having Shining Path rebels drain their resources with no improvement in the quality of life for the highland farmers—no one was getting more land, more animals, or a redistribution of wealth—people started to get impatient with the movement.

This impatience was met with violence, and the Shining Path began to turn on the very people it was supposed to be helping. As the Shining Path became more violent, the people rebelled more openly, forming militias to combat out of control Shining Path leaders, which only made the Shining Path react with a newfound ruthlessness and terror.

The military and the central government in Lima had successfully ignored the Shining Path movement in its early days. They were unsettled in 1980 when Shining Path rebels hung dead dogs from lampposts in Lima with signs that read, DENG XIAOPING, SON OF A BITCH.* But the reference to the leader who took over after Mao's death and who led China through market-economy reforms was confusing and didn't make sense to most people, so they didn't give it much attention. The Shining Path was trying to use their displeasure at the direction Deng Xiaoping was taking China after Mao's death—namely opening it up and working toward globalization—as a warning to their own government, but few people in Lima understood this. They only saw the act for its face value, a gruesome and strange way to try to get people's attention.

What finally prompted the government's involvement was an event in 1983, when the Shining Path systematically murdered seventy unsuspecting

---

* Carlos Ivan Degregori, *Shining Path of Peru* (New York: Palgrave Macmillan, 1994), 52.

peasants in a small town named Lucanamarca. The massacre was in retaliation for the murder of a Shining Path leader who was terrorizing the town. A local militia group had carried out the murder in an attempt to protect their town. The killings, especially of innocent people, were meant to show the people and, more importantly, the Peruvian government, that the Shining Path was, as their leader Guzmán put it, "a hard bone to chew."* The military finally acquiesced.

When the Peruvian military got involved it only worsened things for Peru's poor. The military killed arbitrarily, often unable to discern between friend or enemy. As one scholar put it, "the armed forces converted the countryside of Ayacucho into an Armageddon."**

Peru's Truth and Reconciliation Commission, tasked with assessing the true damage caused by the Shining Path, found that of the 69,000 people who were murdered or who disappeared, the Shining Path was responsible for 54 percent, the Peruvian military for 44.5 percent, and a small fringe movement called the Túpac Amaru Revolutionary Movement was responsible for the remaining 1.5 percent. While the Shining Path movement is little known outside of South America, it was an unforgettable bloodbath for many of Peru's most vulnerable people. The Shining Path still exists today, but is only a tiny skeleton of what it used to be. The primary operations of the Shining Path now happen in remote jungle areas and involve the lucrative drug trade.

⁂

AUGUST 12, 2013
DAY 16 OF THE EXPEDITION

Deborah's warning came through the line of the satellite phone, "Be extra careful down there in case there is a backlash against the killings."

Be extra careful?

---

*   Degregori, *Shining Path of Peru*, 149.

**   Carlos Ivan Degregori, *How Difficult It Is to Be God: Shining Path's Politics of War in Peru, 1980–1999* (Madison: University of Wisconsin Press, 2012), 22.

How exactly are three foreign kayakers at the bottom of a bare-rock river canyon with only spindly cacti to hide behind going to be inconspicuous and extra careful? How were we to tell the difference between your average highland farmer and one who is getting ready to partake in whatever backlash there may be?

The sun crested the mountains just as I hung up with Deborah and the sandflies came out in droves so thick that they obscured the air and forced me to give my full attention to something besides the Shining Path. The little bloodsuckers relentlessly attacked any exposed skin—they aren't particular; an earlobe or a fingertip serves equally well as a leg, arm, or butt cheek.

My method for mentally dealing with the threats of this expedition seemed to be putting off the worry until I was standing face-to-face with whatever it was I was supposed to be worrying about. This is not, perhaps, the smartest way to approach things, but it seemed to me the only option for not driving myself insane with apprehension. So I forgot about the Shining Path and instead concentrated on stuffing all my gear into my kayak as quickly as possible so I could get off that gnat-infested beach.

Our first few days after leaving West and Cesar consisted of fun, but not overly taxing whitewater. The scenery was incredible as we descended farther into one of the deepest canyons in the world. The ever-changing geology left us guessing at the magnitude of the tectonic forces that created this place. One minute the rock would be lying flat just as it was deposited layer by layer. Then we would paddle around the corner to find parts of it had been thrust upward and now rested at a 90° angle to its flat counterpart just upstream. Entire sections of the mountains we paddled through had broken off and fallen from their original homes. In some cases, the river had been diverted and flowed through these relatively new clefts.

We encountered a family of goat herders who were ferrying their goats across the river on a homemade raft they'd constructed out of eight logs tied together with rope. Midge was very confused when my rapid description ended with, "Watch out for the rafting goats at the bottom." The herders had hiked six hours to get to the river from their home and said it would be another day and half to get out to the road where they could sell their goats.

Our only annoyance during those otherwise peaceful days was paddling past the Cobriza copper mine where the project managers were hell-
bent on giving us gifts and using us as subjects in their pro-environment
campaign, as if to say, "We aren't totally killing the environment—see,
we are friendly to kayakers!" After being stopped by a radio-wielding
worker, we sat by the side of the river for an hour waiting for the managers
to arrive. This publicity stunt on the part of the mine was arranged by
Deborah and was presented to us in a way that made us feel we had no
choice but to comply. When they finally showed up, we were presented
with wrapped gifts—handwoven Alpaca wool hats and scarves for all
three of us.

I wanted to say, "While we desperately needed these three weeks ago
when temperatures never got much above 40° Fahrenheit, now that the
weather is quite hot and the predominant fauna is cactus, we probably don't
need them so much . . . but thanks anyway for giving us yet more crap to
carry in our kayaks!" I'm sure they would have loved it when I threw in,
"Plus I'm a vegan so I don't even wear wool!"

The hats and scarves were a nice gesture, and I was being a grumpy jerk,
so instead of verbalizing my thoughts, I graciously accepted the gifts. We
put them on and posed for photos while we sweated under the wool. I am
still waiting to see our images on a Peruvian billboard that brags, "See,
these international kayakers like mining, so it must be good for you and
for the environment!"

After the mine incident, we dropped into a canyon made up of some of
the most beautiful polished white granite I've ever seen. The rapids were
challenging but all runnable, and we had one of our best days of kayaking
yet. After five hours, this canyon opened up and we found ourselves at
Campo Armiño, a workers' camp for the water reentry point from the
Tablachaca Dam. Tablachaca is the largest dam on the Mantaro and supplies 30 percent of Peru's energy. The diversion tunnel cuts thirteen miles
through a mountain and the water is put back into the river at the power
generation station. Campo Armiño is the last real civilization, if you
can call it that, before the Mantaro meets the Apurímac to form the Rio
Ene—also known as the end of the whitewater. Lucho called us at 2 A.M.
telling us he was waiting outside the main gate with our box of food. Don

then dragged himself out of bed and jogged up to the gate in his boxer shorts to retrieve it.

We were stopped by a worker and told we must exit the river and we knew why—not far downstream was the construction site for yet another dam, the Cerro del Aguila hydro project. The Cerro del Aguila, or Mountain of the Eagle, project is the final phase of Peru's Mantaro River major hydropower scheme. We had met with engineers in Lima about coordinating our passage through the construction zone. Since we'd started kayaking, Deborah had traded many emails with the head engineer and the project manager, both of whom had warned us (more like tried to dissuade us) about paddling through the construction zone because they felt it was simply too dangerous. Although Campo Armino is government owned and Cerro del Aguila is private, the two groups had apparently been talking, and the guys at Armino agreed to put us up for the night while they made a plan with the Cerro del Aguila folks to ensure our safe passage the next day.

A nice, but overly talkative man named Hugo Chavez—not the infamous Chavez of Venezuela—who claimed to be an engineer from the new Cerro del Aguila project told us it was five miles downriver to the new dam site. He said he had told the workers there to stop blasting at 11:00 A.M. the next day. Assuming the gradient would be similar to what we experienced the day before—steep, but not crazy, creating nice Class IV to V whitewater—we decided we would leave at 9:00 A.M. to time our arrival appropriately.

About ten minutes after leaving Campo Armino, we paddled past the tunnel and water reentry point from the Tablachaca Dam. The tunnels were running at nearly full capacity and added another 3,200 cfs (i.e., a *lot* of water) to our already substantial flow. We immediately felt the push and had to adjust our paddling style accordingly. Instead of easily maneuvering our kayaks around boulders and into and out of plentiful eddies, we were now fighting what felt like an out of control torrent. It took much longer to move from one side of the river to the other and required five times the effort from the day before. Not long after the added water, the gradient steepened significantly and we knew we would never make the five miles in the two hours we had allotted. Within twenty-five minutes of getting on the river, we had already portaged once and had been forced to scout nearly every rapid we encountered. It was our first truly difficult Class V section of the trip.

We reached the construction site after an exhausting two and a half hours. We made three portages and had scouted 90 percent of the rapids we encountered. While the previous days had held hard whitewater, it was lower volume, slower, and the river had lots of eddies that made things a lot easier on us.

We arrived at the construction site and saw many workers standing on the shore looking for us. We all waved at each other in greeting and they motioned for us to go on past. There was a bridge over the river here and two jumbled but fairly straightforward rapids. The bottom rapid had a large and difficult-to-see hole. Don was out in front and saw it at the last minute and frantically pointed Midge and me away from it. I made it past the hole, but Midge was absorbed in his own thoughts and did not notice Don frenetically pointing him around the hole.

Midge dropped directly into the maw and gave the workers an impressive show when his bright blue eight-foot kayak was violently flipped end over end, cartwheeling in a chaotic blur of color. Midge eventually pulled his spray skirt and swam into the turbulent river. Fortunately, there was a big eddy before the next big rapid and Don and I were able to get Midge, his boat, and his paddle to safety. The workers all cheered for us as we got Midge back into his kayak. If they didn't already think kayaking was a crazy sport, they surely did now.

We couldn't believe how easy it was to get through the Cerro del Aguila construction zone, Midge's swim notwithstanding. After all the warnings from the project managers about how dangerous it would be—and hearing West's stories about the rock fall and blasting he'd experienced there the year before—we had expected much worse. We decided that construction must have progressed enough that the all the horror stories we'd heard were a thing of the past, and we paddled away, happy to have overcome another major obstacle in our journey to the sea.

Maybe this really isn't going to be as bad as those days in Lima made me believe, I cautiously thought to myself.

The rapids stayed consistently hard after the construction site. It was late afternoon and we were all tired, but we could not find any place to camp. The cliff walls either came straight up out of the river offering no shore whatsoever, or when there was shore, it was a jumble of boulders with little or no flat ground.

A massive rapid finally forced us to stop. The camp wasn't ideal—it was a big gravel bar without much sand or flat ground, but it was a far better option than running the big rapid in fading daylight with equally fading energy.

We boiled water and prepared our dehydrated meals as two men moved their cows across a suspension bridge high above the rapid. The bridge was probably three hundred feet above the river with two cables as the foundation and two more cables for handrails. A hodgepodge of spindly sticks and twigs had been tied perpendicularly to the foundation cables. The men, one pulling a rope tied around the cow's head and the other pushing on the cow's butt, painstakingly crossed three cows, one at time. Depending on the stubbornness of the cow, each crossing took ten to thirty minutes and they worked well into the darkness. Life moves at a different pace when you are many days' walk from the nearest road.

We were worried about being spotted by the men—you know, in case they were part of the backlash against the military who killed the Shining Path insurgents and decided they could take out their anger on kayakers. But the men never noticed us, they were so engrossed in their problematic task.

I walked down the bank as far as possible to scout the rapid while my Backpacker's Pantry Louisiana Red Beans & Rice rehydrated itself. A quarter of the way into the rapid, our gravel bar gave way to a bedrock wall that ran the length of the rapid and supported the cow bridge. The rapid was huge. It would be the biggest we had run so far and it was dangerous, with the flow of the left half of the river coursing into a nasty sieve where the river flowed underneath a pile of massive boulders. (Remember that large-scale spaghetti strainer that water can fit through but a kayaker cannot?)

I took my time scouting.

It would be possible to portage. We would have to do some rope work to get up and around the bedrock canyon and it looked like that would take two to three hours. I thought I'd better look harder at the rapid; running it would be much easier and much more efficient than portaging. I did eventually find a line that I thought was manageable for everyone on the team.

I respected Don and Midge's desire to lay down while the food cooked. They expressed their fatigue through a strong desire to stop moving, while my exhaustion manifested itself in a profound restlessness. Even though we wouldn't be kayaking this rapid until the morning, I somehow felt a need to figure it out now.

It is a tough position to be in when you are the only one to scout a rapid. You must weigh the difficulty of each move in the rapid against the team's ability. You need to factor in the dangers of a missed line, the possibility of rescue, and the feasibility and difficulty of the portage. Many people don't realize how much of a team sport kayaking is. It seems so individual since everyone is in charge of their own craft, but in moments like these, my scouting and decision-making skills could mean life or death for Don and Midge. We all put a huge amount of trust in each other on the river. It's a bond that is rarely replicated in normal life situations.

I ultimately decided we could to it. As long as everyone made the entry move, the line I picked was far enough away from the dangerous left side of the rapid that even if things went wrong—if someone flipped over or was not exactly where they should be—the river would push all parts to the right side, the safe side, of the river. I went back and told the boys we were good to go.

"Okay, boys, this rapid is huge, but it is runnable and we should do it—"

Midge interrupted, "Can we portage?"

"Yes, but it would take the better part of tomorrow. See that cliff over there?" I asked pointing across the river. "We will have to walk upstream, ferry across the river, go up and over that cliff, and then rappel down the other side." I added, with exaggerated seriousness, "Midge, you can do this, it's what you trained for ten years to be able to do. The crux is one move." Midge was getting his head around the idea of running this rapid so I continued. "Midge you will use those sparrow-knee arms of yours"—this is how he described his own biceps—"and paddle like hell through that wave there," I said, pointing to a fifteen-foot-tall breaking wave. "Once you break through that, the current will deliver you to where you need to be."

I told the guys we could recap in the morning and that we should just eat dinner and get some rest.

I didn't sleep much that night as I was replaying the information about the Cerro del Aguila dam site in my head. Somehow it didn't all add up with the experience we'd had yesterday. My mind flashed back to the meeting with Señor Rojas, the chief engineer for Electroperu. He clearly told us there were *two* construction zones for the Cerro del Aguila project. Electroperu owned the three dams that already existed on the Mantaro River—dams whose reservoirs we'd already paddled through and whose concrete structures we'd already climbed over. Rojas told us that a private company—Kallpa Generación S.A.—was building a fourth dam, Cerro del Aguila, down in the canyon section of the river. He explained that they had two construction sites, one for the dam itself, and one for the turbines where the power would be generated and the water put back into the river. Yesterday, we had asked Hugo Chavez, who claimed to be a top engineer for the project, repeatedly about the second site, but he maintained that there was only one. Maybe Señor Rojas had been wrong—it wasn't his company after all—but something did not quite feel right. My gut feeling told me Rojas was more trustworthy than Chavez.

West had spoken of a deep canyon—thousands of feet deep—with rock blasting going on far above their heads. They never did see the source of the blasting. He had been there one year prior when construction had just begun and we assumed the blasting he experienced was for the road they needed to build to gain access to the dam site. The construction site we passed the day before had been too easy. It was in a comparatively wide-open place, and the canyon walls were not tight or tall. We could not see how rock fall from above could have been an issue for West.

My strongest reason for concern was that West had given me the GPS coordinates from the place where he had experienced the blasting and his coordinates lay downstream of us. Although Hugo Chavez held fast to his position that West's coordinates were wrong and did not coincide with his dam site, I had my doubts.

In the morning, I asked the guys, "Do you guys remember Señor Rojas telling us there were two construction sites for the new dam? I think we should call Deborah and ask her to find out one way or the other before we leave camp."

"Don't call Deborah!" Midge interjected in a panic-stricken voice. "If there is another construction site, we don't want them to know we are coming. They will either stop us from paddling through or will want to invite us to their camp for presents, water, and tuna fish, you know how much I hate tuna fish, Darcy."

"Midge," I said, "don't you remember West's stories of the dynamiting, the rock fall, and the horrendous day they spent somewhere in here?"

"What if he was wrong?" Midge countered.

He had a point. We'd found a few instances where West's memories and perceptions of the river (especially when it came to whitewater) were different from the realities we found on our own descent. Plus, we knew the canyon they were prepping for the dam would undoubtedly look different now that one more year of their dynamite work had passed. Still, I didn't think West would just make up stories about hiding in a cave waiting for the dynamiting and rock fall to stop. West had been meticulous in his note-keeping and in his recording of GPS waypoints, and I had a feeling he was right about this one. I needed to find out. I wasn't really in the mood to die this early because we were too stupid or stubborn to do our homework.

"And what if they tell us we can't paddle through?" Midge asked.

It had become clear that Midge would either successfully kayak the Amazon from source to sea, or he would die trying. That is how deep the obsession ran.

"That is a risk we will just have to take. In my opinion, it's preferable to dying," I said, getting out the satellite phone and searching for a signal. I could see the disapproval on Midge's face. I dialed Deborah's number. Midge could die in the construction zone if he wanted, but I wasn't going to join him if I could help it.

I managed to get a satellite signal and reached Deborah. I passed West's GPS coordinates along to her and she told me she would call the Cerro del Aguila office in Lima to see what she could find out. Our plan was to eat breakfast and then call her back before we shoved off.

Midge again tried to convince me not to call Deborah back, he was so afraid they would block our passage and ruin his complete Amazon descent.

My desire not to die under a pile of dynamited rock debris won out in the end and, after a small fight, I insisted on calling Deborah back.

She confirmed that there was, in fact, a second construction site downstream, and that it coincided with West's GPS coordinates. The people in the main Lima office again tried to persuade Deborah to dissuade us from paddling through and then issued this written warning: "Regarding our telephone conversation I'd like to reiterate our opposition to the passing of the kayak expedition along our works area. We are having explosions in areas close to the river at our dam and plan areas, and rocks could fall over the kayakers. It is mandatory for us that in our area of works no fatalities occur. Regards. Jorge Mónaco, Project Manager at Cerro del Aguila."

Well, I thought, if it's mandatory that no one dies, we should be good to go, right?

Right?

Deborah, ever persuasive, insisted that we must paddle through their construction zone and got them to agree to stop blasting. She told us the construction itself spanned a three-mile distance and wanted to know how long it would take us to paddle that far. Put another way, she wanted to know for how long she should ask them to stop with their dynamite work.

She relayed that Jorge had explained that nearly two thousand workers were employed there and that any stoppage of work would be costly because he would have to pay people to stand around while we paddled through. They had agreed to stop, but wanted to stop for as short a time as possible to minimize their losses. Adjusting our time frame from the day before, we estimated two and a half hours to cover the three miles. We had done five miles of very difficult whitewater in two and a half hours the day before and so figured this was a safe guess. Deborah relayed the information, and told us to call her again when we were within sight of the construction.

Bewildered at the fact that Hugo Chavez had adamantly denied the existence of a second construction site, we packed our boats and wondered what exactly we would find downstream. As we got into our kayaks, we redirected our attention to our immediate concern, the enormous rapid that we would start our day with.

I explained the line to Don and Midge and they were both game to follow me through. As we set off—me first, Midge second, Don third—I felt confident in my decision of telling them to run, but a little voice in the far recesses of my brain whispered, "I hope I've read the water correctly." I quickly pushed this doubt out of my mind and snapped my neoprene spray skirt onto the cockpit of my kayak.

Equally important as physical aptitude when running hard whitewater is the ability to keep your mental state balanced. The most technically solid paddler in the world can make dire mistakes if they panic or even just slightly lose their mental composure. It's difficult, especially in Class V whitewater, not to let doubt or fear dictate your decision-making. Unfortunately, this happens all the time to even the best paddlers; it's an extremely difficult problem to overcome.

The ability to distinguish between rational thoughts and panicked thoughts driven by fear can mean the difference between success and failure, even life and death, when it comes to making sound choices on the river. Managing doubts, fears, and uncertainty in a way that still allows for rational decision-making requires years of training and a Zen-like attitude when standing at the brink of a gigantic rapid. When done properly, it feels like you are standing outside of yourself, detached and making decisions for a stranger, not for yourself anymore.

The three of us checked in with each other one last time, making sure everyone was ready. I had succeeded in pushing the uncertainty from my mind, and I was focused. We dropped into the heart of the rapid. Everyone easily made it through the lead-in. I looked back at Midge and, with a nod of my head, told him this was the meat of the rapid and pointed right. We would need to paddle through a constriction and then a series of towering fifteen-foot breaking waves in order to escape the current that was careening toward the sieve on the left bank. The waves were even bigger than they looked from my perch on shore, but they were not nearly as violent as I expected. Paddling like mad, we all made it past the breaking point with the leftward flowing current. Once safe from the pull of that current, the only goal was to stay upright through the conflicting currents, waves, and boils in the final pinch of the rapid. Midge flipped over, but as I predicted, the water helped him get to safety.

He rolled up and shouted, "Now I'm awake!"

We sat in the calm water below the rapid letting the adrenaline course through our veins and relishing the high. There is no feeling in the world like inserting yourself into the raging, violent chaos of a Class V rapid and emerging out the other side alive and happy. This is the addictive part of kayaking. Living on the brink of death, whether it be for a few seconds, a day, or a week, will make you feel more alive than anything else.

We stared directly up at the cow bridge and celebrated an exciting start to our day. Then we paddled around the great bend of the Mantaro where the river turns 180°, doubling back on itself, first flowing northwest, then changing course and heading southeast. It was pure bedrock in there and utterly stunning with walls so closed in that they often blocked out the sun.

Part of the reason that this area was selected for the Cerro del Aguila hydro project is that it lies in the Villa Azul Batholiths. The river has carved its way all the way down to the solid bedrock, so solid that it has no problem providing "competent rock quality" for the new dam.* Earthquakes are common in this tectonically active part of Peru, so when building a dam and subsequent powerhouse, you want to make sure to build on solid rock, not boulder piles that will continually shift and move.

What bedrock usually means for kayakers is an intimidating, walled-in river bed. Since the river had long since stripped away any boulders and other debris that normally clutter the shore of a river, we were down to the essential building blocks, the sheer-walled, smooth rock canyon that is the foundation for the Rio Mantaro. Getting out of your kayak to look at a rapid is often difficult to impossible. The lack of a typical rock-filled shore where kayakers can usually scout or portage difficult rapids raises the stakes. We got lucky in this part of the Mantaro—the rapids were difficult but all runnable.

Our GPS showed that we were getting close to West's coordinates, the location where he had heard the blasting. We were all on the lookout for signs of construction. Eventually we turned a corner and spotted a tiny

---

* Selim M. Sayah, Sante Bonanni, and A. Fenelli, "Cerro del Aguila 510 MW Hydro Plant: The New Peruvian Challenge," May 18, 2014, http://www.researchgate.net/publication /262379686_Cerro_del_guila_510_MW_hydro_plant_The_new_Peruvian_challenge, accessed August 3, 2015.

building on top of the cliff easily five hundred feet above us. It was hard to make out the details, but it did not look like your typical Andean house constructed of stones and mud; it looked more like a metal construction trailer. Assuming that the trailer must be associated with the dam site, we pulled over and got out the satellite phone.

Finding a signal was difficult at the bottom of this canyon. I finally found a patch of sky wide enough to get a few bars and called Deborah. I told her we had arrived, and she said she would make the final call to the operators at the site and that I should call her back in ten minutes. We ate some food and relaxed in the sun as we waited. When I called Deborah back, she said that blasting had stopped and we got the okay to head downstream.

"You have two and half hours to get through there," Deborah reminded me just before she hung up.

Chapter 7

MIDGE'S ESCAPE

"One cannot answer for his courage when he has never been in danger."

—François de La Rochefoucauld

AUGUST 16, 2013
DAY 20 OF THE EXPEDITION

Three and a half hours of being one mistake away from death—or worse, one stick of dynamite away from death—had left all our nerves frayed and our energy sapped. I was horrified, but not terribly surprised, when Midge narrowly missed the must-make move above the gigantic hydraulic. When he fell into the huge hole in the rapid Don and I had scouted for him, I was certain he wasn't going to make it out of that canyon alive. All I could do was concentrate on my own line through the rapid and leave Midge to fight for his life.

We all knew that paddling into the Cerro del Aguila construction zone against the advice and wishes of the company was a risk. Somehow, we'd convinced ourselves that it was a reasonable risk, one in which we would prevail. The reality of the canyon was far worse than any of us expected. The rapids—more man-made than natural—were gigantic and dangerous and the portage routes held the constant threat of rock fall and landslides on the unstable slopes.

I was scared, but I was also angry. How could I have gotten myself into this position? Didn't I know better than to take this big of a risk? My plan to use the Amazon expedition as a springboard into a normal life was completely stupid and useless if I died in the process. But both my fear and anger were quickly superseded by an immediate need to focus on my own survival, so that's what I did.

I watched from twenty feet away as Midge fell into the corner of the hole and his eight-foot kayak immediately started looping end over end in the powerful hydraulic. Frantically, I got Don's attention by blowing my whistle to alert him to what was happening. Using hand signals, Don indicated from his position in the eddy that what lay around the corner was bad. We should not chase Midge farther downstream.

I safely passed the hole and, as I did, I looked down into its gaping mouth and shuddered. The turbulent backwash of the hole was tossing Midge around as if he were a child's tiny toy. I had roughly two seconds between seeing Midge drop into the hole and the moment when I needed to paddle away from the rock fall cascading down the cliff directly above me. It's amazing how quickly the mind works under intense pressure. In those seconds, I managed to consider the following:

Assess the hole.

Terrible, gigantic, I'm not even sure if Don could paddle his way out of that thing, and he is the hole-escape master. Midge is screwed.

Assess the Rescue.

This rapid is just as pushy as we expected; Don is telling me not to go downstream past his eddy. Am I willing to risk it to try to save Midge once he swims out of his kayak?

The nightmarish rapids that we had already portaged upstream flashed through my mind. Assuming they had to be similar downstream, I thought, No, I can't risk it, I will almost certainly die, too. Better one person dead than two. My mom will be really pissed at me if I die.

This is it. I am about to watch Midge die.

Time was up.

I had to turn and paddle away from Midge and away from the rock fall. My first emotion after realizing that Midge was about to die was guilt. Not sadness, regret, or anger. Just guilt that my last interaction with Midge had been one of impatience and irritation. Why couldn't I have been nicer, more understanding?

As I was pondering all this, the hydraulic did the unthinkable and spit Midge out into the downriver current at just the moment it should have sucked him into its depths. For some reason, the water did not do what I thought it would do, what Don thought it would do, what it should have done. Instead, it released Midge, spat him out down the river, free and safe from its grasp. I was unsure if shock or relief was the tingling feeling I had throughout my body, but when I saw his upside-down kayak floating down the rest of the rapid, my brain kicked into action again.

"Roll up, roll up!" I yelled uselessly, since he would never be able to hear me with his head underneath the water. But his mind was telling him the same thing and he did roll up. He was enthusiastically greeted by our cheers; and then Don and I both screamed at him to catch the eddy.

He did.

Once at the bottom of the rapid, we all sighed a huge breath of relief. What I was sure was going to be a tragedy had reversed course. We sat in our kayaks, bobbing around the eddy catching our breath and being thankful that we were all alive and together. I have no idea what went through Midge's mind as he dropped into that hole, but when I saw his kayak cartwheeling in the hydraulic, I was certain he would swim and subsequently drown when Don and I weren't able to chase him downstream. The fact that the three of us were safely sitting in the eddy together took a while to sink into my brain, which was still busy trying to figure out what we were going to tell Rachel—Midge's girlfriend—about the circumstances of his death.

Midge would later say that years of Don drilling him with hole escape tactics had probably saved his life. His mind was replaying Don's words— "don't get established in the hole" and "use your momentum"—as the massive hydraulic tossed him around.

Peering around the corner, we saw another enormous rapid, but none of us cared, because we also saw that there was a break in the cliff walls. Things momentarily opened up and, on the downstream end of this break, we saw a road leading to a stick-and-cable footbridge that crossed the river. Beyond the foot bridge, the river canyoned up again, but all signs of construction faded. I believed if we could make it past that footbridge, roughly half a mile away, that we would be safe from the construction zone. For the first time in hours, I was hopeful that we'd make it out of there alive.

We felt so good about our situation that we even let Midge have a long snack break. He deserved it after what he'd been through. While the boys snacked, I decided to go look at the next series of rapids. What I saw as I climbed the boulders dampened whatever relief I had felt moments before. We had at least three more gigantic rapids before we got to the bridge and what finally did look like the end of the work zone. I was exhausted, too, and just wanted to be finished with this day and with the relentless whitewater and claustrophobic canyon. Every muscle in my body, down to the little connective tissues between my ribs, ached and pleaded for mercy. My mind was buzzing, replaying each rapid, each step, and trying to erase images of what would have happened in an alternate reality where the hole didn't let Midge go, where I tripped on a portage, or where Don missed an eddy above an unrunnable rapid.

I had to muster whatever reserves I had left and keep moving. I walked down the rocky river bank and found us a sneak line through the first rapid. This line led us to another eddy where we could climb out of our kayaks and scout the next two rapids. After snack time was over, we got back into our boats, and I led Don and Midge through the sneak.

"Jesus, Darcy, you call that a sneak?" Don growled at the bottom of the rapid.

Midge was too tired to admonish me, but I could see the disapproval in his eyes.

They were right, the "sneak" was a big Class IV/V line, but it kept us safely out of the main channel of the river where things were substantially worse. We all had to shift our definition of what was reasonable in order to make it through this day.

In the eddy below the sneak, Midge opted to rest while Don and I scouted—a fine idea, we all agreed. This time, scouting required climbing the steep bank three hundred feet up to the level of the road and then walking down to the footbridge to fully assess the two rapids and what lay below the bridge. Looking at the overall scene from up near the bridge,

Don and I thought about how incredibly lucky Midge was that he got out of that hole and stayed in his kayak. Had Midge swam from his kayak, he undoubtedly would have swum three more Class V/VI rapids and well past the footbridge we now stood on. Rescue in the short space between that rapid and the next one that we snuck would have been extremely difficult, probably impossible. Swimming those next three rapids would likely have killed him.

Don and I walked around on the newly built road and walked all the way to the bridge. It was not a road bridge, but a replica of the cow bridge we had seen earlier that morning. It felt like an eternity ago that we were celebrating our breakfast rapid, staring up at that bridge, but only eight hours had passed since that moment. It had taken us four and a half hours of kayaking Class IV and V rapids to get to the start of the construction zone. We'd spent another three and half hours battling our way down through the construction to get where we were now, still not out of the work zone. In those eight hours we had been transformed. Now instead of cheering, excited people, we were beaten down, exhausted, and weary.

I took a few steps out onto the sticks that made up the bridge's floor, hoping to lighten my outlook as well as to gain a little more empathy for the cows. Although there were handrail cables, the bridge was sketchy and after getting only a quarter of the way across I turned back and ran for the safety of the shore. Don emulated my experience but added a little commentary as he retreated, shouting, "Fuck that!" For the first time in hours we laughed.

I looked downstream and relief flooded my body. The view was fantastic: a sheer-walled bedrock canyon continued downstream as far as we could see, but the rapids were Class IV at most. Best of all, there was no hint of construction. It was a beautiful, natural river, and it could not have looked better. If we could just make it through the last two big rapids, we would be free from the construction zone.

Don and I decided that we all needed to portage the rapid below where Midge was waiting. It was runnable, but too big and too dangerous for the three of us in our worn-down condition. We would portage as far as possible until the cliff walls would force us back into our boats before the third and final big rapid. This rapid was also runnable, and was steep and big, but at least it was relatively short. More importantly, there was no reasonable way to portage it. We hiked back to where Midge and our kayaks were waiting and explained the plan. We all got back into our kayaks and ferried across to the river left side where we would start our portage down the bank.

We grunted and swore, but spoke little as we made slow progress. The boulders were big pickup truck–sized affairs and hauling our heavy boats across them—often times we had to pass the kayaks up and over the giant boulders—took a long time. As if shoving an eighty-pound kayak up over my head to Midge wasn't strenuous enough, when it slipped and landed on my shin I thought my head might explode with all the stress of the day. It boiled to the surface and nearly erupted as a fit of rage before I closed my eyes, fought back the tears, and forced myself to calm down.

Fatigued, we reached the end of our portage route and prepared to seal launch into the final colossal rapid. With no good place to get back into our kayaks at river level, we found a huge, flat boulder sitting about fifteen feet above the water. We got into our kayaks on this rock, and then pushed and scooched our way to the edge until we finally slid off, free-falling for a couple of seconds before splashing into the water.

Plopping one by one into the churning rapid, the powerful current immediately swept our kayaks downstream, making the transition from falling through the air to rushing down the river a violent one. Shortly after our entry point, the river squeezed into the entrance of the bedrock canyon, hurtling us downriver through huge compression waves that broke against our faces and slammed against our chests. We all struggled with the pushy water and the towering waves, but we emerged at the bottom upright and smiling. We high-fived, hugged awkwardly in our kayaks, and marveled at our luck of having come through that canyon in one piece.

We paddled through the pleasant Class IV canyon and began looking for a camp. After close to forty minutes the canyon opened up, but the rapids got hard again. We knew we needed the next possible camp; we were all too beaten down to take on more hard rapids. We found a tiny little beach comprised of sand and pebbles.

We pulled our kayaks onto the beach and collapsed in exhaustion. Our camp was not spectacular, a tiny slab of sand, maybe five feet by fifteen feet and then a patch of rough gravel above that. The lack of real estate was compensated for by the gargantuan granite boulders that constituted our patio. Rounded over millennia by the relentless force of water, they were smooth to the touch, feeling more like a polished writing desk than a hard piece of granite. The fact was that none of us really cared what our camp looked like. We were free from the fear and uncertainty of what we named the "dam canyon." We were safe and we could relax.

We had kayaked for ten hours that day and were in the construction zone for almost five hours, which means we moved at about half a mile per hour through the dam site. We all agreed that no other day of kayaking, or any other life experience, even came close to that one in terms of danger and stress. Sitting on the smooth rocks feeling the pain and fatigue in every part of our bodies, Don spoke first. "Midge, amazing job today, man. I was fucking scared and pushed by those rapids, and I can't even begin to imagine how you felt, but you pulled it off. Hat's off to you."

"Thanks, man," Midge replied, and then we went back to our silent and private contemplation of the events of the day.

All I could say was, "I am so glad I am sitting on this beach with both of you right now," and then I started doing camp chores.

We purified water and set up camp. It was hard to get our bodies back in motion, but it was getting dark and we had some things to do. We considered just going to bed without dinner—we were all so exhausted that the task of boiling water and waiting twenty minutes for our food to rehydrate seemed like far too much effort. Plus, it was nearly dark and we could just crawl into our tents and pass out. But some deep sense told us we must replenish the calories we'd burned for whatever tomorrow may bring.

We ate in silence, listening to the sound of the river coursing past our camp. It was at once soothing and disquieting. The river was so peaceful here, but just a few miles upstream it was a chaotic, raging torrent indifferent to the little humans trying to kayak down it. After dinner, I laid down on my sleeping pad and thought about what might have happened if we had listened to Hugo Chavez's declarations that there was only one construction site. What if I hadn't called Deborah and she hadn't gotten the workers to stop their dynamite? I shuddered and then pushed the thought out of my mind.

∽

AUGUST 17, 2013
DAY 21 OF THE EXPEDITION

I woke up feeling the terror and effort of yesterday in every muscle of my body. But I faced the river with a renewed sense of hope since I knew I'd be dealing with natural forces rather than with human desires to control those forces. Immediately after leaving camp we encountered a two-mile-long series of stacked rapids with relentless holes, undercut boulders, and challenging routes. Although the river was unnerving, there were no construction workers waiting impatiently to use dynamite on the cliffs above our heads, there were no dump trucks in the river, and now we could take as long as we wanted on any given portage or scout. We let Midge have snack breaks as often as he wanted.

I sat down on the rocks and looked around during one of the scouts. I allowed myself to forget the burden of time frames or progress, and I simply tried to appreciate the geological wonder surrounding me. We were supposed to be worried about narco-traffickers hiding in these remote stretches of the Mantaro River, and we were getting close to the Red Zone—a place I still wasn't sure I wanted to paddle through—but on that rock, none of it seemed real enough to worry about. I knew scary people were out there, but in this moment, all I could see were contorted granite walls formed by eons of earth-twisting pressure, another big rapid, and the blue skies above. Then an Andean fox ran by and I wondered how tough his life was in this barren river canyon.

I remembered that I was scouting alone and Don and Midge were waiting in their kayaks to hear my report. I walked back up to Don and Midge and told them it was a big rapid, but there was a good line. I explained the route, got in my boat, and led them through. Just one more Class V rapid in a mounting list that we had run.

The gradient of the river bed was relentless and while the rapids were huge, most of them had lines through them. That afternoon, Don did a lot of solo scouting while Midge and I waited for his reports. A master at picking clean lines in huge rapids, Don led Midge and me blind through some of the biggest and hardest whitewater Midge had ever run. I knew that, for this day at least, Don was happy with his decision to stay. Midge rose to the occasion well in an incredible display of how far his hard work and dedication to this Amazon project had taken him. We ran many rapids that day that were nerve-racking for Don and me, and so we could only imagine how Midge felt. Yet through it all, he kept a good attitude and pushed himself forward over horizon line after horizon line.

Despite my tendency to focus on Midge's mistakes, quirks, and flaws, he pulled off an incredible feat. The Mantaro River contains weeks of intense, dangerous, and exhausting Class IV, V, and V+ rapids, where even the smallest mistake can have deadly consequences. Ten years earlier, Midge had never sat in a kayak, but he dedicated himself to building the necessary skills and making sure he could keep a cool head in the midst of the whitewater terror—this, by far, is his most laudable accomplishment. Fear plays a powerful role on the brain and Midge masterfully managed his own fears and physical limitations in the whitewater.

Midge accomplished what only a very few elite kayakers in the world ever will. To date, only five paddlers have kayaked the entire Mantaro River—Rocky Contos, James Duesenberry, and then David Midgley, Don Beveridge, and me. Many members of West's team, notably Rafa Ortiz, Juanito De Ugarte, and Tino Specht, kayaked portions of the river while they supported West and his raft team, but because of time constraints they were unable to complete the river. West Hansen descended the entire Mantaro, but for much of the hard whitewater he was in a raft with Juanito.

Later that day, while taking our time on a long portage, I was in front and saw that we needed to pass the boats down a steep incline. I was impatient to keep moving so I set my boat on a ledge, preparing to jump down and set up a passing line to be ready when Don and Midge arrived. I even did a little nudge test to make sure my boat was solid—bump, bump, looks good, doesn't seem to be going anywhere. I turned my back to jump down to the lower landing and heard a swoosh near my ear. I spun my head just in time to see my orange kayak whizzing by. I got my hand on the back of the boat but wasn't quick enough to close my fingers around the grab loop. I watched helplessly as my boat slid into the powerful Mantaro River and was quickly swept downstream.

I had let my guard down too much.

Don was right behind me and saw what happened. In a quick exchange with him, I told him, "I'm all good but going after the boat."

He yelled after me his favorite quote at times like this, "Sometimes we have to go slow to go fast, Darcy!" meaning I should take care not to fall and break my leg in my chase. Before he could finish, I was off, sprinting as fast as I possibly could over the rocky shore of the river thinking "don't break your leg, don't break your leg."

I watched every single step I took at high speed knowing that a fall could be disastrous out here, but also knowing that running too slowly could be equally devastating now that I had dropped my boat.

"I'm going to lose all my food" was the commanding fear in my brain.

"I can't even eat Don and Midge's food if it comes down to it. I'm going to be incredibly hungry if I don't get this boat back."

I had been a vegan for nearly thirteen years before the expedition began and I hoped to keep it that way throughout the trip. We brought enough dehydrated meals for the first fifty days of the expedition. After that, we thought we'd pass villages and towns frequently enough to resupply with food. I hoped I could find enough food to make it through. I had the capacity to be tough about not getting enough to eat if it meant upholding my morals. I went a week in Cuba subsisting on nothing but bread and tomatoes, and when we finally found a woman who had beans and rice I told Don we were staying with her two days minimum. I was mentally prepared to go off the vegan wagon if things got dire—if I was truly starving to death and couldn't find food. But being careless and dropping my boat was not an acceptable reason to falter. I had to get that boat back.

As I sit here now, with access to grocery stores and normal food, I wouldn't even look twice at one of my unappetizing vegan dehydrated meals, but at that point in the expedition calories were like gold and our diets were already insufficient. We each ate one dehydrated meal in the morning, giving us 500 to 1,000 calories (depending on the meal), then one at night, giving us an additional 500 to 1,000 calories. For lunch we usually had one Clif bar and one Shot Block, giving us a combined added 450 calories. While 1,450–2,450 calories are plenty for sedentary people, it falls short when you are kayaking difficult whitewater for eight to ten hours per day. I was already constantly hungry and losing the rest of my food was just not an option. We were still days from our resupply point.

As my fear of hunger pressed me on, my kayak politely eddied out for me. With renewed hope, I gave my last reserves of energy only to get within fifteen feet of my kayak before the river surged and pushed it out of the eddy. I had run out of river bank and energy, and I was staring at the sheer face of a rock wall. I would have to climb up and over a substantial cliff to continue my downstream run. I also noticed a small pool in the river ahead of me before another imposing horizon line.

I began to scramble up the cliff. While I knew that my boat was surely lost, I decided I needed to "dig deep" as my coaches used to say, and keep trying. Just then I heard hooting behind me and turned around to see Don in the water chasing my kayak. While I was sprinting down the shore lamenting the loss of my Backpacker's Pantry Chana Masala, Don had finished the portage, gotten in his kayak, and started paddling after my boat. I climbed the cliff as he paddled downstream and I saw him make contact with my boat.

Between Don and the next horizon line I saw only one marginal eddy.

He will never catch that eddy with my swamped kayak clipped onto his life jacket, I thought. The current is swift and that's too much weight to pull into that tiny eddy.

The worst raced through my mind. It is dangerous to clip onto another kayak in whitewater. Rescue life jackets are equipped with a tow tether and a carabiner that, among other reasons, are meant to clip onto an empty kayak to tow it to shore. There is a safety feature that allows the towing kayaker to execute an emergency release of this tow tether in case they get into a bad situation—if the kayak they are towing gets hung up on a rock or tangled in a log jam in the river—but it is still always something of a gamble to clip on. Sometimes the release mechanisms fail, or the kayaker can't get to it in time. Paddlers have died trying to rescue gear when the boat they are towing gets entrapped somewhere and they can't release from it.

Don, now attached to my kayak, was careening toward what looked like a huge rapid. Never one to tolerate losing gear on his watch, Don will often perform superhuman efforts to recover anything that is lost. I knew that in a situation like this—deep in a remote Peruvian canyon with very little egress options—that Don would do anything to save my kayak, and I did not like that he was doing it above what looked more and more like a dangerous rapid. I reached another cliff, topped out, and expected to see Don getting pulled into the potentially unrunnable rapid by my out of control kayak. To my relief, I could no longer see Don. I sat and watched the horizon line waiting to see him, but he never appeared and neither did my kayak. This meant he caught the eddy.

Don was safe, and I would eat again after all! I climbed over the cliff far enough to get visual contact with Don who was standing on shore with my kayak. In my best sign language, I profusely thanked him—I got down on my knees and bowed toward him, arms outstretched showing my utmost gratitude. Then I motioned that I was heading back upstream.

I left my paddle up at the site of the boat-dropping and hadn't seen Midge in over ten minutes. I started walking back upriver. I was exhausted and walked slowly. I found Midge sitting on a rock upstream of where I'd dropped my boat blowing his whistle and looking rather unhappy.

Immediately when he saw me he started yelling, "Never leave a man behind!" and asking, "Why the fuck did you guys just run off and leave me here?"

Hot, sweaty, spent, and now flabbergasted, I explained, "I thought saving my boat and being able to paddle out so I wouldn't have to try to hike out among the cocaine producers and Shining Path militants was more important than coddling you through the—"

He stopped me short, "You dropped your boat? I had no idea!"

I started laughing as I imagined what must have gone through Midge's head when he had no idea what was unfolding and he just thought his two kayaking partners had wordlessly abandoned him (and my paddle) on the side of the river.

We portaged the rapid just below where Don saved my kayak—it was enormous. Had he not gotten my boat to shore where he did, I would have lost it for sure. I would have been faced with a formidable retreat from an incredibly remote and deep canyon. I forced myself not to think about what would have happened had Don been pulled into the rapid attached to my kayak. I offered to share my vegan dehydrated meal that night, but Don politely declined and opted for his Chili Mac with Beef instead.

It was only after my belly was full, or full enough, that I remembered that my passport and all my money were also in my boat as it was traveling down the river by itself.

Chapter 8

UNCONSCIOUSLY ENTERING THE RED ZONE

*"I knew it like destiny, and at the same time, I knew
it as choice."*

—Jeanette Winterson

AUGUST 21, 2013

DAY 25 OF THE EXPEDITION

S hit!" I said angrily as another military helicopter flew over our heads.
"We really are stuck on this beach in the middle of the fucking Red
Zone like the stupid, gringo idiots that we are."

Midge, ever the optimist (or in my opinion, delusional), countered with,
"Stop worrying, Darcy. Cesar will be here any minute."

I chose to ignore Midge and go back to my own sulking.

Don, Midge, and I paddled into Peru's Red Zone twenty-five days
into our trip. The Red Zone is a loosely defined geographical region that
is infamous for violence, drug trafficking, illegal logging, and justifiably
distrustful indigenous people. We began to feel the effects of a legacy of
violence as we approached the true flatwater. The people we saw on the
lower Mantaro had become more skittish. In the upper reaches of the river
the people were outgoing, curious, talkative. Down here, while we might

still get the occasional wave, most people quickly darted back into the forest after seeing us.

All too suddenly, I found myself longing for adrenaline and fear of the whitewater variety. We now had a new threat, one much more mysterious, unpredictable, and dangerous than the river. After weeks of debating the risks versus rewards of paddling through the Red Zone, I realized I hadn't actually made the decision that I was willing to risk the dangers of this place. I just paddled into it without making a conscious choice and I was furious at myself.

Two weeks earlier, I spent the better part of an afternoon convincing the hairdresser in the town of Huancayo to cut off all my hair. Huancayo was one of the many towns we paddled through in the first ten days of the expedition when we were traveling through the relatively populated highlands. Most towns had been pretty tiny, but Huancayo was huge—450,000 people live there—and I easily found a beauty salon to fit my needs.

The woman working there didn't want to do it.

"Your hair is too pretty," she told me, but I was adamant.

I speak fairly good Spanish, but in this tiny Peruvian beauty salon, I found my Spanish vocabulary fell pitifully short of describing what it was that I feared about being a woman going into the Red Zone. I told her about the people who might murder us, and then, when I realized I didn't know the Spanish word for rape I fumbled around with phrases like "unwanted sex." I got flustered as I realized the look on her face was one of, "Why the hell are you going to this place to begin with?"

I wanted to say, "Right! My question exactly, lady. Let's you and me head over to the bar and forget this whole haircutting and Red Zone thing altogether. My treat."

I agonized over the decision of whether to see the expedition through and paddle through the Red Zone with Midge, or play it safe and walk away after the whitewater. Was kayaking the Amazon really worth dying for? Two of the last six tourists to paddle down the rivers of the Red Zone had been killed, and one more was shot, though he was lucky enough to escape his assailants and survive.

These weren't great odds.

But something pushed me forward and drove me to grab one of the fashion magazines in the beauty salon. I thumbed through until I found a picture of nerdy-looking twelve-year-old boy and demanded, "Make me look like him!"

No guts, no glory, right?

Let's do this thing—the haircutting at least.

She finally gave in and cut off all my hair, shaking her head throughout the entire process.

Especially after witnessing the drastic act of me cutting my hair, Midge began to realize just how worried I was about paddling through the Red Zone. As we kayaked away from Huancayo, he mentioned that if I wanted to bail after the whitewater, he would understand.

"This is my life goal, Darcy," he said. "If you really think there is a good chance you'll die, you definitely do not need to come with me."

I said I'd think about it, which I did on and off, but mostly I pushed thoughts of the Red Zone to the deepest recesses of my brain. I knew it would take us at least two weeks to get there from Huancayo, so I figured I had plenty of time to make up my mind. I kept hoping that I would have some epiphany and wake up one morning and declare, "Yes! It's worth the risk, I'm going." Or, "Nope, not worth it, I'm content walking away from this expedition and going home."

Neither happened.

I didn't deal with it until I found myself sitting in the heart of the Red Zone on a beach waiting for Cesar. Our plan was to meet him at the confluence of the Mantaro and Apurímac rivers at 10:00 A.M. He had left more than a week earlier to help West get our sea kayaks to the town of Puerto Ene and to find a motorized canoe that would be willing to travel down the river with us. The canoe would carry Cesar and our gear, but we primarily hoped that the driver would be a local and would help us out with any uncomfortable situations that might arise among us, the Asháninka, narco-traffickers, or anyone else we needed to be cautious of.

Our hope was to meet Cesar early enough to transition into our sea kayaks and still have enough daylight left to paddle downstream to a suitable camping spot. Recent news reports from Lima had pointed to this confluence area—now Peru's number one cocaine-producing region—as the new focal point of the battle between the military and the drug traffickers, and we decided it wasn't a place for three gringos to linger.

The area is referred to as VRAEM—Valle de los Rios Apurímac, Ene y Mantaro—and, as of this writing, has the highest density of coca crops in the world.* At the height of the Shining Path insurgency, in the mid-1980s through the early 1990s, this region exported coca paste to Colombia, where it was turned into a far more valuable substance—cocaine. Backpackers used to hike the paste out over the mountains by the duffel bag–load.

Pablo Escobar, "The King of Cocaine," died in 1993, and Peru quickly filled his void in supplying the demand for cocaine in the United States. By 1995, 70 percent of the cocaine sold in the United States came from Peru.** It was around this time that the Shining Path forged their lasting relationship with the coca growers, cocaine producers, and narco-traffickers in the Amazon regions of Peru. With so much money at stake, the narco-traffickers needed protection. The Shining Path needed money, and in each other, these two outlaw groups had found the perfect partnership.

Today, there are more sophisticated processing plants in the jungle where the Peruvians make the cocaine themselves. They gave up on the back-packers, and started using Cessna airplanes that can carry up to 350 kilos of processed cocaine per load, making it a much more profitable endeavor. Using tiny, hidden airstrips, the drug traffickers are flying up to thirty tons of cocaine out of the VRAEM region each month.*** The Peruvian military had recently stepped up efforts to curtail this profitable drug trade. In one airstrike alone, military helicopters blew up fifty-seven airstrips. Critics say their efforts are futile because almost as quickly as the military can blow up landing strips, the cocaine bosses can order another one built. Labor is cheap in the jungle, especially when you have a gun to your employee's head.

Ollanta Humala, Peru's president from 2011 to 2016, made a concentrated effort to eradicate any remnants of the Shining Path movement. He wasn't proud of this part of his country's history and he was determined

---

* "Peru Aims to Tire out Drug Traffickers by Destroying Air Strips." *Peruvian Times*, January 8, 2014, http://www.peruviantimes.com/08/peru-aims-to-tire-out-drug-traffickers-by-destroying-airstrips/21135/, accessed January 10, 2015.
** United Nations Office on Drugs and Crime, World Drug Report 2010, https://www.unodc.org/documents/wdr/WDR_2010/1.3_The_globa_cocaine_market.pdf, accessed March 19, 2016.
*** Ibid.

to try to erase it. This became increasingly obvious to us as we entered the Red Zone. Sightings of military helicopters became frequent.

Our last night sleeping on the Mantaro River, two Black Hawk helicopters flew over our camp. They were flying low and without the aid of their lights. Judging by the number of passes they did, they were clearly looking for something or someone. We assumed these two choppers were part of this ongoing campaign and that they were most likely looking for cocaine production sites or rebel camps. The nearly full moon illuminated the night sky, and I lay terrified in my tent, thinking with each pass they'd mistake us for Shining Path rebels or drug traffickers and open fire on us as they had done to the two Shining Path leaders days earlier. I laid there and prayed they'd see our kayaks and realize we were tourists. After four passes, the helicopters left and did not return.

We arrived at the confluence around 10:30 A.M. with the naïve hope that we would find Cesar sitting in a motorized canoe waving his greetings to us. Cesar wasn't there. None of us were surprised, but that didn't mean we weren't disappointed. We found an island near where the two rivers met and uneasily started to cook lunch. We got out the satellite phone and called Cesar's cell phone to see where he was.

Time is a point of contention between North Americans and Peruvians. While we are used to living our lives on an uptight schedule where everything is ruled—down to the minute—by time, many Peruvians consider time to be a very vague concept that is usually meant to be ignored. Even bus schedules run on a haphazard when-the-driver-feels-like-it kind of schedule, rather than one ruled by time as we know it. I knew this well from years of living in Ecuador, where the same rules apply, but I still somehow expected Cesar to be waiting for us.

In the Spanish language, there is no verb *to drop*. Instead they say, "It fell." Where I would say "I dropped the plate," Spanish speakers say, "The plate fell." When problems do arise, they are attributed to some force outside the realm of control. On the phone with Cesar, we heard a story of road construction, then it turned into a roadblock, then something about how the dugout canoe was going to be late anyway, so it was okay that Cesar was late, too.

"Don't worry," he said. "I'm arriving, I'll see you soon."

When pressed about what "arriving" meant, we learned that he was more than two hours away, and we would just have to wait. We sat on our gravel island trying to be as inconspicuous as three white people with brightly colored whitewater kayaks could be. We quickly discovered that there was very little noticeable activity near where we sat. We saw two fishermen in a canoe paddle past our island but that was it. We assumed there were a lot of illicit activities happening just beyond the cover of the thick, green jungle and we just hoped that they would keep on doing their thing and leave us alone to do our thing, which, for the moment, was waiting.

We sat anxiously and impatiently. We weren't yet accustomed to waiting around, though just a few months later we would be extremely well trained at the practice. For the past twenty-five days, the only reasons we stopped were to scout a rapid, eat, or sleep. Now we just sat and stared at a seemingly endless green expanse sliced through by two rivers, each claiming to be the source of the Amazon.

Sitting on that gravel bar was a victorious moment for Midge. He knew with certainty that he had completed and survived Phase 1—the whitewater. This was the phase Midge was convinced he would die on. Against all odds, he had somehow managed to survive, and he felt euphoric.

We had just entered Phase 2—the phase I felt we were *all* most likely to die on. I still hadn't concluded whether the glory of becoming the first woman to kayak the Amazon was worth the risk. Was the potential freedom from my itinerant lifestyle worth tempting fate in the Red Zone? Writing this now, it seems like an obvious NO, kayaking the Amazon isn't worth dying for. But it was different then. I'd invested a lot of time and suffering already. I'd had a harrowing day in the dam canyon and had come out alive. I thought I'd be letting myself down if I quit. Plus, I felt like I'd already come so far, though the reality was, the expedition was barely getting started.

We started talking about the miles we'd done while we passed the time on the gravel bar. We all became a little dejected as we did the math. We had descended over 13,000 vertical feet in twenty-five days. This meant we had lost more than 85 percent of our gradient in less than 17 percent of our trip. For the rest of our voyage, the average river gradient would be less than two inches of elevation loss per mile paddled down the river. A good whitewater river usually has a gradient of 50 to 150 *feet* per mile. We were in for a long, flat paddle out.

Cesar did eventually show up in a dugout canoe, but he promptly told us not to put anything in this canoe because it was not the one that would be coming downriver with us.

"Where is the canoe that's coming with us?" I asked.

"I don't know," replied Cesar. "I haven't found one yet. Probably I can find one in Puerto Ene."

"What?" I was pissed. "You've had more than a week to get this arranged and you still don't have a canoe?"

"Don't worry, I will find one."

Clearly, I was worried.

Our desires to make a timely transition were up against Cesar's very Peruvian attitude of everything will work out somehow, no sense in worrying about it. There was nothing we could do, but to go along with Cesar's non-plan.

We paddled another twenty minutes downriver to the tiny town of Puerto Ene where Cesar had arranged for the sea kayaks to be delivered. We all wondered why we hadn't just planned to meet Cesar there, but second-guessing past plans was futile and we just needed to focus on making the transition into our sea kayaks and moving down the river. We hit the beach of this small town—roughly one hundred residents—and, as we were prone to do, immediately drew a crowd. They asked the usual questions.

"Where are you going?"

"Where did you come from?"

"How much do those kayaks cost?"

Little did they know, that the real spectacle was about to begin.

An old beat-up Toyota truck pulled up with three massive cardboard boxes tied to the roof. The boxes were five feet longer than the truck and hung awkwardly over the front and the back of the truck. We greeted the driver, who promptly presented us with a papaya. None of us particularly like papaya, but after twenty-five days of subsisting on processed dehydrated food we were like greedy little kids shoveling the fresh fruit into our mouths as quickly as possible to make sure we each got our fair share.

The relatively fragile carbon Kevlar racing sea kayaks had made an arduous journey from Miami Beach, Florida, to Puerto Ene, Peru. They traveled by shipping container, tractor trailer truck, West's rental minivan, and now this guy's Toyota truck, no doubt costing Midge thousands of dollars in import and transportation costs—not to mention the cost the of the high-tech racing sea kayaks themselves. In order to help the kayak's chances of survival, the manufacturer had wrapped them in bubble wrap and then also filled the cardboard boxes with biodegradable packing peanuts. The mayhem we caused by unpacking these seventeen-foot sea kayaks on that small beach was impressive.

The grown women of the town were immediately drawn to the bubble wrap. Every woman over the age of twenty-five grabbed a piece and stood watching us intently, while meticulously popping individual bubbles. The children went for the packing peanuts and had a heyday with this new toy. The grown men jumped right into the action, helping us unload the kayaks and trying to contain our mess as much as possible.

When we unpacked the two KayakPro Nemos (Darcy- and Midge-sized kayaks) we discovered that one of them was missing the rear hatch cover. Whether Peruvian customs lost it or KayakPro just did not supply it we will never know, but what mattered now was that we had one kayak with no hatch cover. The rear hatches can hold up to twenty-nine gallons of gear—or water—so leaving it uncovered was not an option.

I looked quizzically at the hole and wondered what to cover it with. Then, some of the men of the village started looking with me and as I explained the problem to them, they set off running into the heart of Puerto Ene. About fifteen minutes later they reemerged with a thick sheet of black plastic and a bicycle tire inner tube—the perfect solution to my problem! We placed the sheet of plastic over the hole then wrapped the bicycle inner tube around the lip of the hatch pulling it taut and tying it as tightly as we could. Peruvian ingenuity continually impressed me, as did their generosity. These guys were monetarily poor and we were comparatively rich with our fancy kayaks and gear, but they refused when I tried to pay them for the supplies.

This was the first of many pleasant interactions we had with the people of the Red Zone as they repeatedly proved to us that the rumors we had heard did not apply to *all* the people living in this region. We had gear spread from one end of the beach to the other; pocketing something would have been easy for even the most inept of thieves, but no one tried to steal anything from us. They were curious, friendly, helpful, and talkative. We found no hints of the foreboding place we thought we were entering.

During our two-hour-long unpacking and reorganizing gear session on the beach of Puerto Ene, Cesar did successfully procure a dugout canoe and an Asháninka driver named Wilson. Wilson would accompany us three days down to the town of Puerto Prado and then we would have to find a new driver. Feeling that having an Asháninka on our team would help our chances of survival, we happily launched our sea kayaks into the Ene River at 2:15 in the afternoon. Cesar was right, everything did seem to be working out.

We paddled away from Puerto Ene, and were sent off with enthusiastic waves and shouts of good luck. What we thought would likely be the most logistically challenging part of the trip—getting the sea kayaks to Puerto Ene intact—was now behind us. The jungle here was beautiful and there were tall cliffs rising straight out of the water reminding us that we had not yet hit the true flats. Small, Class II rapids kept our excitement up as we quickly learned that these racing sea kayaks were not nearly as stable as our whitewater boats. It took an absurd amount of concentration to not capsize in what were comparatively tiny rapids.

We noticed that our sea kayaks' lack of a back band (support for the lower back) was going to be extremely problematic. Without a supportive back rest like our whitewater kayaks had, we had to constantly engage our stomach and back muscles to remain in an upright sitting position with our legs stretched out in front of us. Sitting on the floor in this position at first does not seem too strenuous, but imagine doing it for hours without a break. Still we had no time to deal with the pain that first afternoon. We were losing daylight and had to paddle downriver to find a suitable camping spot before dark. It was imperative, everyone told us, not to be out on the river after dark.

The three of us, Cesar, who was now officially our Red Zone guide, and Wilson, our wise-beyond-his-years twenty-one-year-old dugout canoe driver, had a team conference before leaving Puerto Ene. Explaining our fears to Wilson and showing him all the permissions we had carried along with us, we devised a plan where the canoe would never be out of our sight, would usually go first in case someone wanted to talk with them (or us), and would be in charge of picking camping spots since Wilson was the local. Wilson and Cesar both agreed that this seemed logical and was the safest way to proceed.

It was a sound plan that lasted exactly zero minutes after the team meeting. We launched and did not see the canoe again for twenty minutes. The river traffic we saw wasn't overly threatening. The only boats that passed us were school buses—motorized dugout canoes full of children. We saw canoe after canoe full of kids aged four to fourteen all cruising back up the river. The kids were friendly and excited to see us. The boat drivers were usually children themselves, often looking like not quite teenagers. They would motor alongside us for a few minutes at a time checking out our boats and gear and giggling when we talked to them in our heavily accented Spanish. Nonetheless, our plan had failed even before it started and we needed to do something about this. When Wilson and Cesar finally caught up we called them over and asked what had happened.

Bewildered, they said in unison, "Nothing."

Cesar followed up with, "We decided to eat lunch in Puerto Ene."

Clearly, we'd had a failure to communicate; so we went over the plan again and asked them to please stay with us.

Things went well for the next hour and a half with Cesar and Wilson staying close. Then we got to a place where the river split into two channels. It was about 4:30 P.M. Wilson explained that, in order to make his camping spot of choice before nightfall, the kayakers would have to take the shorter right channel. The dugout canoe could not come with us because there were places too shallow for him. This seemed odd to us, as the canoe did not seem to have a keel much deeper than our sea kayaks. We figured he could just pull the motor and drift with the current (there was still current up here) through the shallows; but he was adamant that he could not do this.

Not wanting to split up, period, especially so close to dark, we tried to come up with an alternative plan. Wilson explained that it was too dangerous to camp anywhere but his chosen spot and that we would never make it before nightfall if we took the left channel with him. Everything from sitting in the heart of the cocaine production zone for two hours by ourselves to now having our escort boat abandon us just before dark left us questioning the point of even making plans.

We split up; the kayakers went right, and the canoe went left. Our channel was enchanting. There was decent current, a luxury that we grossly underappreciated at the time. We saw huge flocks of macaws, guans, kingfishers, and cormorants, and the fading daylight illuminated the rainforest in a warm and inviting manner. The three of us were so enthralled with our new surroundings that we forgot we were in the Red Zone, forgot that it was getting dark and we still were separated from Wilson and Cesar. Snapping out of our trance, the need to paddle fast and find our canoe became critical.

We saw the place where the two channels came together and we saw that Cesar and Wilson weren't there. There was a different boat at the confluence of the two channels. It was a much larger dugout canoe and it was tied to shore. We could see a man and a woman on it and we approached cautiously. Just as we started talking to the couple, Wilson and Cesar showed up. This was our camp spot. It is apparently a popular night fishing location for a nearby village that doubles as a sort of rest area for boat traffic. This "rest area" had no amenities, not even a little thatched roof shack for the fishermen. It was a seemingly desolate beach but a place where people knew they could find a safe refuge in this part of the river.

A group of three fishermen arrived as we set up camp. They were friendly but terse, as they had to get to work. They spread out along the beach, sitting roughly 150 feet away from each other, each of them wielding a flashlight. At various intervals, they would flash their lights at each other in a Morse code–looking sequence of flashes that came in series of ones and twos.

Flash-flash, flash-flash, flash I was certain meant, "Kill the girl first."

I passed most of the night in sleepless torment. I lay in my tent watching for the next flashlight signal, waiting for one of the fishermen-turned-murderers to approach our tent. I kept peering out the mesh at the bottom of our tent looking for feet, a machete, or a shotgun.

Nothing happened.

The fishermen continued to fish until 3:30 A.M. We did not get up to see if they pulled in an impressive haul or not. The important thing is that they were really fishing, and they had not, in fact, come to kill us. We survived our first night in the flatwater. The only casualty was my sleep, thanks to my paranoia.

The rules of camping and river life were very different in the Red Zone, and for the rest of the Amazon for that matter. In the remote upper canyons of the Mantaro we easily found uninhabited beaches or rock ledges to camp on. We rarely saw people. Starting at Puerto Ene, everything was different. The river was now heavily populated—we would see multiple villages each day—and it now became imperative to camp near other people or in their villages. Because suspicion of outsiders runs rampant in this region, we relied heavily on the permission letters we acquired in Lima. Our permissions also acted as a way of notifying villages along the way that people would be passing through and that they were river runners, not Shining Path, not loggers, not cocaine producers, and not government resource scouts.

We were originally against the idea of notifying would-be murderers or robbers about our presence because we were extremely naïve about the work-ings of this part of the river. In Lima, we had made the decision to ask them not to radio our whereabouts to all the villages in the corridor. It just seemed like a bad idea to advertise, "Three vulnerable gringos are approaching, pre-pare yourselves!" Annoyed, the people issuing our permission papers agreed they would advise the people of the Red Zone not to radio news of our progress, but assured us that everyone would know we were coming anyway.

Even without radios, word travels fast among the small river communities that are all connected by the river—everyone's lifeline in the Red Zone. Each village expected us as we paddled up and most welcomed us to camp on their beach or recommended camps to Cesar farther down the river. As long as we produced our permission papers, we were treated as family. We often camped on fishing beaches where fishermen worked all night long. It was hard for us wilderness lovers to get used to this mentality, but we soon realized that, in the Red Zone at least, there really was safety in numbers. We would follow this motto throughout the rest of our trip, seeking out seemingly friendly locals and asking permission to camp at their village or on their land.

Our first twenty-four hours in the Red Zone was a strong argument against all I had feared and expected from this place. Every single person had been extremely friendly. It was beautiful, the birdlife was incredible and abundant, and it certainly didn't feel like a fearful place full of murderous people. I began to let my guard down a little and thought maybe my being there wasn't such a terrible idea after all.

Chapter 9

THE ASHÁNINKA

"No, no, my friend. You are kind, and you mean well, but you can never understand these things as I do. You've never been oppressed."

—S. Alice Callahan

AUGUST 22, 2013
DAY 26 OF THE EXPEDITION

We were in a tiny town called Queteni Colonial and the guy selling the cold beer out of a room in his house said to me, *"Buenas tardes, señor."*

I couldn't have been happier.

Ordering our beers, my voice gave away that I was not, in fact, a señor, but rather a señora.

He was mortified, but I tried my best to explain. "No, I'm so happy you thought I was boy!"

He was clearly confused.

I continued my clarification. "I cut off all my hair in Huancayo hoping that the 'bad people' here in the Red Zone would mistake me for a boy—us for a group of three men. It just seemed safer that way."

My voice trailed off. It was an awkward conversation, me trying to explain to a stranger why I found his home region so terrifying that I cut off all my hair and decided to dress in drag for half a year.

As he passed me the beers, he said in a quiet, uncertain voice, "Okay, gracias, señor . . ."

As I talked more with the beer man, I think he began to understand or at least pretended to. He acknowledged that he lived in a dangerous area, and warned, as everyone had, that our next couple days of paddling downriver would lead us into even more unsafe terrain.

It had been an interesting few hours leading up to Queteni Colonial and many of the safe, welcoming feelings about the Red Zone I'd had from the day before had vanished. Just before town, we stopped at a new military base to check in and show our paperwork. The Red Zone has had virtually no police or military presence. The new Peruvian government, however, was not proud to be the world's top cocaine producer; not to mention the fact that it still hadn't completely gotten rid of the Shining Path insurgents who started their bloody civil war. Consequently, they were in the process of building two military bases along the river. While it's a start, two bases to control hundreds of thousands of square miles of jungle is more a symbolic gesture than anything else.

Two men, one with an M16 and the other with an M60 machine gun, checked our passports and our paperwork. The men were neither welcoming nor mean, just very military-like as they barked orders at us, demanding our documents and an explanation of what we were doing. They made us get out of our kayaks, but then did not search them. After ten minutes, they were seemingly satisfied with our papers and sent us away with a warning that it is very dangerous downstream and that we must be careful.

Great, I thought. Two big military guys with even bigger guns are telling us to be careful. Our only weapons were our paddles, some little pocket knives strapped to our ankles, and our permission papers. I started wishing the guys with the guns were coming with us.

A few hours earlier, I'd nearly been crushed by thousands of tons of mahogany and other trees I couldn't identify being moved down the river in an ungainly gargantuan log raft. Hundreds of trees ranging from a few feet in diameter to monsters that would rival redwoods with their girth were lashed together with rope creating a forest platform wildly careening down the river. We assumed the trees we saw floating in the river had been harvested illegally. Roughly 80 percent of the high-value lumber coming out of the Peruvian Amazon is illegal.* The poaching of these forests is too lucratively tempting on the black market, as wood from a single big-leaf mahogany tree can bring in $11,000 USD.** The log raft pulled over before the military base. I don't know how they got through, but a combination of bribes, falsified papers, and threats of violence seems to be the norm.***

The allure of money, combined with the lack of law enforcement presence in these areas has made the Peruvian jungle a region where the person with the most firepower wins. Like the people in the cocaine industry, the loggers act with impunity.

Less than a year after our trip down the Amazon, four Asháninka community leaders were murdered by illegal loggers because the Asháninka were drawing international attention to the fact that these criminal loggers were destroying their land. The loggers brought the men out to the soccer field and shot them in front of the entire village, sending a clear message to others who thought about calling attention to the illegal logging. It took family members six days to travel upriver to the town of Pucallpa in a motorized canoe to report the crime. Nothing ever happened to the murderers. This is life in the Red Zone and the reason that most people feel they must take their safety into their own hands, as they've been accustomed to doing for centuries.

But for the moment, we were in a different world. Drinking beers on the sandy beach at Queteni Colonial—our first truly cold beers in almost a month—it seemed that life just couldn't get any better. The entire village, about fifty people, came down to talk to us. All the normal questions

---

*   M. Pereira Goncalves, M. Panjer, T. Greenberg, and W. Magrath, "Justice for Forests: Improving Criminal Justice Efforts to Combat Illegal Logging," World Bank Study, Washington, D.C. 2012, http://siteresources.worldbank.org/EXTFINANCIALSECTOR /Resources/Illegal_Logging.pdf, accessed January 12, 2015.

**   Frank Bajak, "Police Meet Widows of Slain Indigenous Leaders," *Merced Sun-Star*, September 9, 2014, http://www.mercedsunstar.com/2014/09/09/3838891_police-meet -widows-of-slain-indigenous.html, accessed September 10, 2014.

*** The illegal wood trade continues seemingly unabated. Between October 2017 and August 2018, Peru's OSINFOR— Organismo de Supervision de los Recursos Forestales y de Fauna Silverstre—identified 25,455 cubic meters of illegally cut wood. That's the equivalent of about 5,000 truckloads of timber and was valued at over $30 million USD. Nelly Luna Amancio, "The Last Trees of the Amazon," Mongabay.com, https://news.mongabay .com/2018/11/the-last-trees-of-the-amazon/, accessed October 14, 2019.

ensued, followed by looks of disbelief when we told them we were going to the Atlantic Ocean. They were intrigued by our stories of ice and snow in the headwaters—two substances totally foreign to them. They eventually got bored of us and said goodnight with more warnings.

"Tomorrow will be very dangerous. Keep your eyes open. The Asháninka down there don't like foreigners coming into their territory."

Don and I set up our tent and crawled in to begin the nightly ritual. For me, getting into the tent was always a struggle. It was a calculated risk. It involved a wild dance of shooing away bugs, telling Don, who was already in the tent, to prepare himself and his stuff, and then a bout of visualization on how best to unzip the tent, jump in, then re-zip the tent.

The unzipping and zipping was the most challenging. It had to be fast enough to limit the number of bugs flying into the tent with me, but slow enough not to jam the zipper, or bring in too much of the sand stuck to my feet. I also had to be careful not to topple the tent by catching my foot on the bottom. The tent was fifteen years old and the fragile zipper was growing weaker by the day from the millions of pieces of sand that were accumulating between its teeth. One errant yank and the tent would no longer be our safety zone, and I would no longer be Don's girlfriend. He really hates bugs.

After tent-entry was accomplished, it was time for the bug hunt. This meant lying very still on our sleeping pads, turning our headlamps on—which of course had been off during entry so as to not lure any opportunistic mosquitos inside—and diligently searching every inch of the tent for an enterprising bug who snuck its way in. I scanned the tent walls each night in a pattern, moving first over the nylon walls, giving careful scrutiny to the corners, then moving onto the mesh ceiling where the little bloodsuckers found better purchase for clinging upside down. I would typically see lots of bug guts, the remains of other intruders, before finding any live bugs. Eventually, I'd find a few.

Squish.

"Sorry, mosquito."

Squish.

"Sorry for you, too."

Killing mosquitos occupies a blurry space in my vegan morality—I don't like killing things. My main reason for being vegan is that I hate the large-scale factory farming of animals that has become so prevalent. I don't believe that people should be able to buy a plastic-wrapped hunk of meat in the grocery store and be allowed to be so physically and emotionally distanced from the process of raising and killing that animal. I'm theoretically okay with the act of killing individual animals for food—hunting a deer for example—but I hate doing this myself. So if I'm not willing to get my hands dirty, why should I let others do it for me? But here, it was a me-or-them scenario. Either I killed the mosquitos, or they'd give me dengue, malaria, or yellow fever. I decided to be proactive in this instance.

"No more bugs, can I have the baby powder?"

I could have never guessed that baby powder would have been one of my most treasured items on the Amazon trip. We only threw it into our bag as an afterthought, "just in case our feet get jungle rot," we thought. Although we bathed in the river daily, it never really made us clean. The muddy water left a dirt residue on us and we'd be sweating again before we fully made it out of the water. The baby powder, covering up the sweat on our skin, at least gave us the illusion of being clean.

Each night before bed, Don meticulously put baby powder between his toes, under his armpits and between his butt cheeks. He was calculating, using exactly as much as he needed, and careful to make a minimal mess in the tent. Then, each night, Don watched in disgust as I mimicked Pig-Pen from the Peanuts comic and proceeded to douse my entire body and all the contents of the tent in a baby powder dust storm. I never figured out why he kept being so careful when he knew what was coming next.

We would both inwardly panic when we ran out of powder. Luckily, baby powder is one of four staples in tiny Peruvian village stores; tuna fish, Inca Kola, and what Don and Midge described as bland, cardboard-like cookies are the other three.

During these nighttime rituals, our orange Marmot tent became a chaotic mess of dirty clothes, smelly sleeping gear, crumpled maps, and baby powder. We tried to stay organized but failed. My sock would inevitably end up under Don's head and his hat under my feet. We hung a string inside the tent to hang and dry our wet paddling clothes, but they never dried. They just made our tent smell more awful with each passing day and made it that much harder to move around in the already cramped tent. Embracing the mess, the sweat, the stickiness, and the stench was our only option, so we tried our best to get used to it.

Some people find a sense of security by being enclosed in a tent. Not me. I wanted to be able to see what was going on around me. Especially in the Red Zone, I wanted to be able to see if machete-wielding murderers were running toward us. I'd much prefer to sleep on a tarp without a tent, but with the Amazonian bug life, this was not an option. Each night before attempting to sleep I made sure the little corner of mesh just above my face was clear—my four-by-four-inch window to the outside world.

"Goodnight, Don."

"Goodnight, Darcy."

"Okay, body, you have eight hours to recover before we get up and do it all over again," I reminded my beaten-down muscles, my blistered lips, and my fingernails which were sun-scorched to the point of irradiation. Then I would settle into my sleeping routine, spending the next eight hours dutifully trying not to touch, and therefore stick to Don, while being vigilant in my watch for bad guys out my mesh window.

My insomnia came in handy that night when I noticed that our motorized canoe looked farther away than it should have. Once my eyes adjusted to the dark night, I realized it had come untied and was floating away. Wilson had gone to town, and Cesar was sleeping on the boat. I ran down the beach in the dark screaming Cesar's name and hooting as loudly as my quiet voice could manage. My yelling finally roused Cesar, who managed to pull the engine to life just before the canoe went down a set of Class II rapids. I didn't take this as a foreshadowing of events to come, though it was the first incident in a string of many.

We were paddling by first light the next morning as we hoped to make it through the upcoming zone of extra wary and suspicious Asháninka. Our goal was the town of Puerto Prado, where locals ensured us we'd be safe. This part of the Red Zone was hit the hardest by the Shining Path conflict. The historical consequences of the Franciscan missionaries' attempts to settle the area and the subsequent rubber boom are incredibly strong in the Red Zone; but for the people there today, these are distant cultural memories recalled only in stories and strange myths. The Shining Path destruction, conversely, is recent and very real. Living Asháninka, many of them not very old, survived this traumatic event.

In 1992 the Shining Path's leader, Abimael Guzmán, was arrested and jailed for life. The movement was losing supporters daily, and remaining rebels were scared. In the region we were about to paddle through, the Shining Path set up what they called labor camps and filled them with the Asháninka people as both a source of labor and coerced support. If someone tried to escape one of these camps and was caught, the escapee would be brought in front of the entire camp. Then his relatives would be asked to step forward. One relative was chosen, handed a machete and told to kill the family member who tried to escape. If they refused, Shining Path soldiers would murder the entire family.

The Shining Path's ideology was supposed to be about defeating the government, killing the bureaucrats, and elevating the marginalized people of the nation. Here, in the jungles of the upper Amazon River, the Shining Path was dealing with a group of people who functioned almost entirely outside of the Peruvian government's rules, programs, or benefits. They were people almost wholly unrecognized and forgotten by the very government the Shining Path was trying to destroy, and they were very poor, monetarily speaking. They were the people on whose behalf the Shining Path was supposed to be starting a revolution. Instead, the Asháninka were the biggest victims; a fact that has deeply confused academics studying the Shining Path movement. More than 20 percent of the Asháninka people were displaced during the war. More than ten thousand were killed, and over thirty Asháninka communities disappeared altogether.[*] Archeologists have unearthed mass graves of Asháninka who died at the hands of these "revolutionaries."

I found many of the Asháninkas' recent actions—the murders of both tourists and Peruvians alike—reprehensible. But considering their history, I could understand their fear of strangers. History had treated them abysmally, and outsiders only ever seemed to bring death to their people. I just wanted to do my best to leave them alone and to get out of their homeland as quickly as possible.

---

[*]   Stefano Varese, *Salt of the Mountain: Campa Asháninka History and Resistance in the Peruvian Jungle* (Norman: University of Oklahoma Press, 1968), 125.

Midge started paddling very slowly and kept saying that he just felt tired. About midday we forced him to eat some Shot Bloks for energy and implored him to pick up the pace—we needed to get out of this zone. Even Wilson, the local Ashaninka canoe driver, was acting edgy. Almost immediately after eating the Shot Bloks Midge started throwing up. He spent the next fifteen minutes hanging onto the bow of Don's kayak hurling last night's dehydrated chicken tikka masala into the river.

Thinking that perhaps Midge had purged himself of whatever was making him sick, we pushed on. Twenty minutes later there was more barfing, followed by Midge frantically paddling to shore and running into the rainforest—his problems had moved south. Midge tried to paddle through his sickness, but by 3:00 P.M. we were nowhere near Puerto Prado. We repeatedly asked Wilson if there wasn't somewhere else that would be safe to camp and he repeatedly answered with a resounding NO. Wilson maintained that the only safe option was to load everyone and the kayaks into the canoe and motor down to Puerto Prado.

Midge was adamantly against this idea, saying it would ruin the integrity of the expedition. We implored him that we could mark our exact take-out spot with both GPS and physical landmarks and then motor back up to the exact spot when he was feeling healthier. We all preferred the idea of camping where we were (had it been safe); but already we had seen a few men with either shotguns or bows and arrows surreptitiously walking the riverbanks. They didn't wave or shout hello, but would peer around boulders every now and then to get a look at us. Presumably they were trying to figure out just who we were, but they could have had other motives. Not to mention the fact that Midge was putting himself at further risk by running into the cover of the jungle every time he needed to go to the bathroom. After a heated argument, Midge relented.

We motored into Puerto Prado just before sunset and parked the canoe near the mouth of a tributary called the Perené River. Where the Perené joins the Ene River, the name changes to the Tambo River, another milestone in our progress, though we couldn't quite tick it off yet. The plan was that Midge and I would go find the hotel—there was rumored to be one here—and Don would wait by the river guarding our kayaks and gear until I came back to get him.

The phrase "I don't know" apparently doesn't exist in the South American vocabulary. If you are trying to find a particular building—say a store, hotel, or immigration office—everyone you ask will offer up directions regardless of whether or not they know where said building is and regardless of whether or not they've ever even heard of the place you are looking for.

Numbered addresses aren't all that common, either, so directions usually involved some version of "go two blocks, turn right at the tomato cart, go one block, turn right again at the guy selling shoes, and then your hotel is just before the row of pig heads and strips of cow meat on display in the sweltering heat."

Okay, they don't say that last part, but replace "the row of pig heads and strips of cow meat on display in the sweltering heat" with "butcher shop" and you get the idea. And so our hunt for the hotel in Puerto Prado began. Luckily, there was only one hotel so finding it was not terribly difficult. Of course the first three residents had no idea their town actually had a hotel, but gave directions anyway, which sent us on a few misadventures through the five streets and forty or so businesses. Midge was growing more impatient by the moment, tormented by his now simultaneous need to throw up and have diarrhea.

We both determined that "hotel" was an inappropriate descriptor when we finally found the building. I'm no snob when it comes to living conditions. I spend a lot of time sleeping on the ground, but even I was dismayed. The floors were dusty, splintery one-by-eights spaced irregularly so that sometimes there was a gap of one inch, or sometimes six inches, requiring patrons to walk carefully. There were beds in the rooms, but Don and I opted to set up our tent on the floor instead. The bathroom had two communal toilets barely hidden by plastic shower curtains. It seemed that they were the only flushing toilets in town as there was a steady stream of users' day and night despite the fact that we were the only guests staying at the hotel. There was running water roughly four to six hours per day. For the rest of the hours, the stuff in the toilet piled up until the water was turned on again.

Don and I felt badly for Midge, who had spent the day of paddling, interrupted at regular intervals first by throwing up, then by pulling over and rushing into the rainforest. But now we *really* had compassion for him. Being sick almost anywhere else on the planet would have been more pleasant than this hotel. Our beach camp from the night before would have been a veritable paradise—at least there was room to roam when Midge's bodily eruptions became urgent. But here, he had to wait in line to use a clogged-up public toilet.

Despite all the hotel's shortcomings, amenity-wise, its friendly owners sold incredibly cold beer. Don, Cesar, and I passed the better part of the evening drinking this cold beer and amazing the owners with stories of the headwaters of the Amazon and the whitewater in the canyons of the Mantaro. They were most amazed that we'd managed to survive the cocaine producing hot spots just fifty miles upstream. Don and Cesar both ordered a plate of salted beef. I ordered my standard meal in small Peruvian restaurants—a plate of rice—after a long and, for the cook, confusing, conversation about whether or not they used butter when cooking rice. "No butter? Great! I'll have a big order of plain rice."

Then a group of five Peruvian navy guys marched into the bar and said they were looking for us. I got nervous. It's never good when guys with guns are looking for you. These guys had come from a mountain base about thirty miles away, near the town of Satipo, where twenty years ago, the Shining Path had murdered sixty-two people and left 2,500 people homeless after burning their homes. They did this in retaliation for rumors that the locals were forming a militia to fight back against the insurgents.

The guys from the navy had heard about the kayaking expedition and wanted to come meet us. They also checked our paperwork, talked to Cesar, and made sure we knew just how dangerous a place the Red Zone is. By this point, I was getting tired of heavily armed military guys telling us how dangerous things were around here.

∽

AUGUST 24, 2013
DAY 28 OF THE EXPEDITION

After twenty hours of purging himself, Midge felt well enough to paddle. He'd managed to keep down a chocolate bar and some water. We estimated it would take us four hours of paddling to make it from yesterday's stopping point back to Puerto Prado—a comparatively easy day. We loaded the kayaks back into the canoe and motored up the river to our exact stopping point—not near it, but the exact spot down to the specific rock that marked the point where we'd gotten out of our kayaks.

After two hours of paddling, we came across a group of about twenty Asháninka men, women, and children who were yelling and waving at us. We knew what their peculiar waves meant. With their palms facing down, arms outstretched then drawn back toward their bodies—almost like they were mimicking a back hoe in motion—they were calling us over to them.

This was not good.

"Shit," we said almost in unison.

Our activities over the past twenty-four hours undoubtedly seemed weird to the Asháninka. Motoring past them heading downriver the afternoon before, then motoring back upriver this morning, then paddling back down the river now. Besides the fact that they have come to view every outsider as a threat, and tourism is not a thing that exists in their territory, we were doing extra-strange stuff. Being singled out as a source of trouble for the Asháninka was the last position I had hoped to be in.

We felt that stopping could be the wrong choice. This village was not one of our official checkpoints. It was a Saturday afternoon so there was a good chance the men would be drunk. If they were drunk, then the best case is that they would hassle us, maybe search our kayaks, but it wouldn't be a pleasant interaction. Worst case, well, we didn't really want to think about that. Remembering that in 2011 Jaroslaw Frackiewicz and Celina Mroz, who were canoeing down the river, were murdered by three drunk Asháninka men with shotguns and machetes, we decided that stopping seemed unwise.

And yet, not stopping also seemed like a bad idea. We thought of Davey du Plessis, a South African who had set out to paddle this part of the Amazon River alone in 2012. He had been shot multiple times with a shotgun by two Asháninka men who pursued him in their motorized canoe. The rumor is that these men wanted him to stop and he didn't. He got lucky and survived, but barely. With shotgun pellets lodged in his arm, neck, spine, face, skull, and one in his heart, he had a harrowing thirty-six-hour journey to get to the hospital in Pucallpa. Incapacitated, he was passed from village to village, being shuffled among people who wanted to help him but who were also afraid of his attackers.

We had a lot of things to consider in the minute that we had to make our decision. Besides the language barrier, being unable to understand each other's backgrounds, fears, and hopes all made this decision a total crapshoot. We had case studies against the wisdom of both stopping and not stopping:

"Maybe they just want to say hi?" said Midge, true to his optimist nature.

Don, ever the realist, pointed out, "Or maybe they just want to kill us."

"They wouldn't do anything bad to us in front of all those kids," Midge countered.

"Their shouts seem rather angry to me," I said.

"If we don't stop, they might shoot us anyway. We can't outrun them. They'll just get in their canoes and motor on down after us," Don added.

"Well, shit!"

Then Midge remembered the canoe. "Where the fuck is Cesar?"

We decided to smile and wave back enthusiastically and pretend we didn't know they were calling us over. We figured this would buy us a little more time. We all looked around for Cesar, Wilson, and the motorized canoe that was carrying them down the river. Finally we spotted them a few hundred yards upriver of us. Annoyed that our safety plan had fallen through yet again, we started waving our arms to get their attention. They finally realized what was going on, cranked the engine to life, and motored over to the beach to talk to the Asháninka. Meanwhile, we had drifted past their beach, and their shouts seemed to be more frantic now.

When the motorized canoe caught up with us, Cesar spoke first, "You must paddle back up the river and go talk to them."

Then Wilson added, "Yes, they are very angry with you. You must go back."

"Great," I thought. Day three in the Red Zone and we already have the one group of people we're trying not to not piss off "very angry with us."

My brain whirled with anxious thoughts of paddling back upstream within range of their crappy old 1950s shotguns—leftover gifts from the Peruvian military when they were enlisting the help of the Asháninka to fight against the Shining Path in the 1990s. We were complete idiots about to paddle to our executions.

With all of this going on in my head, we began a quick conversation with Cesar and Wilson. Both thought it was reasonably safe to go back; they agreed that the Asháninka just wanted to talk to us, to assure themselves that we weren't dangerous. We turned our seventeen-foot sea kayaks around—an extremely slow process—and paddled back up a giant eddy to talk to the villagers.

In preparation for all the dangerous situations we might encounter on our source-to-sea descent, we had thought of a number of safety measures. We had two satellite phones to call the outside world in case of an emergency. We each carried a SPOT device that would, in theory, alert the closest rescue organization if we pushed the SOS button. We bought Global Rescue insurance that guaranteed the armed forces of whatever country we were in would come to our aid if something went wrong. We had emergency teams in place in the United States who were ready to act if we sent them a specific message. And, we had gunshot wound treatment kits.

I quickly realized that none of this would help if the Asháninka decided to open fire on us. Okay, maybe the gunshot wound kits would, but if all three of us were shot and bleeding to death, we might not have time to dig them out of our dry bags. Plus, we would have to fight over who got to use them since we only had two and there were three of us.

We were really out there. Even if we did call for help, the reality is that it would most likely be days before any rescue team could reach us, if they came at all.

We approached with trepidation, having no idea how they might welcome us. We were not greeted by a wall of shotgun fire so that was a good start. Still, we were scared. A man, who appeared to be the leader, began speaking to us in Spanish, his second language, and ours as well. During a fifteen-minute oration, he lectured us on why they needed to be vigilant to protect their people and we began to learn that they were as scared of us as we were of them.

"We need to protect the children, in particular, because many gringos come to steal their organs," the chief slowly explained.

When the confused looks on our faces made him think that we did not understand the Spanish word for organs (*organos*), he paused and thought for a while and then said that the white people come to steal the "hearts of children" and "other important parts."

He pointed emphatically to the young children hiding behind their mothers on the beach and said, "You see them? They are so young, you can easily hurt them. We are the only ones who can protect them."

I can only imagine what was going through the kids' minds as they listened to one of their leaders explain that people like us come to murder them and steal their body parts. It must have felt like watching some overly personalized horror movie.

We knew the people of this region were afraid of outsiders, among other reasons, because of this conviction that white people are child kidnappers and organ thieves. We had read numerous accounts about this belief, but we thought they were written by travelers trying to embellish their stories, trying to make the Asháninka seem more mysterious and dangerous than necessary. Yet, here we were, hearing firsthand from the chief of the village that this was, in fact, something they understood as a real threat.

This idea of white people as child-stealers likely comes from the Franciscan missionaries' actual horrific practice of kidnapping Asháninka children. Citing the "natural evils of the Andes Indians" as the reason for the Franciscans' failure to convert the Asháninka adults, they decided that Asháninka children were the only ones who might be saved. The Franciscans stole the kids and moved them far from their families, stripping them of their culture in the hope of converting them before their native ways became too entrenched.* They might not have been stealing their actual organs, but they were certainly stealing their souls.

In addition, the chief continued, they needed to ensure that we were not drug traffickers, military people looking for drug traffickers, government logging scouts, illegal logging scouts, Shining Path terrorists, military rooting out Shining Path terrorists, or engineers sent by the government to plan dams on their river. We were beginning to understand the untold threats that the Asháninka faced. They were truly afraid of every human who was not Asháninka (and some who were). As we sat there getting lectured, we learned more about their fears from hearing their words and seeing their physical reactions than we ever could have from all the reading we had done about them before the trip.

---

*　Stefano Varese, *Salt of the Mountain*, 82.

I noticed that the women and children had all huddled toward the back of the group and there was a row of men standing in the front, closest to us. Some of the men were clearly drunk, although the chief did not seem to be. I tried to smile and wave at a couple of the women thinking that our shared gender would give us some kind of bond, but I failed. I hadn't spoken yet, so maybe my haircut was fooling them. Some scowled at me, others just hid themselves from my gaze. It was an intense, yet impersonal hatred, and it confounded me. This was the first time in my life that I had caused such fear or hatred in another human being, and it was certainly an uneasy feeling. This was only our third day in the Red Zone and we had already confirmed that many of the rumors we had heard about this place were true. My comfort level at being a tourist in this place sank to a new low.

As I was considering our unfortunate position, the chief's voice got a little louder and commanded my full attention once again. Feeling that he had sufficiently educated us about the innumerable dangers they faced from outsiders, he turned to the problem of us not stopping when they asked us to.

"We are not angry at you," explained the chief, and this was a huge relief to hear. "You didn't know any better. But Cesar, he should know better. We will have to punish him."

Whatever relief I had felt a moment before evaporated. The blood rushed out of my face as I considered what sort of punishment the Asháninka felt was worthy of Cesar's mistake. Tension flooded our sandy beach and everybody waited to find out what would happen next. The rest of the Asháninka seemed as on edge as we were, although I'm sure they didn't care nearly as much as we did if Cesar would live or die.

"What do you think punishment means to them?" I whispered to Don as quietly as I could as to not draw attention to myself.

"I don't know, but I'm sure it can't be good."

One of the men who seemed drunk began tugging at my SPOT that was attached to the front of my boat. He demanded to know what it was and wanted to know why it was flashing.

He asked brusquely, "Is it filming us?"

He seemed satisfied with my explanation that it was a GPS, not a camera, and that we were using it to track our progress down the river.

He pointed at the sky and said, "So the satellites, they know where you are?"

"Yes!" I shouted emphatically hoping this might deter any murders he was planning, "Many, many people know where we are."

He then turned to Don's GoPro camera, wanting to be sure that it was turned off. My fear escalated. Why could they possibly care if we were filming unless they were about to do something really awful to Cesar?

Cesar Pena had been through the Red Zone the year before with West Hansen's expedition. West didn't travel with the same permission letters we did and his group was subjected to numerous searches and interrogations, some of them at gunpoint. Nothing serious had happened to the team on West's expedition but living with the constant threat that things could go terribly wrong was too much for Cesar. When he returned home to Iquitos, Peru, he vowed he would never travel through that region of Peru again.

Given nine months to forget this vow, and in serious need of money, Cesar agreed to accompany us and travel through the Red Zone one more time. His normal work as a guide for jungle trips out of Iquitos had recently dried up, and he needed a job. He had a wife and three kids to support, so Midge's invitation to accompany us from Puerto Ene to Iquitos would give Cesar more than a month of much-needed income.

I could not help but feel guilty for talking him into coming with us. I was certain he was regretting his decision with every fiber of his being. What good would the extra money be to his family if he did not make it out of here alive?

When I had been slugging back tequila shots in Ecuador and shaking Midge's hand committing myself to try to become the first woman to kayak the Amazon from source to sea, I had never considered a scenario like this one. We were selfish foreign explorers wanting to kayak the Amazon River. What would we gain from doing this?

Fame?

Accolades?

Or, more likely, nothing at all.

Now, our desires to paddle this river, for reasons that I still can't quite understand, were about to get a father of three murdered.

Chapter 10

LEGACY OF THE SHINING PATH

"Fears are educated into us, and can, if we wish, be educated out."

—Karl Augustus Menninger

We sat in our kayaks and waited an uncomfortably long time before the chief finally stopped deliberating and issued Cesar's punishment. I listened breathlessly as the chief announced, *"Como su castigo, tendrá que hacer cincuenta planchas."*

"What?" I asked Don. "Did I just hear him right? That means he has to do fifty push-ups, doesn't it?"

But then I remembered how widely Spanish can vary from one country to another, or even one region to another. For example, *coger el bus* in Ecuador means you are going to catch the bus. In Mexico, however, this would be the vulgar equivalent of saying, "I'm going to have sex with the bus." So then I began to worry that *plancha*, which in Ecuadorian slang means push up, but literally means sheet, iron, or griddle, was the chief's way of saying they were going to cook him up, iron him flat, waterboard him, or some other horrible form of torture.

I anxiously looked at Cesar and his embarrassed smile told me I'd heard the chief right—fifty push-ups was his punishment!

"Can you do fifty?" the chief asked Cesar in a mocking tone.

Cesar replied, "I used to be Peruvian military." And he got down on the ground to begin.

Cesar did his push-ups while the men counted. Around forty he began to falter and finally pulled off forty-nine, but then collapsed onto the sand. The chief said something about Peruvian military being weak and everyone laughed, including all the women and children. Then he told Cesar to get to his feet.

It was strange transitioning to laughter and lightheartedness after being certain I was about to watch something awful happen to Cesar. I was more relieved than anything else, but still felt edgy and wanted to get off that beach as soon as possible. The Asháninka said goodbye and wished us well. I paddled away wondering what the hell had just happened. The Asháninka came across so angry and fearful, yet at the same time so playful and jovial. I couldn't reconcile the conflicting emotions they had inspired in me.

∽

AUGUST 25, 2013
DAY 29 OF THE EXPEDITION

The next day a massive rainstorm swelled the river and carried us quickly to the town of Poyeni, our next official checkpoint and where we hoped to get permission to camp for the night. When we pulled into Poyeni, we found Tomas waiting for us on the bank. He was the appointed guard for the day and wore his old shotgun slung over his shoulder resting on his back. He was friendly, but serious, as he cut off our questions and told us to produce our passports and our permission papers. We showed him our permission papers from C.A.R.E. (Central Asháninka del Rio Ene) and C.A.R.T. (Central Asháninka de Rio Tambo), our letter of introduction from the Peruvian ministry of tourism, and our passports. We were nervous and on our best behavior after the push-up incident. Once he had looked everything over, his face broke into a huge grin, he introduced himself, and he asked if he could show us his town.

Tomas led us up a slippery mud trail. We hiked for ten minutes and climbed about three hundred feet in elevation to a cloud-shrouded view of the confluence of the Tambo and Poyeni rivers. We were looking out over a vast expanse of rainforest and braided riverbed. It was thick jungle as far as we could see. It was our first view from any vantage point besides the river bottom in nearly a month and the new perspective was refreshing.

The view helped to bring home what we had undertaken. We had already been kayaking for twenty-nine days, but had only put a tiny dent into our total mileage. I could no longer see any hint of the rocky, desolate canyons we had spent the last few weeks navigating. It was as if that part of the expedition existed in a different era. Now our world consisted of lush jungle, heat, humidity, and the legacy of the Shining Path. The Atlantic Ocean was still a few lifetimes away, too far even to begin to think about. I stood at the edge of the cliff looking out over the beautiful, seemingly wild rainforest and tried to contemplate what this whole thing meant.

Would kayaking the entire length of the Amazon change me? Everyone told me that surely it would. But they had never done anything like this so how would they know? I had to admit that this expedition had already given me a thorough education about the Asháninka people and had opened my eyes to an unstable and unpredictable region of my planet that I could have never understood without seeing it firsthand. However big I thought my problems were, they paled in comparison to what these people along the river had been through. But was I really any different, aside from having this new perspective?

The question that most concerned me was whether I was more prepared now to tackle my own challenges of quitting my vagabond lifestyle and becoming normal. Why was this so important to me anyway? I liked to think that I didn't care what other people thought of me, but it was obvious that I did. Otherwise I wouldn't feel the need to constantly prove myself to the world. If I truly didn't care, I certainly wouldn't feel the need to give up my enjoyable lifestyle in exchange for a settled existence that pleased others.

The last twenty-nine days had been stressful and trying, but I still felt more comfortable in situations like these than I imagined I would sitting through an interview or surviving a week at a desk job. A nine-to-five office job, a mortgage, and a 401(k) still seemed frighteningly inaccessible. I didn't even have a clue where to start in order to get these things. That probably wasn't a good sign for my anticipated transformation. The hardships of the Amazon trip should have made me happy to give up this way of living, but so far, that wasn't happening. A perverse part of me enjoyed the suffering.

I kept staring out over the watery expanse as I tried to convince myself that my plan to quit adventuring made sense. One huge perk of walking away from this life was that I would never have to sit in front of a group of frightened Asháninka again and fear for my life. Giving up Class V kayaking could have its advantages, too, I told myself—I don't necessarily love the feeling at the top of a rapid when flawless execution is essential; that a mistake could be fatal. It is incredibly stressful.

More than once I'd said, "I wish I could be content doing that," as Don and I paddled away from a perfectly good fishing hole. We'd wave goodbye to the couple sitting in their folding lawn chairs, fishing poles in one hand, Budweisers in the other, as we headed downriver into the Class V maelstrom. Meanwhile, they would continue to sit peacefully at the put-in. But these people never get the feeling I get at the *bottom* of a Class V rapid.

I implored my brain to get on board with this scheme, to grow up, settle down, and start a new career after the trip was over.

My reflections were cut short by Tomas politely demanding, "Let's get moving. You have a lot of people waiting to meet you."

Our first order of business, Tomas informed us, was to see the chief of the *ronda*. In our naïveté, we had a vague idea of what this meant, but weren't even sure what a ronda was. We had heard many stories from previous trips down the Amazon that *ronderos* were drug lords, drug traffickers, or crazy gun-toting indigenous people. The man we met in Poyeni didn't fit any of these descriptions. He was lounging on a platform raised off the ground by about two feet. The structure had no walls, but there was a tin roof overhead that protected him from the sun and the rain. He listened to a small radio and did his best to feign interest when Tomas introduced us to him.

"Welcome to Poyeni," he stately flatly. "What are you doing here?"

I started to explain, but Tomas cut me off. "They are traveling down the river, trying to go all the way to Brazil. They'd like to stay here tonight. I've seen their permission papers, they are okay."

"Alright, you may camp down by the river tonight."

With that the chief of the ronda stopped paying any attention to us whatsoever and resumed his relaxing afternoon of listening to the radio. His disinterest was a huge relief. I've been waylaid for hours by curious locals who want to know every single piece of information about your life, your sport, the materials of your clothing, your financial status, your marital status, your child-bearing potential. It had been a long couple of days and I really wanted to relax. The fact that the chief of the ronda wanted nothing to do with us was some of the best news I'd had in days.

Next we had to meet the president of the rondas, not to be confused with the chief, although we were getting more confused by the minute. The president was very interested in us, but luckily he was also interested in drinking beer and he promptly marched us to the nearest store. The beer store was someone's house that had a four-foot-long storefront built into the front porch. With a loud banging on the wall, the president of the rondas shouted, "Buenas Tardes," a few times in a loud voice to get the owner's attention.

On our walk over, we had picked up an engineer who was from the next village up the river but who was in town working on a city planning project. He decided he would also join us for a beer. The president ordered beers for everyone except Tomas (who got a Coca-Cola since he was on guard duty), and they began peppering us with questions. In between their questions, we were able to shout a few of our own. Don and I were trying to figure out what, exactly, a ronda was, and Midge kept interrupting us to try to get us to ask Tomas if Midge could hold his shotgun. We tried our best to ignore Midge, feeling it was an inappropriate request.

The president of the ronda turned to us with a strange seriousness and spoke to us about his desire to develop tourism in the area. The main thing he wanted to know from us—a sample of the tiny number of tourists that they had met in their lifetimes—was what he could do to help the area's damaged reputation. I thought, for starters you could stop murdering the few tourists who do come here, but of course I kept this suggestion to myself.

As we talked about how best to get tourists to come to a notoriously dangerous part of the world, the people of Poyeni filed past, giggling at us and waving hello. A few of the braver kids even came up to shake our hands and to get a closer look at Midge, who was wearing red and orange striped pants and a white and red checkered shirt, and who had a huge furry beard and by now was holding Tomas's shotgun while drinking a beer. Persistence is one of Midge's strong points, but Tomas had agreed only after he'd emptied the shotgun of all its shells, wisely knowing that Midge should not be trusted with a loaded weapon.

The people of Poyeni had structured their society around both a chief of the ronda, who served more as the chief of the town, and a president of the ronda. The ronda itself was set up to protect the people of the town, posting guards and keeping an eye out for strange activity—three gringos kayaking down the river, for example. Rondas were created in the late 1980s to fight back against the Shining Path insurgents. Since the Peruvian government wasn't helping the people defend themselves against the *Senderistas* (Shining Path rebels), the people decided they had to take their safety into their own hands. They began forming *rondas campensinas*, vigilante groups to help keep their families and villages safe. Today the rondas keep a watchful eye out for all kinds of threats to the safety and sovereignty of the people trying to carve out a peaceful existence in the Red Zone.

Roughly three hundred families live in Poyeni, and it truly is an idyllic place. Their schoolhouse and yard were painted gaily by children, and the streets had center medians full of plants and flowers. We never saw a single car in the town, but the streets were built wide and sturdy to accommodate whatever vehicles might happen to pass through. Though life here felt peaceful, the residents lived in a constant state of low-level fear, never knowing when or how the next threat might appear.

The next morning, we woke up before dawn as we had become accustomed to doing. This was imperative to having a good morning bathroom experience. The sand flies, while relentless during the day, disappeared almost completely at night, so one could go to the bathroom before daybreak without getting attacked in unpleasant places by these bugs. The other obstacle to morning toileting was that boat traffic on the river got very busy each morning as day was breaking. Once the boats started running, it was hard to get a private moment on the wide-open sandy beaches, and we tried to avoid walking into the jungle before daylight for fear of what we might discover there or what might discover us. Our beach at Poyeni was extra difficult. Since it was a relatively large town, Poyeni served as a transportation hub for the surrounding villages and the motorized canoes began arriving before daybreak.

I was on what I thought was a private patch of sand. I heard the motor and by the time I made out the shape of a large motorized canoe, it was almost upon me, about to beach right where I was going to the bathroom. With pants around my ankles, I waddled into the nearby jungle with as much speed and agility as possible given the circumstances.

Later that morning, a group of workers wearing orange safety vests and hard hats shouted at us from shore, "*Oye! Pela Caras!*"—"Hey! Face Peelers!" The term *Pela Cara* is deeply associated with the organ-stealing white people that the Asháninka chief had explained to us. Pela Caras were originally rumored to be white, tall men who come and peel the faces of their victims to use the skin and fat. What they were using this for is unclear. Along the river, the story has morphed and they now believe that Pela Caras come and steal children to harvest their organs and sell them on the black market. When the Pela Caras are done, they dump the bodies of the children into the river with their organs replaced by money. The money is supposedly to bribe the families not to report the crimes.

I didn't like being called this.

By the 1990s both indigenous people living in the highlands of the Andes and those living along the headwaters of the Amazon had begun referring to the Shining Path insurgents as Pela Caras or Pishtaku (which in Quechua means "to cut the throat") as they often had lighter skin than the indigenous people. These terms, and their dreadful connotations, persist today. I wanted to paddle over and explain who we were, that we were nice people, and that the last thing we would do is peel off their faces, cut their throats, or steal their organs, but I knew this was unrealistic. We just waved and paddled by, doing nothing to dispel the myth.

∽

AUGUST 26, 2013
DAY 30 OF THE EXPEDITION

Besides being seen by the locals as organ-stealing child murderers, our group was straining under the pressure of proximity. By day we were each other's only company, and while we often had other people to talk to at night as we camped in villages, the three of us ate together, slept within fifteen feet of each other, talked about bathroom routines freely, and had lost all normal boundaries that dictate human interactions. We also hadn't taken a rest day—we'd been paddling thirty days in a row. Certain personality traits were coming out under the stress of the expedition and little fights were erupting daily.

Midge makes a lot of money from his exceptional computer programming skills, and he enjoys many of the opulent benefits of being wealthy—vacationing in the Alps, eating out in lavish restaurants in London, and buying expensive Scotch. At the same time, he feels at home in the poor person's world because he came from a family of weavers. He can chug a Pabst Blue Ribbon beer or sip expensive Macallan Scotch with equal vigor.

Midge is a self-admitted computer geek. When he walks into his office, he sits down at a desk that features a coffee mug that reads I ♥ PIVOT TABLES. Don't worry if you don't know what a pivot table is, it just means that you don't belong to an elite group of data organizers.

He can be a lot of fun and even has the capacity to care about his friends, but he can also be a self-absorbed, unapologetic asshole. When he's in one of these moods, if something doesn't directly benefit him, then he won't do it. Once in this mind-set, there is no arguing him out of it.

Midge relies on his self-diagnosed Asperger's as an excuse for his "behavioral problems," as he calls them. Whether or not his self-diagnosis is accurate, it is evident to all who spend more than a couple of minutes with him that he lives in a different world.

I like Midge.

Even as I write these negative things about him, I admit that I like and admire him. He is undeniably smart. He also has a crazy streak which led him to the Amazon River in the first place. I can't think of another person in my world who has so wholeheartedly dedicated themselves to an endeavor while having no prior skills or experience to encourage such a dream. For this, I have nothing but admiration for Midge. He can be fun to talk to and, when he's in the right mood, he can be charismatic. It was somehow easy to enjoy his company despite all of what I perceived to be his negative qualities.

Don takes pride in his whitewater and survival skills and in his life's work as a kayak guide. He doesn't make much money, but he lives a life that most people only dream about. He owns very little, but in turn, nobody owns him. He has no debt, so he funnels all the money he makes into "living the life." He travels to exotic locations, kayaks more than two hundred days a year and has relatively few worries. Of course, he may pay for his lifestyle choices when the realities of not having a retirement fund present themselves, but for the time being he has an enviable existence. He likes to joke that he'll make an excellent Walmart greeter when he's too old to kayak. Due to his own financial circumstances, Don was happy that Midge was footing the bill for this expedition, but this was also a point of contention, gnawing at Don's own insecurities.

I am incredibly impatient. As much as I try to combat this, it still dominates my personality. I want things done in my time frame, and can get pretty irritated if my schedule isn't being met. Though spending large amounts of time in South America has partially cured me of this scheduling hang-up, I still cling to pointless desires to get things done quickly.

After nearly a decade of training Midge and helping him build the skills to survive the whitewater in the Amazon's headwaters, Don and I knew a lot about him and he about us. As we learned about each other's quirky personality traits, we did our best to develop strategies to deal with them. But spending a few weeks at a time in Ecuador with each other, where we all had our own separate rooms to go back to, was different than the intense exposure of spending every waking hour together on this expedition. There is only so much people can withstand before the tension gets out of control.

We reached Atalaya on the thirtieth day of the expedition and were planning on taking one much-needed rest day. Besides the fact that our backs were sore and cramped from the lack of back bands in our sea kayaks, we were sunburned, grumpy, and exhausted. We had scrapes and cuts from the whitewater canyons that wouldn't heal because they were persistently wet, and we were emotionally drained from the stress of the past few days. On top of all that, we had painful rashes on our butts from sitting in wet kayaks ten hours per day. We were also freezing cold—an irony in the jungles along the Amazon—from our third day in a row of paddling in the driving rain. Midge refused to put on any of his warm paddling gear and was nearly frozen as we pulled into Atalaya, adding hypothermia-induced grumpiness to our list of mounting tensions.

With teeth chattering, the three of us worked our way through the maze of brightly colored motorized canoes that blocked access to the beach. We bickered as we walked through town dodging speeding moto-taxis—motorcycles that have been converted into taxis by putting two wheels in the back and a bench seat big enough for two people behind the driver.

Midge insisted that we find him a hotel with Wi-Fi, which proved challenging in Atalaya. We finally found the one hotel with Internet in town. The hotel had one room left; the rest were occupied by oil workers conducting explorations in the area. Without a moment's consideration, Midge took it.

Midge had gotten to be annoyingly demanding, especially when we were in or near towns. When we got to Atalaya, Midge asked us to do his laundry for him.

We said no.

In normal circumstances, we probably wouldn't have minded helping him out, but there was something so grating in the way he asked that our immediate reaction was, "Thanks, but I think we'll pass on the opportunity to do your laundry." I'm sure my own irritable mood added a filter to Midge's request that made it sound much worse than it actually was. No doubt we left Midge bewildered that we wouldn't do him this one simple favor.

I was working under the assumption that we were a team of three, not Midge and his two servants. I think the former is how Midge viewed the relationship most of the time, but his view was skewed whenever he was overly tired, when too many things needed to be done, or when he felt like checking out. This conflicting understanding of our roles came out the most when logistical tasks needed to be accomplished or when we faced obligatory social interactions to show our gratitude to people who had helped us out along way.

Midge did the majority of the pre-trip planning—purchasing whitewater kayaks and sea kayaks, arranging for the shipment of kayaks to Peru, buying topo maps of the whitewater sections from Peru's military (the keeper of maps for remote regions of the country), getting West to come to Peru to help us, and much more. But his actions suggested that he expected Don and me to deal with most of the logistical headaches once the trip started, such as working out the permissions we needed from the navy and the indigenous people to proceed down the river. It's possible that in his mind he was paying for our expenses in exchange for these duties, but this wasn't part of our spoken agreement. In many ways, this division of labor made sense, as Don and I speak Spanish and Midge does not. Yet I was always surprised when he refused to participate in these sorts of tasks.

Midge stated that he would have nothing to do with the meetings with the navy, the coast guard, and the local indigenous groups that Cesar said were mandatory before heading down the river. Never feeling the need to explain his actions—probably rooted in his deep disregard for other people and other people's opinions of him—he just stated flatly, "You can go if you want. I'm not going."

It's not that Don or I *wanted* to go. There were a million other things that sounded more appealing—sleeping, showering, eating something besides dehydrated meals, to name a few. To me, all these meetings represented a variety of ways to help ensure our survival; I felt it was necessary to go.

Midge didn't appear to believe in the dangers that everyone, both locals and foreigners alike, warned us about. Just as he hadn't believed (or at least was unwilling to acknowledge in any form that I could understand) that his life was in danger in the dam construction zone or in the treacherous whitewater that pushed his kayaking skills well beyond their limits, he was equally incapable of acknowledging the dangers of the Red Zone. I'm still unsure about Midge's perceptions of the dangers we faced. Maybe he felt he was too significant to succumb to these dangers, or maybe his way of coping with the fear was to deny the emotion entirely.

Don and I spent our rest day with Cesar, talking to various indigenous groups, the coast guard, and the navy. We also found a new motorized canoe to come downriver with us. Our refusal to do Midge's laundry, his refusal to come to any of the meetings, and a short but loud shouting match between Don and Midge over finances had left all of us angry. Don and I never knew the exact dollar amount of the expedition, but I have no doubt that the figure would sound astronomical to us. I'm not sure if Don felt guilty that Midge was paying for everything, or if he was chagrined that he could never afford a trip like this, but either way, the finances created a thick layer of pressure. There was palpable tension as we started paddling again; our day off hadn't done us much good.

Leaving Atalaya was as much of a scene as arriving. When we tried to put our sea kayaks back into the river, we found the waterfront so clogged with passenger dugout canoe traffic that we had to slip one at a time between the big motorized canoes. We paddled through a jumble of boats until we finally broke free from the traffic jam. Most of the dazzlingly colored canoes were already loaded up with local passengers who gawked at us and took photos with their cell phones.

We did not make it far past town when we came upon a floating barge that served as the coast guard office of Atalaya where we needed to check in one last time before leaving. I'd been working with Guillermo (the guy with the navy connections from Lima) trying to get us a navy or coast guard escort for the remainder of the Red Zone. Guillermo was involved in the logistics, and some of the whitewater paddling, during the first full descent of the Amazon with Joe Kane and Piotr Chmielinski in 1985. He liked to pay attention to all major river expeditions in his country and was eager to help however he could—mainly through his ties to the navy. He felt strongly that the Red Zone was sufficiently dangerous these days that, while a navy escort wasn't required, we would be a lot better off with one. I had traded numerous emails and phone calls with Guillermo over the past few weeks and he told me he was working on the escort.

The military would not travel upriver from Atalaya to help us for a variety of reasons that were never made clear, but which probably involved too much danger and an unwillingness to stir up whatever equilibrium existed on the Ene and Tambo rivers. Guillermo had thought that once we reached Atalaya, we could pick up an escort. Although the dangers seemed to significantly diminish below Atalaya, we figured we'd take an escort if they were willing to provide it. We checked in with the officials here, letting them know we were heading downriver, and we asked about the possibility of an escort. They told us it was not up to them and they could do nothing until they received orders from the bigger base downriver in Pucallpa. Not knowing whether these orders would ever materialize, we decided to continue downstream.

We left town and paddled past the confluence with the Urubamba River, which nearly doubled the volume of water. Now the water we kayaked on was called the Ucayali River. For the next two days, when the three of us did talk, it was curt and reserved. Every interaction between Don and Midge ended in a snide comment. Neither was willing to be up-front about what it was that was making them mad, but they each had to get in as many derisive quips as possible. It was driving me insane. I asked the guys to paddle over and we floated together as I broke the silence.

"Okay, guys, let's just get it out in the open."

My suggestion was met with silence.

"Come on," I said. "Don, just explain what is bothering you."

Then Don laid into Midge. "You act like we are your employees. You treat us like shit. I know you are paying for everything, but you are also using that as leverage to act like an asshole. Plus—"

Midge cut him off mid-sentence shouting, "You could try appreciating the fact that I'm paying for everything!"

To which Don yelled back, "And you never fucking listen!"

"Wait!" I shouted above both the guys, a difficult feat for me. "Midge, just let Don finish. Hear him out, then you can talk."

Surprisingly, Midge agreed and quietly listened to the rest of Don's complaints, which revolved around the fact that Midge made Don feel inferior, like his servant, and Don wanted him to stop acting that way.

"Okay, Midge, your turn. What are we doing that is pissing you off so much?"

Midge was unusually impassioned as he explained, "You guys don't give me any credit for doing anything for, or on, this expedition. All you've done for the last month is point out the ways in which I've failed to prepare, but you've never once said thanks for the things that I have done."

"That's because you keep telling us to do this stuff for you," Don interrupted.

Again I stepped in. "Don, you had your turn, now we have to listen to Midge."

"This is exactly what I mean," Midge continued. "I successfully imported the sea kayaks, I arranged for West to help us out, I found Deborah in Lima, and I got Cesar to come with us through the Red Zone. I just wish you guys could acknowledge this."

It was my turn now, and I explained, "Midge, it's not that we don't appreciate what you've done, but you are right we could tell you thanks more often. But our issue now is that you don't seem to be interested in participating in our safety through the Red Zone. You expect Don and me to take care of—"

"Bullshit!" screamed Midge in a surprising display of emotion for him. "I hired Cesar to come with us, I hired the motorized canoes, all to make you guys feel better about coming with me through the Red Zone. It is fucking expensive, and this is exactly what I mean. You think I've done nothing, but I have done a lot."

I was surprised by Midge's passionate response. I guess it was easy to fall into the trap of believing his Asperger's explanation and to take that one step further to assume that he didn't experience strong emotions himself. "Okay, okay, Midge. Thank you for hiring Cesar and the canoes, both are great to have along. For my part," I continued, "I wish you would try to act a little less entitled and a little more like part of the team. Every night at camp you finish your dinner, say 'I'm all done now,' and hand me your trash. I'm not the garbage lady."

We felt better after we all had yelled at each other for a while. Even if none of us really felt like our problems were resolved, we did feel we had relieved a huge pressure just by vocalizing what we were each pissed off about. On a deeper level, we were happy to ignore our issues a while longer, and act cordially toward each other because we all believed that life would be much better once we met up with the *Perolita*—a larger support boat that was going to meet us in Pucallpa. We all pinned our highest hopes on this boat to provide every kind of relief.

Not long after our fight, Midge declared that he only wanted to paddle six hours per day despite new warnings about the rise of violent river piracy in the area we were paddling into. He had some logic to this wish—he knew we still had a long way to go and he did not want to develop tendonitis or some other detrimental condition that might ruin his chances of finishing. I felt strongly that we should wait until we reached Pucallpa, were out of the Red Zone, and theoretically safer to implement the six-hour-per-day rule. I did not want to spend any more time in the dangerous areas of the river than was absolutely necessary.

Midge was visibly tired and I sympathized but, for me, it was imperative to get out of the Red Zone as quickly as possible. But Midge was adamant. That afternoon Midge demanded we stop at 2:00 P.M. As if to add credence to my position, some guys from a nearby rice farm motored over to talk to us. They asked why we were sitting on this beach, and told us repeatedly that we must be careful, this is a very dangerous zone.

"Are you sure you want to camp here?" they asked us, adding, "It's not safe."

I fumed at Midge. Each day after six hours, he decelerated to a pace so slow that it was hard to tell if he was actually moving or not. I begged him to paddle a little bit longer.

"Midge, please. As soon as we are out of the Red Zone, we can paddle one hour per day for all I care, but please don't do this here."

My pleading was useless; if anything I think it made him go slower. I'm sure his pace was a passive-aggressive expression of displeasure over my pushing him to go farther.

The sun had become a real issue as well, adding to our difficulties. To prevent malaria, we were taking doxycycline, which causes "a heightened sensitivity to the sun." The doctors felt we'd be okay just using extra sunscreen. I guess they didn't believe us when we told them we'd be out in the sun every daylight hour. The sun sensitivity meant that my lips got insanely sunburned and no amount of SPF lip balm or sunscreen could stop the blistering. The sunburned blister on my bottom lip had become a giant bloody mess and I knew I could not paddle the remaining three thousand miles to the Atlantic like this. Don and I had scoured the stores of Atalaya in vain for a bandana; just as I was about to buy a baby's skirt to wear around my head, Don found a cloth napkin that I tied onto my sun hat.

Another consequence of our sun sensitivity was that our fingernails started to get irradiated. We didn't know what was going on at first. Midge and I succumbed to it before Don, and we both felt like we had thousands of tiny needles jabbed under our fingernails. Touching anything was painful and if we caught a fingernail on something, it was excruciating. I snagged my index fingernail on my spray skirt one morning while gathering up my gear and Don stood over me, dumbfounded, as I rolled on the ground in agony, unable to speak.

Don didn't understand what we were whining about until his fingertips started turning a very weird shade of orange. It looked like he had put bad tanning cream on only the top half of his fingers. Then his fingernails started disconnecting from his fingers—like what happens when someone hits their fingernail with a hammer and it dies and falls off. He then understood why even something as simple as getting dressed in the morning could cause unimaginable pain. We tried paddling with socks over our hands, duct-taping our fingers, and I even paddled in my pogies—neoprene mittens that kayakers use in extremely cold water—despite the 90° heat. We eventually started wearing driving gloves that Midge's girlfriend, Rachel, had delivered to us from England.

Four days downstream of Atalaya and ten days into our journey through the Red Zone, Guillermo came through and the Peruvian navy started escorting us. By the time the navy started accompanying us down the river, we had already passed the spot where just weeks before the eight Peruvian settlers had been murdered by the Asháninkas, the spot where the Polish kayakers were murdered in 2011, and the place where Davey du Plessis was shot in 2012. We were grateful nonetheless.

We'd heard a shotgun firing the night before the navy joined us. That, mixed with countless warnings from locals about robberies along the river and Midge's new paddling regime of only six hours per day, made us feel more vulnerable than ever. The two navy patrol boats each had fifty caliber machine guns mounted to the bows, and each marine held his own assault rifle. We figured the *assaltantes* would not mess with us now.

Since there were two patrol boats, one would motor around checking the paperwork of barges and other large boats, and the other would float along behind us, growing increasingly annoyed at our slow pace. We tried not to worry about the boat full of irritated marines as we paddled past dolphins, squirrel monkeys, jabiru (storks), and hawks along the river. Our spirits were high, we were temporarily getting along, and everyone seemed happy to be on the river.

Our excitement about the escort was all too short-lived. As our daylight started fading and we began looking for a camping spot, the marines let us know that they had not come prepared to camp. They had planned on traveling from town to town and being able to stay in a hostel or someone's house, buying food from each village. Clearly there had been another failure to communicate. Upon their suggestion that we all load up and motor an hour and a half down to the next town, Ipiria, Midge flew into a rage and said there was no way he would do that.

Don and I were in an awkward position. We agreed with Midge that it was ridiculous to waste an hour and a half motoring down to a town when we were prepared to camp out. This would also mean that we would then have to spend two or more hours motoring back up against the current in the morning; but at the same time, we did not want to upset the guys with the heavy artillery. Plus, we felt bad that they were so unprepared to camp. We were in heavy mosquito territory now and without their mosquito netting, they would have a rough night, not to mention that they had no food.

Midge made his intransigence clear.

The commander of our escort was professional. He hid his irritation and recognized that he had orders to protect us. His solution was that the boat with lower ranking soldiers would stay on the beach with us and the other boat would go to town.

Trying to assuage their disappointment as much as possible, Don gave them a bottle of Pisco. Cesar and Socimo, our new canoe driver, motored off to try to find a little store that would perhaps sell at least some tuna fish and crackers for the marines. They came back an hour later with no food, but with two cases of beer. The two marines chosen for guard duty that night could not drink but the rest imbibed. Since Cesar had found no food, we pulled out a few extra dehydrated meals for them to share. They were gracious about it, but I felt confident that after trying the food, they would have preferred to go hungry. What started out as a tense evening ended up being fun as we drank a couple beers and learned about the lives of some of our protectors. Most were from the coast or the highlands and looked upon their station in the jungle with a mixture of disdain for the heat and humidity and awe at the adventure they were having. Midge joined us, too, and the entire hodgepodge team of kayakers, marines, and motorized canoe drivers had a good time together. The next day we easily made it to Ipiria, and when the marines asked if we could spend the night there, we obliged.

Our next major milestone would be reaching the town of Pucallpa. Pucallpa was significant for two reasons: one, it meant we were *mostly* done with the Red Zone. The river was reported to still be dangerous a few more days downstream of Pucallpa, but once we reached that city we would be out of the heart of the Red Zone's worst areas. Two, we were meeting our next support boat, the *Perolita*, in Pucallpa.

An important part of Midge's plan was to hire a support boat for as much of the flatwater as possible. He was looking for a boat we could sleep on, with a local crew who knew the lower river with its myriad channels, tides, and other hazards. He also hoped that the added protection of a larger boat with three or four crew members would keep us as safe as possible in the pirate-ridden lower Amazon—proof that he was concerned about our safety, and that I wasn't giving him enough credit. Before we signed on to Midge's full Amazon expedition, he spent hours wooing us—or more accurately Don—on our porch in Ecuador over gin and tonics.

"Don," Midge would say, "what part of 'air-conditioned gin palace' do you not understand?"

I'm pretty sure this was the only reason that Don agreed to do the entire trip. Don hates the heat, bugs, and flatwater, but he really loves air conditioning and gin and tonics.

The reality was slightly different. There would be no gin palace, but we had found a somewhat suitable replacement.

It was amazingly difficult to find a boat captain that was willing to help us. There are a handful of tourist boats on the Amazon, but not nearly as many as I'd expected. The captains we did find would only agree to help us for one or two weeks at a time, preferring to stay in their known parts of the river (for good reason, we would later find out), and they all asked an astronomical amount of money—more than even Midge was willing to part with. Through a travel agency called Rainforest Cruises, we finally found the *Perolita*. It was a boat based out of Brazil, but was willing to jump through the somewhat insane bureaucratic hoops to motor into Peru to meet us. They were also willing to go downriver "as far as possible" with us and for a more affordable price.

The *Perolita* was a forty-foot, two-story boat with two cabins and a kitchen downstairs, and a covered deck upstairs. While they wouldn't supply endlessly flowing gin and tonics, they would provide us with meals, a place to sleep, and the added security of traveling with a boat that could, in theory, anchor anywhere and would post a guard twenty-four hours per day. We were all looking forward to a level of safety and comfort that wasn't possible while hiding behind a mesh tent on the wide-open beaches of the Amazon.

While Peru's Red Zone stuck out in my mind as the scariest part of the flatwater, there were plenty of other zones throughout the Brazilian Amazon that were dangerous. The people in the lower river live in constant fear of what they call assaltantes, or river rats. These river pirates, known for robbing, raping, and murdering people, are a serious concern for local residents and tourists alike. The lower Amazon River is full of thousands of river channels impossible to effectively police. The river pirates know where to hide and are virtually impossible to find once they've slipped into the watery maze. They do what they want and most of them get away with it.

The region is home to an extremely lucrative drug trade, and the river rats want in on the action. Some river rat gangs have grown to huge numbers that vie for control of the drug trade. While big drug money is the prized objective, river rats confine their daily work to easier targets— namely river ferries traveling up and down the Amazon transporting locals. Rape is a constant threat for women passengers on these ferries. Robberies are also common. Though most people using river ferries don't have much to steal, it's a convenient way for the pirates to get food and a little extra cash. Tourists, seen as having lots of money, are an obvious target for river rats, and police who get too close to shutting down either a drug cartel or a river piracy operation are frequent targets as well.

In 2001 Sir Peter Blake—a New Zealand yachting hero—was murdered near the mouth of the Amazon River when pirates boarded his yacht. They presumably wanted to rob him, but when he tried to defend his boat, they killed him.

The team about to start their paddle across Lago Acucocha—the headwaters of the Amazon River in Peru. From left to right: Senor Matteo (landowner), Don Beveridge, Darcy Gaechter, and David Midgley. *Photo by West Hansen.*

ABOVE: Don and Midge paddling across the pristine waters of Lago Acucocha, Peru, on their way to the far shore to start hiking up the mountain to find the source of the Amazon River. *Photo by Darcy Gaechter.* BELOW: Don and Darcy showing off their frozen socks and shoes after an unprepared-for night out near the headwaters of the Amazon River in Peru. *Photo by David Midgley.*

Darcy standing on the banks of the Mantaro River, Peru, near the headwaters of the Amazon. *Photo by Lizet Alaniz.*

ABOVE: Darcy and Don padding through the San Juan Mine in the upper reaches of the Amazon in Peru. *Photo Lizet Alaniz.* BELOW: Darcy gets a little help from the locals while portaging the Malpaso Dam on the Mantaro River, Peru. *Photo by Don Beveridge.*

ABOVE: Darcy taking a break from hauling her kayak up and over gigantic boulders during a portage on the Mantaro River, Peru. *Photo by Don Beveridge.* BELOW: Darcy following Don through one of the granite canyons in the whitewater section of the Mantaro River, Peru. *Photo by Darcy Gaechter.*

Sea kayak delivery to Puerto Ene, Peru. *Photo by Darcy Gaechter.*

ABOVE: Midge trying to recover from his stomach illness at the "hotel" in Puerto Prado, Peru. *Photo by Darcy Gaechter.* BELOW: Midge holding Thomas's gun. Thomas was the appointed guard of the town of Poyeni—inside Peru's Red Zone—the day we showed up. *Photo by Darcy Gaechter.*

ABOVE: Plants can grow anywhere in the Amazon River Basin! *Photo by Darcy Gaechter.* BELOW: Darcy and Midge paddling the huge Amazon River below Manaus, Brazil. *Photo by Don Beveridge.*

Midge emerging from one of the frequent storms we encountered on the lower Amazon River in Brazil. *Photo by Darcy Gaechter.*

Midge waving at a passing supertanker. Boat traffic increased as we made our way down the river. *Photo by Darcy Gaechter.*

Local Brazilian girl seemingly unfazed by the proximity of the logging barge passing her. *Photo by Darcy Gaechter.*

Darcy making friends with the locals near Santarém, Brazil, after we asked if we could camp on their land. This is before we got into the tidal zone, but notice how tall the house on stilts is to accommodate high water season. *Photo by Don Beveridge.*

ABOVE: A small village in the Para Bay, Brazil. This is inside the tidal zone where the tides rise and fall roughly fifteen feet twice a day. This was the type of place we had to seek out when we needed to wait out the incoming tide in the lower Amazon River as there was no more dry ground. This village's main economy is producing acai and harvesting fresh water shrimp. *Photo by Darcy Gaechter.*
BELOW: Shrimp traps at a family's house in the Para Bay. This is where I bought the souvenir for my parents just before we crossed the Tocantins River, Brazil. *Photo by Darcy Gaechter.*

ABOVE: Don and Midge waking up on our basalt rock at Pontu Taipu when we couldn't find a proper camping spot. *Photo by Darcy Gaechter.* BELOW: The team at the Atlantic Ocean in Brazil. Left to right: Don Beveridge, David Midgley, Darcy Gaechter.

Midge sitting in silent contemplation on a beach overlooking the Atlantic Ocean. No doubt he was feeling the satisfaction of a decade of hard work paying off. *Photo by Don Beveridge.*

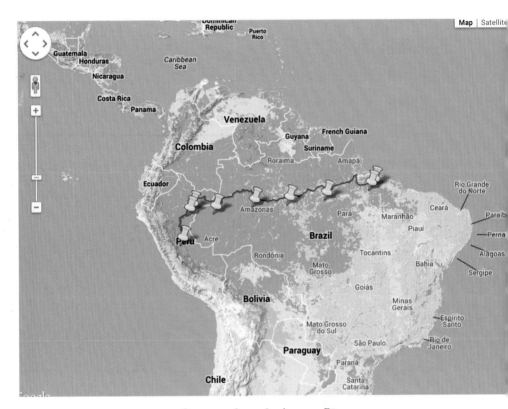

Our route down the Amazon River.

In 2016, the police chief from the town of Coari, Thyago Garcez, disappeared after he and his fellow police officers got into a firefight with drug traffickers. His body was never found. No one was arrested.

In 2017, a fight broke out in a Manaus prison between rival gangs, each fighting to control the drug trade. Fifty-six people were killed inside the prison, and dozens more died outside in riots that followed. Countless other locals have died and suffered at the hands of these river rats.

In 2017, four years after our expedition, a British woman named Emma Kelty was murdered near Coari in Brazil. She was attempting to paddle the river solo, and a young gang of six murdered and robbed her. Shortly after Emma's murder, a rival gang killed one of Emma's murderers in order to steal the cell phone, tablet, and GoPro camera that Emma's attackers took from her. Three people were arrested for Emma's murder; two of them were seventeen years old. These pirates are often kids who have known nothing but a life of fear and violence, and this makes them all the more dangerous. Life feels cheap to them and murdering a tourist or police chief doesn't feel very extreme.

There is no doubt that we all placed a lot of hope for safety and comfort on getting to the greatly longed for *Perolita*. For now though, we had to continue concentrating on surviving the rest of the Red Zone.

Four days after implementing his six-hour paddling rule and driving me, Don, Cesar, and all the navy guys absolutely crazy, Midge got a major burst of energy. Cesar, my coconspirator in trying to get Midge to paddle faster, had bought Midge a few beers during lunch, and in an alcohol-fueled frenzy, Midge had decided to break his six-hour rule when he realized we had a real chance of making it to Pucallpa. The navy guys were ecstatic because as soon as we made it to Pucallpa and hooked up with the *Perolita*, they'd be done with us.

We paddled well after dark—eleven hours total that day. We saw the lights of the comparatively huge town of Pucallpa nearly an hour before we reached the port. We excitedly paddled toward shore scanning all the boats and wondering which one was the *Perolita*. As we got closer, Cesar listened to a voicemail from Deborah:

"The *Perolita* is not in Pucallpa. I don't know where they are and no one can get in touch with the captain."

Chapter II

THE MIDGE WARS

"It is with rivers as it is with people: the greatest are not always the most agreeable nor the best to live with."

—Henry van Dyke

SEPTEMBER 3, 2013
DAY 38 OF THE EXPEDITION

I have a terrible habit of anthropomorphizing everything. As a consequence, I found myself irritated on behalf of our kayaks for the abuse they were enduring. Every passerby gave them a firm kick to find out what they were made of. Most of these kayak-abusers then proceeded to grab the rudders and shake them violently, wanting to know if they would fall off, I could only guess. My annoyance wasn't based solely on my empathy for the kayaks. The weeks of expedition paddling were also taking their toll and I was pissed off at the *Perolita*.

We were in the town square of Pucallpa, Peru, and it was 9:30 at night. Midge and I stood with our kayaks and pile of gear, still wearing our sweat-crusted button-up sun shirts and our ridiculous-looking floppy hats. None of us had enough energy left to emotionally deal with the disappointing news about the *Perolita*. Besides all the physical discomfort that we believed the *Perolita* would alleviate, we also thought that the boat might deliver us from some of the isolation of our undertaking. Three people spending all day everyday together gets unhealthy after a while.

Most of the time on the Amazon, we didn't wake up thinking, "Yep, we are living the dream, this is so wonderful, I can't wait to get my ass bitten by sand flies while I poop, then eat another bag of 'Kathmandu Curry' for breakfast, then sweat and paddle and live in monotony for the rest of the day. And maybe, if we're lucky, we will have another big fight!"

More accurately, we were constantly convincing ourselves of reasons to keep going. We all had a million reasons to quit; that would have been the easy thing to do. It was finding reasons to stay that was difficult. The *Perolita* had been that reason for us for weeks, and now we'd lost that, too.

When we'd reached Pucallpa, the marines helped us carry our kayaks up to the main town square and within minutes Midge and I drew a remarkably large crowd. Don left Midge and me to guard the gear while he tried to find us a hotel. It was rumored that there was a nice one in town. We were exhausted, but giddy with the anticipation of taking a shower and sleeping in a bed. I kept imagining laying my head on a pillow.

Midge and I were busy answering the locals' questions, enduring their stares and awkward touching of all our stuff. For the next hour, we fielded such questions as: "Where is the motor?"

We basked in their disbelief when I told them, "There isn't a motor," and then pointed to my bicep and said, "This is the motor."

The youngest kids tentatively climbed into the kayaks while their parents shouted more questions at us: "Where did you come from?"

"Where are you going?"

"What do you eat?"

"Where do you sleep?"

"How much do these cost?"

"Are you married?"

"Where are your children?"

In the middle of what felt like a twenty-questions game show, I started to feel smothered. With fifty or so Peruvians standing around us in an ever-tightening circle, a minor bout of claustrophobia set in. My eyes began to dart around the crowd looking for a weak link, someone I might knock over and plow through if I needed to escape.

I had just zeroed in on a scrawny-looking teenaged boy and had decided I could run right through him if need be when I noticed three men dressed as women. A good distraction. Cross-dressing men aren't altogether uncommon during certain South American festivals or holidays. In Ecuador, for example, many men dress up as women and dance in the streets on New Year's Eve. They often block traffic and only allow vehicles to go once the "lady" has done a comical lap dance on the hood, and the driver has given a "donation." But I didn't notice any parties or festivals going on. The most flamboyant cross-dresser had two balloons serving as breasts shoved into a tight, black spandex tube top. Two more balloons acted as a voluptuous buttocks underneath a tight green miniskirt. All three were wearing a preposterously bright shade of red lipstick. I couldn't help but laugh, which brought them closer to me.

As they were touching my clothes, the kayaks, and our life jackets, I slyly got out my tiny GoPro camera and started filming. I turned my back to the cross-dressers and stuck the camera under my armpit toward them. I tried to stand nonchalantly so they wouldn't discover my documentation of their attire, but it didn't work. They busted me. Instead of getting angry, they started hamming it up for the camera, showing me balloon cleavage, shaking their butts, blowing kisses, and doing other things they saw fit for cross-dressers to do. When the show was over, we began talking and then they looked me up and down and said, "What about you?" They were referring to my own, less showy cross-dressing—my short haircut, loose pants, slouched shoulders, and button-up shirt. I didn't feel like going into the whole rape and murder in the Red Zone thing so I just said, "What? I'm a kayaker."

Don showed up in a military truck to relieve Midge and me from our inquisition. We loaded the three kayaks and all our gear into the truck and stashed it in the garage of our hotel. We decided we would take two rest days here to let our bodies recover and to figure out what had happened to the *Perolita*.

Don found an amazing hotel. It really did have beds with clean, white sheets and actual pillows. The hotel had air-conditioning! There were toilets and showers in the rooms and there was hot water—an extravagance we hadn't had since leaving Lima forty days earlier. There was even a restaurant and bar; and, better yet, they said they would still serve us food even though it was almost 11:00 P.M. by the time we got there. There wasn't much for a vegan on the menu but they did cook me a giant plate of French fries and served me vegetables and hummus on the side. The boys ate hamburgers and we all indulged in ice water, which, at the time, seemed like a minor miracle. Midge also treated us to gin and tonics, beer, and a few shots of tequila. We figured getting drunk was an effective way to forget about the fact that the *Perolita* was MIA. Strangely, after the last week of fighting, the three of us got along great. Despite the disappointing news about the *Perolita*, Don, Midge, and I had fun together, laughed a lot, and stayed up well into the night talking. It felt like we might be putting our disagreements behind us.

We woke up in the morning indescribably happy to be in beds and to have eaten a real meal the night before. That morning, the three of us probably would have consented to spending the rest of our lives in that hotel in Pucallpa—it really felt that good. But we knew we needed to try to figure out what happened to the *Perolita* and to keep pressing forward with the expedition, so we dragged ourselves out of bed down to the lobby and started making phone calls.

∽

SEPTEMBER 6, 2013
DAY 41 OF THE EXPEDITION

We paddled away from Pucallpa two days later. Don, Midge, and I had come to terms with the fact that the *Perolita* was still unaccounted for, but the navy guys and Cesar were inconsolable. They had all thought their duties with us would be finished in Pucallpa and they weren't pleased about the change of plans.

There was only one thing that could lift everyone's mood at times like these. Our new canoe driver, Edwin, motored over to us and pointed at a rumpled patch of water in the river. We saw nothing, though we could hear a faint farting noise. We strained our eyes. Still nothing. Just a *phffft* sound off to our left, then again to the right.

"Dolphins!" Don finally shouted.

Then we saw them; giant, fat, pinkish Amazonian river dolphins. Watching the ungainly animals surface then make a breathing noise that sounds ridiculously similar to a fart cheered everyone up. We huddled together and watched and even the marines found the lumbering animals to be endearing.

We crawled into our tent on the third night after leaving Pucallpa and listened as a fishing boat pulled up to our beach with a radio blasting the Uruguay versus Peru soccer game. Our military escort was, once again, mad at us for not making it to the next town where they could have watched the game on TV. While the radio broadcast was a mere consolation prize, I hoped that hearing the game would at least cheer them up a little bit. I feel asleep to the shouts of the announcer on the radio yelling, "Goooooo ooooooaaaaaaaaaaaaaaaaaaalllllllllllllllllllllll!"

When I woke up again, everything was silent. The game was over and everyone was sleeping. Almost everyone. I got out of the tent to pee and as I squatted on the sand behind the tent I was greeted with an intensely bright flashlight beam in the face. This navy contingent was more diligent than the last couple groups had been.

"What are you doing?" demanded the young solider.

"It's me, Darcy, I'm just peeing."

The flashlight immediately snapped off and the embarrassed officer walked away saying, "*Lo siento, señorita.*"

At 4:00 A.M. I got out of the tent to pee again, this time without a flashlight greeting. It was still completely dark, but I could see ominous, low clouds. I got back into the tent thinking about the single cloud from the night before.

Then the wind began.

We lay back on our sleeping pads loving the breeze. It felt so good. The constant heat of the Amazon was wearing us down as much as the paddling was and we enjoyed this break.

Don and I had a brief discussion about breaking camp before the rain hit so our tent and gear would not get wet, but then we decided that risking the morning mosquitos was not worth it. We decided we would just put the rain fly on and deal with the wetness, assuming this storm would be like most of the others—we would get rain for twenty or so minutes and then it would pass. Just as Don got out of the tent with the fly in his hand the wind turned into a gale. With each gust, our tent flattened around me, the poles completely unable to withstand the force.

"Should I get out and help you?" I shouted to Don.

"No. Stay in there and try to hold the poles up."

Arms stretched out straight above my head, I sat in the tent and tried to hold the poles to their original form, but the wind was winning. While my efforts helped, the tent was still collapsing around me, and I tried my best to keep our poles from snapping. Meanwhile, Don held the half-fastened rainfly in one hand—he had only managed to get two of the corners fastened and was trying to hold up the poles with his other hand. It was pouring now and in seconds he was drenched. It was not long before I, too, was drenched, as was everything inside the tent.

The problem was that we didn't understand the scale of meteorological energy in the upper Amazon Basin. We had spent the previous evening admiring a lightning storm that seemed to originate from a single giant, black cloud. This cloud was bigger and blacker than any we had seen before and that's why it was so impressive. The best thing about this cloud was that it was a long way away.

Tiny streams had formed on the sandbar we were sleeping on and many of them were flowing directly into the tent. After another couple of minutes, there was a six-inch-deep puddle inside the tent. We were on a slight incline and everything down near the feet area was floating in water. Where our heads had been was soaking wet, but at least there was no puddle, and I tried to push our belongings up to that zone.

After ten minutes of me sitting in the puddle trying to hold the tent up and Don standing in his boxers taking the full brunt of the wind and rain, the storm intensified and we decided we needed to try to pack everything up and get moving. I packed away our sleeping sheets and pads while Don continued to stand in the rain and hold the tent up. My paddling clothes, long-sleeved shirt and long pants, had been down by my feet and I had not rescued them before the puddle developed. They were floating inside the tent—a phenomenon I'd never before experienced in my thirty-five years of camping. Despite the fact that just the day before I had written in my journal, "It is so hot now, we spend all day drenched in sweat," Don and I were both freezing. The rain and the wind had changed the temperature by what felt like 30° or 40° Fahrenheit. I was dreading putting on my soaking wet clothing, but it was time. I extracted them from the puddle, wrung them out as much as possible, and reluctantly put them on my shivering body.

I climbed out of the tent, and Don and I struggled to pack it away against the wind. While we were trying to force the tent into a dry bag, I noticed that Don was shivering and his lips were blue. I had never seen Don truly cold before and I found it ironic that I was watching him develop hypothermia in one of the hottest places on the planet.

I groped around in the wet sand wearing even wetter clothes trying to find my Crocs.

"How hard can it be to find two pink Crocs on this flat sand beach?" I muttered to myself.

"I've got one over here!" shouted Don just as I had decided the wind must have carried them off and that I should give up the hunt. I looked up and saw him extract one of my Crocs from a newly formed lake on our beach. Five more minutes of searching led me to my second Croc, which was floating down a tiny streambed created by the predawn deluge.

We found Midge in an equally miserable state. He had pulled out his bivy sack when it started raining and had huddled in the fetal position inside it but to little avail. His teeth were chattering when he climbed out of his hiding place.

The wind had stopped now, but the rain was still coming down in thick sheets. We decided we were too cold and it was too wet to try to cook breakfast and we would just start paddling. Don and I took the time to dig out our paddle jackets to protect us from the rain, but Midge said he was too cold to bother with it and he took off down the river. I then extracted my hat, lip protecting napkin, and sunglasses from the mound of sand they were buried under and got ready to paddle.

Midge was way out in front of Don and me and was paddling fast to warm up. Don and I paddled together and, as we warmed up, our attitudes improved and we started joking about the situation. Laughing at ourselves was usually just what it took to make light of our challenging situations on the Amazon, as in life. Nothing, it seems, is ever as dire as it may feel in the moment.

Over the course of my life, I've come to realize that things are always going to go wrong. Nothing and no one is perfect, and challenges in all aspects of life will be a constant. No matter how good you have it, life is just one perpetual stream of problems, and how you choose to react to those problems truly dictates your level of happiness. Trying to avoid problems (I'd spent the better part of my life doing this) will get you nowhere.

It never fails me to remember that, however bad my troubles may seem, they pale in comparison to millions of other people around the world. I usually have enough to eat, and, unless I'm purposefully putting myself in danger on a river or a scary region of Peru, my existence is relatively safe and secure. And, yet, I still have problems that seem very real and very serious to me. But remembering the fortunes I do have helps me approach my problems more productively.

Laughter helps too. It can be hard to find humor in a difficult situation, but if I try hard enough I can usually find something. In this case, laughing at myself for wallowing in a waterlogged tent while Don succumbed to hypothermia in the Amazon Basin was immediately soothing.

I also knew then that Don was happy to be on the Amazon, even at this low point in the expedition. Despite being cold and hungry, he was enjoying it. This was a huge comfort.

We ended up paddling until 6:30 that night—twelve hours total—in an effort to make it to the town of Contamana where there was a military base, a hotel, and the promise of perhaps drying out our gear. Being cold, it turns out, was another motivator for Midge when it came to breaking the six-hour rule. We made it just after dark. Conveniently, the military base was another floating barge moored at the edge of the town, and they allowed us to leave our kayaks there while we schlepped our gear up to the hotel in town.

Once everything was laid out and drying in our hotel room, Don took stock of his now painful fingers. He was going through exactly what Midge and I had just a week before, only on a more intense level. His irradiated fingertips were incredibly painful to the touch and he realized that both of his index nails were peeling away from the skin of his fingers. The nail on his left hand was barely hanging on. He taped up his fingers while I devoured a vegan dehydrated meal, and then we set off around town to find a restaurant for Don, Midge, and Cesar.

Once we were all fed, Cesar suggested we invite the navy guys who had been escorting us out for a few beers on us to show our appreciation. Although we were completely exhausted, Don and I understood that this symbolic gesture was necessary.

Midge refused to go. He said he'd pay for the beers, but he was going to bed.

The navy guys drove Don and me to the edge of town to their favorite bar. The military guys were much more relaxed now and seemed to enjoy talking to us. It was a complete turnaround from how life had been on the river. While they were guarding us they hardly spoke to us; they were reserved and were usually annoyed with our pace. Professional resentment was the overwhelming feeling we got from them. Here in the bar we were all friends, and despite our extreme desire to sleep, Don and I were happy to be in their company.

We learned that at least some of their grumpiness wasn't totally our fault. Many of these guys were young—nineteen or twenty—and this military stint was the first time they'd been away from home. They didn't know when, or if, they'd go back home and many of them were trying to figure out what was next in life. Most of the marines came from the highlands where the climate and the food is much different; where there are no mosquitos, no oppressive heat, and fish didn't constitute the staple of their diet. They were all fighting their own battles to survive in their new environment, and it was refreshing to hear young guys with guns talk so vulnerably about their own quest for a place in this world.

Around midnight Don and I excused ourselves, explaining that we had to get some rest for the next day of paddling. All the guys were understanding and hailed us a taxi. We left Cesar with a handful of Midge's money to pay for the beers and the boys indulged for another couple of hours before calling it quits.

The next morning we finally got a hold of Francisco, the captain of the *Perolita*. The reasons that no one could get in touch with them for six full days remain a mystery as they were in cell service that entire time.

It was a fitting start to what would be prove to be a trying relationship. The important news, however, was that they were making their way upriver. He said he would go as far as Orellana, but no farther. We thought we were still two days from Orellana, but this was good news nonetheless.

When I shared the news with the navy crew they seemed angry, probably at the prospect of having to come with us for additional days. They wanted me to call Francisco back and to tell him to come up the river farther. Latin Americans have a strict hierarchy and since Francisco was the employee of our paddling team, it was unacceptable for him to tell me where he would meet us. The navy officer demanded I call him back and tell him that he was to motor upriver until he found us. I was reluctant to do this, assuming Francisco had his reasons for not wanting to come farther upriver, but I eventually gave in. I called Francisco back and he was, of course, resistant. I ended up feeling like a pawn stuck in the middle of a fight between the navy and a private boat captain, and I passed the phone over to the navy captain. He yelled at Francisco for a few minutes, then handed me the phone back and said, "They will come farther up the river to meet you."

We set off paddling, and the navy escorted us. In the late afternoon, a small metal motorboat with two men in it—one dressed very nicely with a white pleated shirt, orange dress shorts, and large sun hat—approached us. It was Francisco and his second mate, Edgine. Having seen photographs of the *Perolita*, we knew this little metal dingy was not it, and we asked where it was. They explained it was moored in the last place where they felt the water was deep enough for it to travel.

For the next four hours we paddled downriver while the navy patrol boat, Cesar and the motorized canoe, and Francisco's metal dinghy tied up together and floated near us. Cesar had bought a lot of beer in Contamana and he proceeded to get stammering drunk. I think the weeks of being in the Red Zone and then feeling the stress of the navy escort—the soldiers constantly telling Cesar to tell us to go faster—had burdened him to the point of mental and physical exhaustion. Seeing Francisco and the *Perolita* as his own personal deliverance from the river hell, he took advantage of the reunion to hold his own private celebration.

We made it to the *Perolita* well after dark. We tied our three sea kayaks to the back deck of the boat and climbed aboard where Mara, the *Perolita*'s cook, treated us to a home-cooked meal. Mara fed Cesar, Edwin, and the marines as well and, for the first time in weeks, everyone felt relaxed and cheerful.

∽

SEPTEMBER 21, 2013
DAY 56 OF THE EXPEDITION

The entire *Perolita* crew was from Tabatinga, Brazil, and none of them had been this far into Peru before. They were just as amazed by the scenery and people as we were. The core crew consisted of Francisco (the captain), Edgine (the first mate), Mara (the cook), and Raimundo (who they called the *commandante*—a required person on any licensed boat in Brazil). They all had kids ranging in ages from two years old to twenty years old who they'd left at home. They'd all come prepared for an adventure and to be a part of something bigger—a foreigner's expedition down their home river. They were all excited to be helping us out and it showed. I was writing things in my journal like, "The *Perolita* crew continues to be amazing" and "Life is pretty easy now that we are on the *Perolita*."

But as I noted earlier, life is nothing if not a string of problems. After ten days of traveling with the *Perolita*, Francisco asked Don and me if we really thought it would take us sixty days to reach the Atlantic.

"Sixty days!" Don laughed, knowing that our pace was anything but impressive since we had hit the flatwater.

Realizing where this conversation was probably going, I thought I'd dash any hopes Francisco had of swindling us and added, "We expect it will take the full one hundred days that we booked you for."

His jaw dropped, "One hundred days? What are you talking about?"

Either Francisco was a con man, or something had been terribly miscommunicated. We booked the *Perolita* through Rainforest Cruises, a travel agency. Francisco had never heard of Rainforest Cruises, and said he'd only dealt with a booking agent named Moacir, a person we had never heard of. It turns out, Moacir is a rich Brazilian living in Manaus who is the go-between for the travel agency and the boat captains, but with our confusion and our language barriers, it took a long time for us to figure this out.

We spent many painful hours arguing and discussing the sixty versus hundred-day problem with the entire *Perolita* crew, Rainforest Cruises, and Moacir. It never got resolved, despite our signed contract stating we had booked the *Perolita* for one hundred days. Francisco maintained that he had never once heard anything about one hundred days. He had always been booked for sixty days, period. Moacir maintained that both he and Francisco knew we paid for one hundred days, but that together they had decided that our estimate was too high and that surely we would do the trip in sixty days. Rainforest Cruises backed us up; they had written the contract we signed, but they were powerless to temper the complaints of the crew.

The *Perolita* crew consented to continue down the river with us—although we told them numerous times they could refund our money and cancel the entire trip—but they never stopped bringing up the time frame and using it to leverage more money, or at the very least sympathy, out of us.

This infuriated me as we kept showing them the signed contract Midge had with Rainforest Cruises (in English and Spanish). Each time we showed it, the crew's eyes glazed over in a refusal to acknowledge the words on the paper and they retreated to their well-worn mantra, "We were only told sixty days, we need more money."

The *Perolita* was a luxury for us, not a necessity. It was supposed to alleviate some of our safety concerns and comfort issues, but as the problems with the crew kept mounting, we all wondered how much benefit we were actually getting from this boat.

As the weeks wore on, Francisco claimed never to have enough money to buy fuel or food when we got to port. It was always some problem with Rainforest Cruises—now his favorite scapegoat—they had not sent the money, or Moacir had not sent the money, or the bank was "bad" and they could not get the money.

I am still unsure if this was Francisco's way of trying to swindle extra money out of us or if he really was getting the financial runaround from his higher-ups in the booking chain. Regardless of Francisco's motives, the constant problems were adding to an already stressful part of the expedition.

On multiple occasions, I wished I was sleeping in the mud being attacked by mosquitos. That would have been more pleasant than what I was enduring: trying to figure out who was lying and who was being screwed and making sure our threesome was not part of the latter. Yet every time we suggested that we part ways with the *Perolita*, they backpedaled, saying they needed the work and if we canceled the boat now they'd be in an even worse place. We felt trapped.

On top of the *Perolita* problems, we had entered one of the worst periods for Don, Midge, and me. Our group dynamics hit a new low. Most of our problems stemmed from the fact that Midge was paddling intolerably slowly. Don and I found it physically difficult to paddle the same speed as Midge. I spent a lot of time drifting in my uncomfortable sea kayak pondering how his pace was possible. I asked if he felt okay, and asked if he could paddle faster. I tried pacing him, but often I lost my temper with him—I was trying to become a better and more patient person, but I wasn't succeeding.

What bothered Don and me the most was that some days Midge paddled incredibly fast, so fast that Don and I struggled to keep up with him. More often, he paddled so slowly that a jungle slug could have kept up with him. The most maddening part about this disparity was that Midge refused to acknowledge the differences in his pace. He upheld the notion that he always paddled at the same rate.

No doubt we drove Midge crazy by constantly pestering him to paddle faster and telling him he would never achieve his goal at this rate. This last point was harsh, but true. One day we paddled only eight miles, and at that rate, the trip would take another five months. Talking to him about what was going on during his slow days ended in failure and frustration. When I would cautiously bring up the subject, Midge would usually interrupt with one of two of his favorite catchphrases, "Darcy, you know I have muscles like sparrow's knees don't you?" Or, "Darcy, you know I'm not a professional kayaker."

I had begun to feel that I might just spend the rest of my life on the Amazon River, and I wasn't thrilled about that prospect.

Midge's new regimen was to leave the *Perolita* anywhere from thirty to ninety minutes ahead of Don and me so that he wouldn't have to endure our constant pleading for him to paddle faster, and so we wouldn't have to endure paddling at his slow pace. It was working well in terms of enabling us to maintain a tolerable level of internal hostility, but it wasn't the safest way to proceed down the river.

Paddling separately did help mitigate some of our problems, but there were other things going on as well. When Don and I caught up with Midge, he would sometimes be very talkative and sometimes hardly acknowledge our existence. Anytime one of our bows passed his, he would scold us and tell us that he had to go first. This was confusing because at other times during the expedition, Midge would happily go last, middle, or first without issue, but for a two-week period, he had to go first. It could have been his way of asserting power of us. Was it passive-aggressive behavior to show his displeasure over something we had done? Or maybe it was simply the fact that he was the youngest of eight siblings and was used to being a brat? It was all very confusing to me, and since I did not have much else to do during the hours we paddled, I mulled over Midge's psychological makeup as we made our way down the river.

Midge had started to set mileage goals for each day and on the rare occasion we met our goal, the three of us would be happy and have fun together. More often than not, however, we didn't reach our goal and we'd pull into camp with Don and me begrudging Midge and Midge feeling our frustration and I'm sure his own disappointment in letting himself down.

Despite losing each other in a couple of huge rain- and windstorms, this routine kept up until just before reaching Iquitos, where we hit the confluence with the Marañón River. The Marañón is what geographers call the hydrologic source of the Amazon (it's the tributary that has the most volume) and it more than doubled our flow. This confluence marks the point where most of the world starts calling it the Amazon River, which set Don off on a sarcastic ramble when he noted it had taken us sixty days to get here: "It's not the end, it's not the beginning of the end, but we have finally made it to the beginning." Which he followed up with, "My apologies to Winston Churchill," for butchering his quote.

While we could still see from one bank to the other, the river was so wide below the Marañón that if Don and I were on one bank and Midge was on the opposite bank, we would be too far away to see each other clearly. That, combined with the now daily storms that obscured all visibility forced us to change plans and start paddling together again.

Paddling together again strained my relationship with Don in ways I could never have predicted. Most of the fighting was between Don and Midge, but I occasionally sparred with both of them, and the fights with Don made me question whether our relationship would survive the trip. I was still trying to be as neutral as possible, but the way this manifested itself was in me being unduly harsh toward Don. When Don got mad at Midge, I would point out Midge's good qualities and mention some of Don's bad qualities, particularly his tendency to be overly negative, in an effort to point out that Don's anger toward Midge was unfounded.

Obviously, this didn't work.

Usually it resulted in a heated argument between Don and me. Don would get mad at himself for being negative, mad at me for pointing it out, and then even madder at Midge because Don believed Midge was the reason we were fighting. Then Don would declare that he was never speaking to me about Midge again, and we'd both go to bed angry.

I realized that I would often let Midge get away with being a total jerk, but when Don turned around and did the same thing, I would be on his case about his actions. It was one thing for Midge to act irrationally—I'd almost come to expect that from him—but I didn't want the person I loved acting like an asshole and lunatic, and that's what I often felt Don was doing.

Sixty-one days into our expedition, I wrote:

> It's interesting how much this trip is trying my relationship with Don. I suppose this was to be expected. Ninety-five percent of the time we are good, but there have been a few instances—such as tonight—that are very straining. It seems to me that, so far, all our blow-ups stem from Don's anger at Midge (which is ever growing) and my attempts to temper things . . . sometimes Don's anger frightens me. Not that I think he will do anything to me, but because I see how much it torments him. I love him very much and want him to be happy, but sadly, I think he is often not happy. This trip and our current life situation—no more SWA, and no other job—aren't helping. He gets unfairly

down on himself and loses sight of the wonderful man he is. Lately I have not been doing a good job of bringing the latter to light as all I do in the "Midge wars" is to keep pointing out the bad things in Don while trying to point out that Midge isn't a total schmuck all the time. But this isn't helping. I really need to stay out of the fighting between Don and Midge. I need to be his support and help him see the good in himself.

I did spend a lot of the expedition wondering why Don was being so negative. Why couldn't he be happy and enjoy what we were seeing and experiencing? I spent a lot of time being angry at him for being angry all the time. My lack of empathy for what he was going through led me to feel that he was ruining my experience with his bad attitude, and I got resentful.

The day after we reached the confluence with the Rio Marañón, the place where the Amazon River officially begins, Don opened up a little to me. During one of my efforts to cheer him up, I was encouraging him to think positively about the expedition, to think of all the ways in which it was strengthening us. He responded was that he didn't feel this trip was building character or strengthening him in any way. He hated acquiescing to Midge's every whim, and he felted trapped in a miserable situation. This was an eye-opener for me.

Don was unable to quit and go home because he felt he had to stay on the river with me. He loved me and didn't want to abandon me on the river, but he was never able to fully accept his decision to stay. I had failed to see how depressed he was to be on the Amazon. I seized the moments when he was smiling, enjoying his surroundings, and being amazed by the trip in order to deceive myself into thinking he actually wanted to be on the river. Considering Don wanted to quit on day seven, I shouldn't have been so surprised that he wasn't overly enthusiastic for the rest of the trip, and it caused a lot of tension between us.

It surprised me how mad I was at Don over this. I felt that Don's non-compliance with my current version of the world was creating a second major problem in my life. I was already weighted down by the decision of whether I was going to give up my awesome, adventure-filled life that I loved but no longer felt comfortable living because of what I worried I was neglecting. On top of that, now the person who was supposed to be my ally in what seemed like a nearly insurmountable decision felt more like my enemy.

This was supposed to be our last big adventure together, and I wanted us to be savoring every moment, every experience, sight, sound, and smell. We'd better soak it all in because after this, we were going to be deskbound and holed up in some city, our fun, adventuresome life nothing but a distant memory. Don was ruining my plan. We weren't supposed to be fighting every day. He figured prominently into the non-adventuresome future I had imagined for us—marrying, buying a house, going off for regular-person job interviews, starting a retirement fund together. We were supposed to fly home and carve out a normal existence for ourselves after this trip; but at this rate, it seemed more likely that we might shake hands and go our separate ways after reaching the Atlantic.

I realized the foolishness in trying to force Don to be happy on this trip. He would have to find that within himself. Still, something had to change as we still had a whopping eighty-eight more days—nearly three months—to put up with each other on this river.

Chapter 12

VOLLEYBALL WILL SET ME FREE

"Our water had always these two moods: the one of sunny complaisance, the other of inconsolable, passionate regret."
—Willa Cather

SEPTEMBER 22, 2013
DAY 62 OF THE EXPEDITION

The shock was immediate when we pulled into Iquitos, Peru, sixty-two days after leaving the source of the Amazon. After weeks in the wild, arriving at a Peruvian city was unnerving. Everything was magnified—the smells, the noise, the heat, the chaos, and the threat of being run over by a motorized vehicle.

The digital thermometer at the navy base read 48° Celsius; that's 118° Fahrenheit. Without the river to cool things down (relatively speaking, the water itself was nearly 70° Fahrenheit by this point), the city was baking in the relentless Amazonian sun. Our noses and lungs were assaulted by fumes from city traffic, rotting fish, and decaying vegetables from street-side markets, plus the sawdust and gasoline from timber mills.

No roads lead into Iquitos; the only ways in or out are by boat or plane, making this city of nearly half a million residents the largest in the world with no access by land. The city streets, nevertheless, are paved, an accommodation to the thousands of moto-taxis that zip around town. These motorcycles hold two to three passengers plus their wares, and they crowd the streets of Iquitos.

Less than five minutes after we'd climbed onto land, Don got sideswiped by one of these taxis. Luckily, the cab only grazed his arm without causing serious injury, but the driver let loose a barrage of insults, clearly expressing his displeasure. Don had been standing on the sidewalk when he was hit, but as far as the driver was concerned, the accident was clearly Don's fault.

Riding in one of these moto-taxis felt like an unnecessary risk. Although they can only go forty miles per hour, that seemed way too fast. Moto-taxis were darting erratically all over the road and sidewalks honking, yelling, and, roughly every few minutes, colliding. Most collisions were minor affairs—one driver coming too close to another guy's motorcycle, scraping off some paint, or jostling loose a load of coconuts—but occasionally there was a more serious crash requiring the drivers and occupants to dismount and debate each other for a while in the middle of the road.

We survived the moto-taxis, but we got lost, hassled by vendors of useless jungle knickknacks, and then later that night, we got robbed. It was the quintessential city experience.

More precisely, Midge got robbed. He had gone to a hotel in town where he could get Internet access while a stealthy thief climbed aboard the *Perolita* and relieved him of $6,000 worth of computers, cameras, GPS units, satellite phones, and other gear. The rest of us were sleeping on board the boat but didn't hear anything. The thief somehow knew only to go into Midge's room, prompting the police to wonder if it was an inside job. Raimundo, who was supposed to be on guard duty when it happened, complained to Midge that his tennis shoes had also been stolen, at which point I thought we might have to physically restrain Midge from pummeling him.

I had failed to obtain my Brazilian visa during our preparatory days in Lima thanks to a maddeningly difficult woman at the Brazilian embassy. She didn't like the fact that we'd be crossing into Brazil in kayaks—this was unheard of and, therefore, unfathomable to her. She refused to issue my visa. Don and Midge didn't need visas because Midge has a British passport and Don has an Irish one. Neither nation requires a visa for Brazilian citizens and, as the woman made clear to me, Brazil is all about reciprocity in visa rules. The plan had been to get my visa sorted out in the immigration office in Iquitos, but as we were paddling down the river, the Peruvian consulate upgraded to an online version of their visa processor. When I got to the Iquitos consulate, I learned that the Internet in town was too slow to support this new program, so they wouldn't be able to process my visa. This meant that everyone had to spend extra days in Iquitos while I flew back to Lima to sort out my visa. Nobody was pleased about it.

We learned that the city has a substantial expat community, with a large contingent hailing from the midwestern United States. In their English newspaper, we read that fake shamans were popping up all over the place and luring unsuspecting "psychedelic pilgrims" into their camps, giving them a hallucinogenic brew of jungle plants called ayahuasca, and then taking advantage of them in their drugged-up state.

Ayahuasca has been used for centuries by local indigenous people for religious and spiritual ceremonies. Recently, ayahuasca tourism has become a big industry throughout Peru and particularly in Iquitos. Taking an ayahuasca trip requires a shaman (or a guide) because trippers lose all ability to think for themselves and even sometimes the ability to control their own bodies. While there are legitimate guides offering their services in this realm who take their role seriously, I wonder about trusting a shaman you found on the Internet to administer a hallucinogenic drug and then guide you properly. But who am I to judge? I was, after all, stupid enough to try to kayak the entire Amazon River.

After deciding we weren't going to be ayahuasca tourists, and discovering that the Internet was so slow in the public cafés that it took ten minutes just to load the Gmail sign-in page, we realized that we didn't want to linger any longer than necessary in Iquitos. None of us appreciated the dose of civilization as much as we had thought we would. I was able to get my visa processed quickly—thanks to Deborah who by then had a friend of a friend who worked in the visa office—and it was a relief to get back on the river. We all missed the daily schedule that had become so ingrained. Kayaking the Amazon was no longer something we did. It had become our entire existence.

Without any conscious effort on my part, I had begun to forget about life beyond the confines of the Amazon. My world had shrunk down to the half-mile-wide strip of muddy, dirt-scented water snaking its way in erratic twists and turns across the entire continent of South America. Its resolute ambition to reach the ocean had become my own.

The day after leaving Iquitos, we paddled past the confluence with the Napo River. The Napo originates in Ecuador and was once, after Francisco de Orellana's journey from Quito to Belém in 1541–1542, considered the source of the Amazon. The Napo was also significant to Don and me because we had spent more than a decade guiding on its whitewater tributaries. For years, our lives and livelihoods revolved around these Ecuadorian rivers. Now, all of that was gone. Our former business, jobs, home, identities—all were in someone else's hands, so far removed from us now that it seemed impossible they had ever belonged to us.

Our friend and ex–business partner, Larry, was still guiding kayakers in Ecuador. Don, Midge, and I huddled our sea kayaks together at the union of the Napo and the Amazon, pulled out a flask of tequila and made a toast to Larry. With a simple, "Cheers to you, buddy," all kinds of thoughts flooded my mind. I wondered how the business was doing without us. Was Larry happy? What were my parents doing? How was their dog? Was my little sister Lacey inching closer to her goal of ending all factory farming of animals? Someone was probably eating a salad somewhere and someone else was lying in a bed with their head on a pillow, having showered in clean water, not the muddy Amazon that was so thick it left a visible residue on my skin.

Suddenly, I hated the Amazon.

I hated Midge for bringing me here, and then paddling so slowly that he was prolonging my time here. Thinking about Larry at the confluence with the Napo opened a floodgate to everything else that was going on in the world. As my mind filled with images of life beyond the Amazon, I began to understand the depth of my self-imposed isolation. When I'd dropped my kayak in the whitewater section, I'd noticed that my priorities had shifted away from things like money and passports. All I cared about when I thought I was losing my kayak was my food. I'd also admitted a few weeks earlier that my main annoyance with Midge's pace stemmed from my eagerness to finish the expedition. But these little jolts of perspective here and there had entered my consciousness fleetingly.

After the Napo confluence, I realized that my yearning to be elsewhere was becoming a real problem. I didn't yet realize how important it was that I continue to shut out the rest of the world. I spent a few days luxuriating in thoughts about riding my mountain bike, skiing, or doing anything that involved using my legs. I'd paddle along daydreaming about eating fresh vegetables or being cold for a few moments. Mostly I fantasized about being able to do what I wanted, when I wanted, regardless of whatever haphazard schedule Midge had concocted for the day. At those moments I found myself prodding Midge to paddle faster, imploring him to add another hour or two of kayaking to our schedule, and then resenting him when he wouldn't.

I had to stop thinking of life outside the Amazon River. I realized that what had started as an unconscious narrowing of my worldview needed to become a conscious effort; otherwise there would be serious consequences to my mental health.

∽

OCTOBER 4, 2013
DAY 69 OF THE EXPEDITION

By the end of that day, we'd been paddling seven hours in a steady, rhythmic wind-milling of our arms when we saw signs of a village: motorized canoes, water jugs along the shore, smoke emanating from a source just out of sight. Eager to feel solid ground under our legs, we paddled to shore and climbed the tall, steep bank toward the town. It was October, low-water season for the Amazon River. The high-water line, at times forty or fifty feet above us, never stopped impressing our waterlogged brains.

Locals walked steep, slippery trails that they cut into the banks annually as the river subsides. From December to July, they could enjoy the convenience of the river's surface sitting at the same altitude as their villages, making the trek for a bath or drinking water a simple stroll along flat ground. From August to November, life was more difficult. Every interaction with the river, and they were numerous, required a treacherous climb using toeholds chopped into the nearly vertical bank with a machete. We were pleased at least to discover that this particular bank was made of solid clay—much different from the sandbanks we'd seen earlier that day calving off into the river, bringing entire trees crashing into the water with them and landing with the furious roar of an avalanche.

We summited the bank and were treated to a mountainless vista that seemed to stretch out into eternity. We could see past the village into a sea of green: trees of all sizes, whose leaves ran the spectrum from avocado green to football-field green. Plants that many Americans would recognize as exotic houseplants filled the ground beneath the trees. A violent rustling of branches in a giant kapok tree—part of the Ceiba family—caught my attention. The kapok's buttress root system stretched well over my head and culminated in a smooth, tall trunk much wider than I could stretch my arms around. The canopy was the most impressive thing about the tree. It splayed out thick and wide, creating an enviable patch of shade in the scorching Amazon sun. Before the advent of synthetic foam for flotation, life jackets used to be made from the fibrous kapok tree seeds, whose waxy coating provided buoyancy. I focused on the motion in the tree until little squirrel-monkey shapes began appearing. I briefly watched the creatures leap from branch to branch, admiring their agility—but I had more pressing things to do, and so I kept walking in the direction of the town.

Thanks to Mara, the *Perolita's* cook, I had recently discovered that the Peruvian women in these tiny villages are superb volleyball players. We'd stopped at a village one night and the male crew members of the *Perolita* went off to play soccer. I asked Mara if she wanted to go play with them and she said, "No, I really prefer volleyball and I never get to play in Brazil." With that, she led me by the hand to a volleyball match happening on the other end of town.

After that, I went in search of a game any chance I got. I walked through neatly kept rows of bananas, papayas, and guayabas on my way to the volleyball court. The tidiness of the village caught my attention. The path through the fruit forest was wide and well maintained; the houses and stores were laid out in straight lines. It felt like one of those perfectly ordered American suburbs—only there were no fancy three-bedroom houses here, no minivans, and no swing sets. Papayas, dragon's blood, and cooking utensils filled the shelves here.

Every house was built on stilts to keep the occupants safe from low-flying bugs, snakes, and other undesirable ground-dwelling critters—not to mention that a stilted house was much more practical during the rainy season, when the village became a sea of mud. The roofs were all made of thatch. Each two-story home consisted of a kitchen and sitting room downstairs and a type of loft upstairs where everyone slept. The upper stories were built without walls in order to take advantage of whatever breeze might blow through in the night. The environment dictated the architecture.

I reached the volleyball court where the air was filled with a buzz of energy. This place had the typical feel of many small South American villages in the evenings. Almost everyone was outside playing a sport, sitting in front of their houses talking, finishing the day's work, or chatting on a cellular phone. But two things stood out as different: the adult women playing sports, and the constant, quiet drone of children fussing. With the women out playing volleyball, there was no one to accommodate the children's needs. For this hour each day, the babies cried while the moms played.

After watching a few volleys, I shyly asked one of the women if I could play. Like always, when I presented my very short self as a volleyball player, skepticism dominated the display of emotions passing across her face as she assessed me. I imagined the bullet points lining up in her mind: Short, skinny, definite issues with fashion. My aqua-blue tennis shoes, oversized brown pants held up by a piece of string I'd found to replace the belt I forgot to bring, dark blue sun-protective shirt buttoned up to the top to keep the mosquitos out, short hair, and backward baseball cap apparently didn't shout, "This girl can play volleyball!" Nevertheless, she agreed to let me play. Her annoyed teammates grumbled as I took the court.

Our caloric intake on this expedition was significantly less than our output. I didn't technically have energy available to burn in a volleyball match that was purely for fun and that would in no way progress me down the Amazon River. The muddy water kept dutifully to its task of eastward progress, taunting me with its undying commitment to reach the Atlantic.

It was as if the river were saying, "I don't have the luxury to stop and play games; why should you?"

Every second that we weren't eating, sleeping, or kayaking had come to feel like an unacceptable waste of time and energy. But I was compelled to play anyway. It gave me a feeling of value that I could find nowhere else on the Amazon. In the middle of our daily trudge and our single-minded focus on the Atlantic Ocean, volleyball allowed me temporary escape, an opportunity to forget the confinement in which I'd voluntarily imprisoned myself.

The opposing team served the ball, and a heated back-and-forth of bump, set, spike ensued. Within seconds of joining the game, I was grateful that I had played volleyball in college, otherwise I could have never kept up with these women. They were strong, athletic, and focused on their game despite the persistent cries of their children. On the third volley, the setter set the ball to me and I spiked it hard into the packed dirt court on the other side of the net. As the ball rolled off the court and into the nearby banana plants, the women on my team all ran over to congratulate—not me—but the woman who had allowed me to play.

The game ended and we handily beat the other team. One woman excitedly ran up to me, grabbed my wrist and placed five Peruvian *soles* (about $1.50) in my hand.

"What's this?" I asked, just as it dawned on me that they were playing for money. This was even more serious than I had thought. No wonder they could ignore their children. They probably needed this money to buy them diapers or toys. As I demanded that my team keep my share of the winnings, they found me to be an even more valuable teammate.

That night, as I lay down feeling even more sweaty and exhausted than normal, I smiled in defiance. The river was just feet from my head, lapping at the shore, beckoning me downriver. The wind was blowing against the current, keeping up with the Amazon's never-ending tug-of-war between air and water. The water wants to move eastward; the air forcefully blows to the west. In the morning I would throw myself back into the middle of this conflict and wage my own battle to gain downriver progress. But for now, I lay content. I had done something besides kayak the Amazon, and I felt like a gleefully rebellious teenager.

I played in only four matches on our trip down the Amazon. I discovered the well-kept secret of tiny Peruvian villages harboring top-notch athletes only after nearing the Brazilian border. The Brazilians did not play volleyball, and soon I was without my distraction once again.

Playing volleyball had temporarily allowed me to be a part of something bigger, even if it was only for a short time. Other adventurers often have a much more social experience. Kayaking or rafting through the Grand Canyon, hiking the Appalachian Trail or the Pacific Crest Trail, backpacking through Europe or South America, you meet other people doing the same thing as you. You make friends, commiserate with them, swap stories and tips, and then you run into these same people over and over again throughout your adventure to share more stories, to celebrate and laugh. Kayaking the Amazon, we had none of that, but plenty of loneliness.

Prior to our expedition, nine people had descended the entire river—Piotr Chmielinski, Joe Kane, Colin Angus, Scott Borthwick, Ben Kozel, Mark Kalch, Nathan Welch, West Hansen, and Ed Stafford. (Ed walked the Amazon, everyone else descended the river in various crafts.)* Some were on foot, some in rafts, some in kayaks, but there were only nine of them between 1985 and 2013. Only a handful of people we met along the way knew of or remembered any of the previous Amazon descenders. To them, we were an island of weirdness in the river sea: two boys and one girl who claimed to have kayaked from somewhere high in the Peruvian Andes and said they were going all the way to the Atlantic Ocean in Brazil. Most people didn't even believe us. If they did, they told us we were crazy and that we were sure to die somewhere farther down the river.

"Really, it's a miracle," they said, "that you haven't died yet."

No one commiserated with us.

And so we paddled, three mentally deranged gringos whom everyone was sure would be swept into the depths of the Atlantic by the strong outgoing tides, eaten by the giant arapaima fish, or simply murdered by the infamous assaltantes. At least we had each other, but it's hard to tell riveting stories to people you spend every day with.

---

* For the full list of Amazon descents please visit http://www.adventurestats.com/tables /RiverAmazon.shtml

Consequently, we spent a lot of time paddling in silence. Sometimes I got lost in quiet contemplation. Other times, I fumed with anger and spent the day trying to figure out how to contain my rage at Midge, Don, the *Perolita*, or just the situation in general. Often, I would stare off down the long line of the Amazon River as it stretched so far that I believed I could see the curvature of the earth, and I would wonder if some particular purpose or meaning would jump out at me. So many people told me this journey would change my life, and I was ready. I was waiting. I'd hoped that kayaking the Amazon would give me all the answers. The problem was, I didn't even know what questions I was asking. I just yearned for some revelation, random as it might be, to emerge from the river and present itself to me.

Chapter 13

WE'LL NEVER MAKE IT

"Midge, this has been your dream for ten years. The nightmare of actually doing it will take much less time."

—Francisco Quessada, captain of the *Perolita*

OCTOBER 14, 2013
DAY 79 OF THE EXPEDITION

Goodbye, I will see you soon," Francisco said as we left the tri-border of Peru-Colombia-Brazil.

By then he knew our facial expressions well and did not wait for us to verbalize our concerns.

"I have to stay behind to look for more money," he explained.

Francisco wisely waited to tell us this news until we'd already launched our sea kayaks and had started to paddle away—an effective strategy to avoid our predictable onslaught of questions, protestations, and arguments. The *Perolita* and the rest of the crew would continue without its captain. By that point, I knew better than to ask unnecessary questions—we could never get a straight answer anyway—so I just kept my mouth shut and paddled away.

"I will catch up with you in two days," he shouted at our backs.

All river traffic must stop where the river flows into Brazil—just like a land-based border crossing—to pass through the immigration office. We had spent three days at the border, passing hours each day in the customs office trying to figure out the easiest and cheapest method for importing our three sea kayaks into Brazil. A violent stomach bug had found its way into my food, making my time at the border memorable, but not in a good way. I struggled each day to drag myself out of bed, back to the office to sit, discuss, and wait, all in agony. I couldn't tell if I had an off-the-charts fever or if it really was that hot in the dusty border town of Tabatinga, Brazil. We finally decided our best option—the option that would get us back on the river the fastest—was not to import the kayaks into Brazil, but rather carry along paperwork saying that we (or the *Perolita* more accurately) promised to return the kayaks to Peru once the trip was over.

The news from Francisco was just another annoyance as far as I was concerned. I had lost my capacity to worry or even give a shit. I was sufficiently confused as to whether I should be more annoyed by Midge's painfully slow pace, his and Don's constant bickering, the incessant wind, the *Perolita* crew's inability to deal with the river conditions we were in, or at myself for letting all of these relatively minor things affect me so much. All I knew was that I was finding it increasingly difficult to stay focused on paddling downstream because so many maddening things were distracting me. I couldn't even read a book anymore during our downtime. There was too much noise in my head.

We didn't see Francisco again for a month.

The river had grown to gigantic proportions. We had constant upriver winds and violent storms had become a daily occurrence. In the month between the Brazilian border and Manaus the storms intensified. We experienced gale force winds, rain coming down in sheets so thick we couldn't see through them, and lightning strikes colliding violently with the river in uncomfortable proximity to our comparably tiny and insignificant sea kayaks.

We learned to anticipate the approach of storms long before we felt any raindrops. The warning was an awful, yet soulful noise. The first time we heard it, we had no idea what it was. An eerie sound emanated from the thick forest on the left bank. It sounded like what you might imagine a ghost army would sound like in a movie about medieval battles. It came from an invisible source and filled the air with a spine-chilling, mournful howl. The sound was otherworldly, and we instantly understood how many of the stories about forest spirits were created along the river. After hearing it a few more times, we figured out that this was the song of the howler monkeys when they felt a storm approaching, and it came to be our signal to hunker down for the impending deluge.

Kayaking the lower Amazon is like driving through Kansas (only a lot greener) at three or four miles per hour all day every day without any real end in sight. The boredom was starting to wear on me. The storms added some excitement to my existence and, especially with the lightning, a welcome surge of adrenaline. But there was a problem with the storms. Midge had already been paddling at an excruciatingly slow pace for most of the flatwater. With the constant wind and the recurrent storms, he seemed to have given up. He was still willing to paddle in the increasingly rare moments of calm, but add any adversity into the mix and it was game over for Midge's motivation.

I had long ago realized that my efforts to encourage, cajole, and even threaten Midge into paddling faster were useless. If anything, they had the opposite effect. I tried hard to give in and paddle at Midge's pace. I reminded myself that Midge is a computer programmer, not an athlete. "Give him a break," I told myself. "If he wants to paddle ungodly slow, that's okay."

Each night I would make a commitment to myself not to harass Midge about his paddling pace. Each morning I'd do pretty well for the first hour, and then my mental outlook would deteriorate. I often kept my promise of not bothering Midge about it, but it tore me up inside. By the end of the day I would be so worked up with conflicting emotions over being extremely angry at Midge for being so slow, frustration at myself for getting bothered by it again, and complete despair over the fact that I had begun to believe this expedition might end up taking us a full year to complete.

I had to actively seek out things that made me happy to be on the Amazon River in order not to a) dissolve into complete insanity or b) hop on the next flight home from one of the many cities along the river that at least had a small landing strip. Fortunately, when I could look past my own pointless impatience, I found a lot to be amazed about on the Amazon.

On day ninety-three of our expedition, we were parked on the river right bank in a spot where the river was nearly two miles wide. We were at the mouth of a small side channel that offered us and the few inhabitants of the place a little shelter from the storms. We welcomed the rain while paddling because it meant cooler temperatures, but the wind was a constant nuisance to both our paddling progress and our ability to find a suitable place to park the boat each night. This night we had found a sheltered camp and I sat back to watch another day end on the Amazon. It was one of those moments that made me feel happy and lucky to be on the water. Thanks to a strong breeze, the air was cool and there were no bugs. I knew this breeze would develop into torrential storm in a couple of hours, but I didn't care. For the time being it was making my existence extremely pleasant.

The sky was heavy with thick cloud cover and so we didn't have an overly colorful sunset, but this one seemed to last an unusually long time. The light grew low and soft and for twenty minutes the muddy water took on a golden glow. I watched the lower sky grow darker shades of blue while the upper layer of clouds grew lighter, almost glowing white. The last remnants of light struggled against the impending darkness, an incredible power struggle to witness.

Down below, another world was unfolding. Fish jumped through the shallows of the river, and an old man came by our camp in a motorboat using his flip-flops as paddles because his motor died. The two families who lived where we were parked occupied two separate floating platforms that each had a house set back about four feet from the edge. These four empty feet functioned as a porch, lounging area, fish-cleaning platform, and garden. Both homes had elevated flower boxes full of herbs and vegetables. The residents sat brushing their teeth, using river water, in the fading light.

We saw pink dolphins every day. They would curiously swim near us and we'd watch them frolic and listen to their fart noises as they surfaced to breathe. The scenery, though I often took it for granted, was amazing. The traffic on the river was always entertaining, the birdlife was superb, and the locals were friendly and talkative.

I felt foolish at getting so worked up over something as trivial as the pace at which I was being forced to paddle down this river. I was lucky enough to even attempt to kayak the Amazon from source to sea. Plus, I still had a paddle and wasn't forced to use my flip-flops to propel me down the river. I wanted to be here, something I realized at some point every day. I enjoyed it often enough. Now I just had to be patient with Midge's pace. How hard could that possibly be?

Two days later, I wrote:

> I wonder how I will look back on this trip in hindsight? Right now, I might say these last few weeks have been one of the more annoying times in my life. Not because of the deed itself—I find kayaking down the Amazon rather enjoyable, every day I get to see amazing scenery and meet incredible people. But a combination of being on Midge's very annoyingly slow schedule and knowing that Don is unhappy have dampened the overall mood of the trip. Midge isn't easy to live with and the constant threat of a conflict between him and Don is almost too much for me to take. The stress of the trip is compounded by literally no alone time whatsoever. I hope Don won't harbor resentment toward me for the rest of his life for "making" him do this trip.

During the day, I tried to take my mind off Midge's slow pace and the constant group fighting by daydreaming about what I'd do next in life. After all, I had convinced myself that this was a huge part of this whole expedition. I was starting to worry that I'd hit the Atlantic and not have come up with the execution of "Plan Normalcy." I hadn't had this sort of freedom, or lack of direction, since graduating from college thirteen years earlier.

I had to keep these thoughts to myself, as bringing up the future had proven to be a sure way to make Don angry. He didn't like his prospects without the kayaking business. He didn't know what other jobs he was prepared for and didn't seem interested in finding out.

My life up until the Amazon expedition had been great, one that I never could have anticipated when I was growing up—as a teenager, I thought I'd be content to never leave Aspen, Colorado. My parents, being smarter, made me leave, telling me I could always come back. I went to college and then graduate school, and after flying the coop, I began actively to avoid the path of least resistance. I'd traveled all over the world and had amazing adventures. There was suffering involved. Living in a tent or a van is hard, and patching together a nutritional vegan diet without a kitchen had its challenges. I lived with the constant worry, or guilt, about not saving for my future. I was left wondering if I was doing the right thing, but all of this did offer a freedom I wouldn't have had otherwise. I wasn't sure exactly how I'd wound up where I was, but I was mostly happy about it.

After kayaking the Amazon, could I really go back and do all those things I was supposed to have done years ago? Yes, I would love to live in a house that was mine. How luxurious to have a bookshelf and to live out of an unpacked house rather than an overstuffed storage trailer and a duffel bag. A permanent address would certainly simplify my life—it's hard to get a driver's license or a credit card without one. And money, yes! I'd love to have money. To be able to eat out and not stress about the cost and to afford to take care of myself when I was too old to work or got injured or sick. On my current trajectory, the best I could hope for (besides an untimely death) was to end up in a government-funded nursing home, if there still is such a thing as Medicare and Medicaid by then. When I put things this way, I could convince myself that I liked the idea of living a more settled life.

But the realities of what it would take—or at least what I believed it would take—to get these securities in place would creep into my mind, and I couldn't imagine myself working set hours at a job I probably wouldn't be passionate about. Only weekends off? A meager one to two weeks of vacation each year? Possibly having to commute in traffic? As soon as I was able to talk myself into it, I just as quickly talked myself back out. Maybe this was just a stupid contrivance I came up with to lend false meaning to this expedition.

I have to admit that part of the allure of becoming the first woman to kayak the Amazon from source to sea would be to validate all my life choices. Now people might understand me better and stop asking all the annoying questions about when I was going to settle down. "Ah," they would say, "I understand why you live the way you do. It was all in preparation for this amazing accomplishment on the Amazon River." In this scenario, I could continue my beloved lifestyle, but with widespread social approval, without all those nagging feelings that I was somehow doing something wrong. This would be an ideal situation. But, conversely, I was sick of letting my silly notions of social approval make me second-guess my lifestyle. Why did I even need that validation from anyone but myself and those I actually cared about?

Whatever the future held, I wanted to be done defending my lifestyle. I realized while paddling down the Amazon that the biggest pressure to conform came from my own mind, and that it takes more courage to change your own outlook than it does to reject societal norms.

I'd already found the nerve to go against most of society's "supposed-tos" and so it seemed trivial defending my decisions to people who can't see the value in them. If they don't get it, that's okay. I might never be one hundred percent comfortable with my choices, but that's okay, too.

These contemplations were a nice distraction from my more immediate problem of Midge's slow pace driving me nuts. Why was I in such a big hurry to finish this thing? Why wasn't I happy spending more time on the Amazon River?

The disconnect in my brain drove me crazy. I wanted to be happy making my way down the river at an awe-inspiringly slow pace, but I couldn't get over feeling that I was controlled, completely, by Midge and his schedule. I'd lost my freedom and that is what pained me the most.

Chapter 14

SWIMMING IN SANTARÉM

"When you blame others, you give up your power to change."
—Robert Anthony

The thirteen days leading up to my breakdown had been stressful, but not abnormally so. The *Perolita* crew was now hassling Don and me daily about their money issues. This was beyond infuriating, because we'd covered it so many times before. We implored them to sort it out with Rainforest Cruises, but they never even called the agency. Instead, they tried daily to swindle more money out of us. Since we were trapped on the boat with them each night, it was difficult to avoid these conversations, and even when we wouldn't engage and ignored them, they kept talking at us. It was usually that they needed money to buy more fuel, and when we asked, confused, "Didn't we just fill up five days ago?" they would say we'd used up all the diesel even though the last fill-up had lasted more than a month.

I hate being lied to.

We told them that if they decided they could not go on for financial reasons that they were welcome to give us a prorated refund and go home. I found myself desperately wanting them to take this option.

They continually answered that they *really* wanted to finish the journey with us. None of them had ever been down the river that far and it was an adventure for them as well, not to mention a paycheck, something that was hard to come by where they lived in Tabatinga. The crew was working hard for us, and we appreciated that, but we didn't appreciate them trying to con us out of more money. What irked me was that they made the decision to continue with us, but could never find peace with that decision. Only in hindsight did I realize that Midge could have said the same about me.

We had meetings with the crew telling them we wanted to cross the river as little as possible. The river was now miles wide and crossing from one side to the other was not only dangerous, but it wasted valuable time and energy that we needed for our downriver progress. Crossing a normal river is no big deal, but the lower Amazon is not a normal river. While we could still see the opposite bank, it had grown to be very far away. One crossing took us nearly an hour, during which we made very little downriver progress.

Some crossings were necessary and we understood that, but in the span of the last two weeks, we had done five unnecessary crossings. The problem was that neither we nor the *Perolita* crew knew what we were doing in terms of dealing with river conditions this immense. Don, Midge, and I were too polite, trying to give them the benefit of the doubt—this was their river after all. We quickly realized that we had just as much experience as they did with this part of the river and many of their decisions were foolish. I began to wonder if they were making us do unnecessary crossings in the hopes of crushing our spirits and making us quit the expedition so they could go home and still get paid.

Finding suitable places to anchor the *Perolita* had also become a daily problem.

Midge was stubbornly opposed to the idea of marking our ending point for the day with the GPS, motoring to a safe harbor for the *Perolita*, then motoring back the next morning to start again at the same point. Part of me doesn't blame him. I understood his arguments for expedition integrity. Plus, there was also the problem of the *Perolita* crew not knowing where good places to tie up or anchor the boat were. They were constantly making guesses—often wrong—as to where we might find a suitable place to stop for the night. If the *Perolita* had it their way, we might have motored around for hours each night looking for a parking spot, wasting valuable paddling or sleeping time.

We anchored in an unsuitable place on night 115 of the expedition. We were asleep when the waves from a passing supertanker clobbered us. The first few waves caused a violent rocking of the boat. The fourth wave nearly tipped the *Perolita* over, knocking most of the dishes off the shelves, leaving them in a shattered mess on the floor.

The crew leapt into action, pulling the anchor and motoring upriver to find a new spot to park for the rest of the night. We motored for three and half hours, slowly plying the banks looking for what Francisco considered another appropriate place for the night. He found one at 2:30 A.M. We tied the boat to a tree and tried to go back to sleep.

Francisco had resentfully rejoined the expedition in Manaus. We'd spent three days in the traffic-congested city visiting the famous opera house—the Amazon Theatre—checking out the air-conditioned shopping mall, and otherwise wasting time while Moacir convinced Francisco to rejoin the crew. Francisco was there against his will; his discontent, which he didn't try to hide at all, grew stronger with every incident like this.

The winds were relentless and strong. Part of the challenge of finding a spot to sleep each night was protection from the often gale-force winds that blew up the Amazon. We repeatedly got blown off our anchor and stuck in the mud. Getting stuck in the mud usually meant two to four hours of backbreaking work in the morning to get unstuck before we could go kayaking.

The winds that pummeled us at night were just as persistent during the day. Paddling against the wind was exhausting, but even more trying was Midge's apparent giving up, his deflation in the face of this type of hardship. If we got a few minutes of calm weather, he would paddle like a crazed man and make good downriver progress; but as soon as the wind returned—and it always did—he lost all motivation and would paddle just enough to keep himself from being blown back upstream.

Midge had overcome so much on this journey. He had not even been a kayaker when he decided he wanted to descend the Amazon. He had pulled himself away from his computer programmer job and was doing the thing of real adventurers. He had successfully kayaked a Class V river that fewer than ten people in the world have kayaked. I could not understand why, now, so close to accomplishing his goal, he seemed so resigned to fail.

No words of encouragement or persuasion could alter this pattern. I tried everything in my psychological arsenal, from inspiration, praise, encouragement, and incentives to pacing, yelling, berating, threats, and sarcasm. Nothing worked.

On day 111, I wrote:

> We'll never make it. This is my official declaration that I am giving up any and all hope and expectations that we will make it to our flights on December 17. So I hope and plan to not stress about it anymore. Stressing about controlling the actions of Midge is akin to stressing about the actions of the supertankers that go past. I control them equally. So this is me letting go. We will get there when we get there and I am not going to be bothered about it anymore.

To have someone constantly begging you, imploring you, encouraging you to paddle faster would be enough to piss anyone off. I've been the weak link before in a group. I've spent my life trying to keep up with the guys, and I usually do, but sometimes I struggle. I know how it feels to know you are holding up the entire group, to try to push yourself harder though you are on the verge of collapse. At times like these, people's encouraging words did little to spur me on toward better performance. Instead, they usually elicited a response closer to "fuck off" than "thanks for your inspiring words, I will go faster now." Despite knowing this, I still tried to boost Midge's morale, I couldn't help myself. When that didn't work, I tried threatening him with the prospect of never realizing his life's dream if he didn't try harder. This tactic also failing, I tried empathizing with him, explaining that I was tired, too, but we had to keep pushing. Sports psychology is not my strong point. I can only imagine the resentment Midge felt toward me during these days.

Three members of the *Perolita* crew were now treating me as their own personal psychologist, talking about problems at home, infighting among the crew, and, of course, the money issue. When they weren't telling me of their own problems, they confided in me that they knew we would not make it to the ocean. We would either die—they felt this was the most likely scenario—or we would paddle too feebly to make it past the wind and waves. Mara's relationship with the male crew members had gone downhill and she now spent most of her time looking depressed and hiding on the back of the boat. She'd taken to needlepointing "Darcy" and a pattern of flowers into a towel she'd bought for me in Manaus. I felt awful for her. But of all the crew members, she spoke the least Spanish. My Portuguese hadn't gotten much better and our communication skills weren't quite up for intricacies of the type of deeper conversation she needed.

We only paddled three and a half miles on day 120. Midge gave up after just over an hour of paddling through strong winds. This killed me. We had hoped to reach Santarém that day, but we didn't even get close. He called it a day before 10:00 A.M. We sat on the *Perolita* rocking in the unrelenting wind and waves for the rest of the day. As I grew more seasick, Raimundo got more drunk. He'd bought beer and booze in Óbidos the day before. The drunker he got, the more forceful his assertions became that we would never make it. I hadn't really liked Raimundo from the beginning, which made it even more painful to listen to increasingly slurred predictions of our failure:

"Just give up. You know as well as I do you won't make it."

"Why are you putting us through this? You can fail now or in two weeks, but you might as well just let us go home now."

"I can't believe you wasted all this time on something so impossible."

I wanted to punch him in the face.

Instead I helped myself to his beers and proceeded to get drunk myself. The truth was, if Midge kept paddling as feebly as he was now, we wouldn't make it to the Atlantic. This reality, more than Raimundo, haunted my thoughts. I felt trapped. I knew I could paddle against the wind and make it to the ocean, but I was beholden to Midge.

Wasn't I?

It didn't feel right to leave Midge. Though he didn't need us now as much as he did in the whitewater, it was still much safer to travel as a team. Midge had swam out of this kayak once in the flatwater and the river conditions were getting more severe. The wind, the various different channels to choose from, and sheer volume of the river made for increasingly treacherous conditions. We knew things would get worse downstream, too, especially once the tides became more problematic. We were already noticing the tides' effect on our progress, but at this point, we could still paddle against the incoming tides which were relatively weak this far from the ocean; this wouldn't be true farther down the river where the force of the tide would be greater than our ability to paddle against it. Not to mention the assaltante factor. Still, I was seriously considering leaving him behind.

We *almost* reached Santarém two days later, with me barking at Midge all day to "keep paddling, don't give up, paddle faster." The wind picked up as it always did in the afternoon, and Midge decided to call it a day a few kilometers short of the city.

We had to motor a short distance to find a place where we could anchor, and I pulled myself onto the *Perolita* in a foul mood. Don was having a good day—our moods seemed to be inversely related—and he joked, "Hey, guys, there's a good-looking airport right over there, we could be drinking caipirinhas on the beach in Rio in a couple of hours if we call it quits."

Don's comment sent Midge into a rage, "Why am I always the one who has to be positive about this expedition? Why is it okay for Don to make jokes like that about leaving, but I have to always try to paddle faster and stay positive?"

Though Midge would never paddle as fast, as hard, or as long as I wanted him to, he had remained fairly cheery for most of the expedition. I had to hand it to him for that. But he let his anger out that afternoon, yelling at me, yelling at Don, and just yelling at the river. I patiently listened and hoped he would blow off some steam and then reinvigorate himself to the task of reaching the Atlantic. Instead, he expressed his frustration at himself for not managing Don's and my expectations well enough, and then he decided to change our plane tickets, pushing them back a week so he would not be forced to meet that deadline.

That night I wrote, "Having a hard time reconciling another month with someone who doesn't seem to want to push for the goal."

After a few more grumblings about how we'd never make it to the ocean if Midge didn't want to paddle in stormy weather, I continued, "Maybe I underestimate his pain and suffering (I hope this is the case) . . . but this trip has been much more of an emotional and mental challenge than a physical one. I am quite up for the physical challenges in life, but I am not sure I knew what I was getting into with this one . . . this has been the worst part of the trip; my life is not my own in so many regards . . ."

I continued, "*Perolita* clusterfuck continues."

And, "Right now I hate David Midgley's intransigence and his pace down the Amazon. He is the man who wanted to paddle the Amazon without taking a single stroke. Now our roles have really switched with Don telling me to be patient, nice, encouraging."

I had a lot to be frustrated about. In hindsight, however, I realized that it was not these external factors that pushed me over the edge. They were all hard to deal with to be sure, but they had existed in some form or another all along. It was not our group's fighting, the *Perolita* crew trying to con us, or their lack of experience on the lower river. It was not the sleep deprivation or constantly hearing from our boat crew that we will never make it.

It was me.

A shift in my attitude caused all my problems.

I started writing things in my notebook like, "I'm getting very anxious to get this trip over with, get home, and get on with my life. It's to the point where every little delay drives me crazy."

I had done a superb job of narrowing my worldview down to this one river until the weeks leading up to my meltdown. I successfully pushed out thoughts of the larger world, hardly even pausing to wonder what friends and family were doing back home. I was constantly daydreaming about what I would do next in life, but all that felt more like a fantasy than anything even remotely associated with reality. The end of our trip seemed so far out of reach that I did not even bother to think about that.

We had one simple goal—kayak the Amazon from source to sea. As a team, we'd discussed how important it was to think of nothing besides this goal. Don and Midge had forbidden each other from saying the word "hamburger." Since they couldn't have one, what was the point of thinking about it?

What had changed in me is that I let thoughts of finishing the trip creep into my mind. After passing Manaus, I felt we were close to the end and

I got impatient. This subtle change was enough to push me over the edge. When I agreed to the Amazon trip, I knew it would be long. I knew it would be hard and monotonous and that lots of things would happen that we could not anticipate. Yet, I had failed to prepare myself for the mental and emotional challenges.

I spent hours in a rage at the dock near Santarém after Midge pushed back our tickets home. I paced around shouting at Don my intentions, "I might just get on a plane and get out of this river hell."

I followed that with the explanation that, "I can't stand paddling with Midge another mile."

"Never mind," I continued. "I'm not going to let Midge ruin my chances to kayak the Amazon. Let's leave him and finish by ourselves."

Don, surprisingly, stood up for Midge.

He told me I needed to be more patient. What was my hurry?

He told me I was unreasonably mad.

Then my anger shifted from Midge to Don.

Why aren't you on my side? I thought.

Then it hit me.

This must have been how Don had felt for the last 120 days. I was rarely on his side and was constantly trying to convince him of reasons to like Midge and to stay with us on the expedition.

I felt awful.

If Don really felt as angry and torn up for the entire expedition as I felt these last couple of weeks, this must have been the most miserable experience of his life. And I, his girlfriend and best friend, wasn't there for him through it.

It was one of the lowest moments of my life.

∞

I didn't sleep that night. Besides feeling like a horrible human being for the way I'd treated Don for the past few months, I laid awake trying to summon the strength and patience to finish the expedition with Midge. So far, I had only succeeded in resolving to make it to the Atlantic with or without Midge. Don and I could ditch him and easily make it. Why shouldn't we? He was a gigantic pain in the ass and we'd be happier and faster without him.

But I knew in my heart it wasn't right to leave him and that finishing without him would make me an even worse person. I anguished over the decision. I was torn between doing the easy thing, leaving Midge and heading to the ocean, or doing what I knew was the right thing. Though staying with Midge would undoubtedly be more difficult.

When we went to bed, the plan had been to start motoring back upriver to yesterday's stopping point at 4:30 in the morning. This way we could get in a few hours of paddling before the winds picked up. The *Perolita* crew didn't wake up until 5:30 in the morning and by 6:45 we still weren't paddling and the wind had started. This little logistical glitch was all it took to bring back my anger, and I started the day in a fury. While physically shaking with emotion, but trying to keep it together, I told Don and Midge to go ahead, explaining I just wanted to paddle alone in the back of the group.

They protested for safety reasons but eventually gave in. They could sense I needed some space. We paddled downriver, Don and Midge a few hundred yards ahead of me in the shockingly blue waters of the Tapajós River. The Tapajós is one of three major clear-water tributaries of the Amazon. It originates in Brazil's ancient plateau that has almost no sediment left to erode. Its waters carry very little debris and the river flows clear, in stark contrast to the sediment-laden Amazon. Where the clear blue water from the Tapajós River joins the muddy water of the Amazon there is a long boundary line of water unwilling to mix together; nearly as impressive as the meeting of the waters in Manaus with the Rio Negro and the Amazon.

Brazilians call their massive river the Rio Solimões above the confluence with the Rio Negro, and, for them, it becomes the Amazon after this union. We'd paddled past the confluence of the Rio Negro and the Solimões twenty-two days earlier, on day 102 of the expedition. The water doesn't mix thanks to differences in density and water temperature. The Rio Negro is 82° Fahrenheit while the Amazon is a chilly 72°. There is a distinct line at the meeting of the waters for nearly four miles downstream of the confluence, and even thirty miles downstream, we could still see a faint line between the two rivers' waters.

The Tapajós, were it not a tributary of the Amazon, would be an impressive river in its own right—it's the world's twentieth largest river by volume. It is far bigger than the Colorado River, yet it pales compared to South America's greatest river, adding only 6 percent of the total flow of the Amazon. It was a pleasant, yet fleeting distraction from my anger.

I told myself I would not cry on our trip down the Amazon. My reasoning: because "that's what girls do" and, as I have been my entire life, I was determined to not fall prey to this stereotype. Yet, there I was on day 124 of our trip on the verge of tears. This only intensified my anger. As a few tears fell down my face, I tried to reconcile them by telling myself they were tears of rage. Still, my already bad mood darkened and my anger boiled inside of me.

I lost control.

As I approached an empty plastic jug floating in the river, I raised my paddle, yelled at the top of my lungs and swung at the plastic bottle with all my strength.

I had survived weeks of Class V whitewater high up in the Andes, I had made it through the treacherous Cerro del Aguila dam site, and I had safely paddled through the biggest cocaine producing and narco-trafficking area of the world. I narrowly avoided being crushed by a raft made of illegally cut mahogany, made it through the last holdout of the Shining Path terrorists, and had avoided being murdered by the Asháninka people who thought we had come to steal the organs of their children.

Since entering Brazil, I'd avoided being run over by barges when storms cut visibility to less than ten feet. I had watched two bolts of lightning strike the river in front of me and a third strike a nearby tree. Perhaps most impressive, I had retained a tiny resemblance of patience after more than fifty days of being asked for more money by our support boat's crew and more than one hundred days of paddling at Midge's pace.

And now I was going off the deep end.

Why couldn't I control my emotions?

My paddle came down hard on the water. I missed the plastic bottle. I leaned so far over my unstable racing sea kayak that, on impact, my kayak turned over. I did not have my spray skirt on, and water immediately swamped my upside-down kayak. Without any outfitting like a back band, thigh braces, or hip pads to keep me in the seat, I went floating out of the kayak. I tried to scooch back into the inverted kayak and attempt to roll up. Although we had done some practice rolling in our sea kayaks and found that it could be done fairly easily, right now it was useless. I was only half in the kayak and actively floating away from it. After two roll attempts, I just let myself float out. I scanned the water as I surfaced. My Crocs, iPod (in a waterproof case), sponge, spray skirt, water bottle, and everything else that was loose in my kayak was floating away.

I swam around collecting all my belongings as some local's words came to my mind, "Do not swim in the river near big confluences," they warned. "There are giant catfish that live there and will eat a human."

I did not believe them at the time, as river people have lots of legends like this one, but now that I was swimming near one of the biggest confluences I had ever seen, those words meant something to me.

I splashed around gathering my belongings and quickly climbed back into the kayak with my newfound motivation to get out of the water. It was easy to get back into the kayak and, in my excitement, I lifted myself up onto it, and then went right over the other side and back into the water. I repeated the process of collecting all my belongings, putting them back into the boat, and then, more gingerly this time, lifted myself into the boat.

Once I was back in the boat, safe from the human-eating catfish, I sat there and laughed at myself. When I was done laughing, I assessed the damage, inventorying my stuff, and found that the only thing I had lost was my bad mood. I bailed as much of the water out of my boat as I could by scooping it out with my hands and attempted to use my sponge to little avail. Eventually I just started paddling to catch up with Don and Midge. Don had the bilge pump and that would be much more effective.

I paddled up to Don with a big, stupid smile, which confused him. He knew what my mood had been when we set off that morning and couldn't understand the change. I explained what happened, and we both laughed. Then Don lectured me about the irony of the situation. Months ago, as a team, we had decided that no one should paddle alone. The river was just too big and the storms that would obliterate all visibility too frequent. It had gotten to the point that losing someone had become a real possibility, so we had decided to stick together. That morning when I told the boys I needed to paddle alone, Don had protested. I assured him I would only stay a few hundred yards behind and that I would be okay. That I had swam (twice) and self-rescued was cause for admonishment in Don's eyes. But my easy answer to him was, "I told you I would be okay, and I am, right?"

I was better than okay. My swimming fiasco was exactly what I needed to put things back into perspective. My rage was fueled by myriad factors, but the most dominant factor was me losing my perspective. There were a million annoyances on this trip and finding ways to deal with them was, perhaps, the biggest challenge; but it was entirely possible to take them in stride and to stay calm. I had temporarily lost this ability and all the irritations came flooding in at once and overwhelmed me into a state of uncontrolled fury.

While writing this book, I read *Bird by Bird: Some Instructions on Writing and Life* by Anne Lamott. One scene describes her little brother, inconsolable because he'd left his school project of cataloguing birds to the last minute. The whole project was entirely too overwhelming, too big even to contemplate. It was hopeless; until his dad came by, laid his hand on his son's shoulder, and said, "Bird by bird, son, just pick one and start there." Well, detailing one bird is manageable. Just as kayaking the Amazon with Midge was manageable if I just remembered to deal with each problem as it came, each mile as we paddled it, and to never think of all of them at once.

Never think of the Atlantic.

Never think of going home.

I felt a strange calm. I felt I could spend the rest of my life on the Amazon River if that's what it took to get Midge to the ocean.

Chapter 15

STICKING IT OUT WITH MIDGE

"Folks are usually about as happy as they make their minds up to be."

—Abraham Lincoln

NOVEMBER 29, 2013
DAY 125 OF THE EXPEDITION

The simple, yet painful, decision to stay with Midge no matter what it took changed everything. I steeled my mind against the temptations of dreaming of home. What did home even mean for me anyway? I didn't have one to go back to. What was the point of ruining my time on the Amazon River agonizing over a concept that was ambiguous at best for me?

With my resolve re-hardened to stick it out with Midge, my attitude improved vastly. I once again loved the Amazon and was grateful to be there. While not much about the reality of the situation was different, my ability to deal with it was renewed. Midge and I even made a deal. In a surprisingly productive conversation about the pace, I agreed to stop harassing Midge about paddling longer hours and he promised to make the most of the hours we did paddle. He even gave me permission to tell him when he was in "slow Midge" mode. Somehow making this deal with Midge, not just with myself as I had done many times, was liberating.

The landscape was changing drastically. The river was impossibly wide with thousands of side channels jutting off everywhere we looked. We often couldn't see the other side of the river, and now a crossing meant a full day's commitment just to move laterally, and not downriver at all. Increasingly larger tributaries joined the Amazon. Strong upstream winds were constant. We saw fishermen sailing up the river in small metal dinghies using blue plastic tarps as their sails. Meanwhile, we battled our way downriver. Making miles had become increasingly more difficult, but I was thoroughly enjoying myself. Each day brought some new wonderment, and I was free from my destructive mind-set that had been torturing me for the past two weeks.

We had entered the tidal zone, which further complicated our downriver progress. We were still six hundred miles from the ocean, but the tides were so strong that we could no longer paddle against them. We could only paddle for the six daylight hours that the tide was going out now. At least this time the schedule was dictated by nature, not by Midge. Often, these hours were split, meaning we'd paddle from 5:00 A.M. until 7:00 A.M., be forced to take a six-hour break to wait out the incoming tide, then paddle again from 1:00 P.M. until darkness fell.

We got good at sitting around doing nothing. I was surprised to find that this didn't bother me much. Sometimes we would sit on a family's dock and talk to them while we passed the time. We sat with one family while they cooked the freshwater shrimp they'd caught earlier that day. I awkwardly explained that I was a vegan and didn't want any shrimp (saying no to free food was a concept that the people along the Amazon always had a hard time grasping). Then the woman asked me if I wanted to hold their pet parrot while we discussed how global warming was affecting their lives. Her daughter tugged at my sleeve wanting me to come to the bedroom so she could show me their TV and stereo.

If there were no villages or houses nearby, we'd just sit on whatever shore we could find. It got boring sitting on the side of the river for six hours with nothing to do, but I had somehow learned to relax a little. I no longer had a time frame to stick to.

The tides, the huge river, and the strong winds combined to make rough seas, or rather a rough river, though it already felt like the sea. Waves were usually three to five feet tall, and often pushed to ten feet during bigger storms. We had to pay attention to our paddling again. No more paddling without spray skirts, no more daydreaming and staring off into the distance. We had to focus in order not to capsize. If we stopped paddling even for a moment, we'd be forcefully blown back upriver, and if we started to get sideways, one of the waves would knock us over.

∾

DECEMBER 11, 2013
DAY 137 OF THE EXPEDITION

We made it to the Para Bay, the southern route of the river on its journey to the Atlantic. The river was mind-numbingly big before the bay, and now it was just plain incomprehensible. I had tried many times to picture in my mind just how big the Amazon River was before we set off on this expedition. I imagined twelve million cubic feet per second of water—one thousand times bigger than the Colorado River as it runs through the Grand Canyon. I tried to see myself in the middle of a river where I couldn't see either bank; this was challenging, as I had nothing in my previous reality to base this on. None of my imaginings prepared me even remotely for the grandeur and vastness of this part of the Amazon. It felt like we were in an ocean; there was nothing riverlike about the Amazon River once we hit the Para Bay.

The color of the water began to change. Blue water from the Atlantic Ocean was making its way this far up the river and gigantic, clear-water tributaries, looking green-blue in hue, continued to dump their water into the Amazon. Instead of the brown, silt-laden highway we'd been following for the last four months, the river was now a beautiful translucent aqua green.

We had been hugging the right shore, unable even to see the left bank after entering the Para Bay. Our plan was to stay alongside the right shore until our ending point, which was also close to the right bank. Our route home—a flight from Belém to Rio de Janeiro—would also take place on the right bank. We wanted nothing to do with crossing this part of the river or being out in the middle with no escape route, no chance for safety. We also needed to stay clear of the shipping lanes.

The Tocantins River flows into the Amazon from river right, dumping its huge volume into the Para Bay. With an average discharge of 480,000 cubic feet per second, the Tocantins River is the world's nineteenth-largest river by volume. We had to cross the 12.5-mile-wide mouth of this river as it emptied into the Amazon. This had been our plan for weeks. We were camped near the town of São Sebastião de Boa Vista and were getting ourselves psyched up for the big crossing. It would be our longest period of open-water paddling. We'd either make the 12.5 miles, or we'd spend the rest of our lives bobbing around the Amazon River delta being carried inward up the Tocantins River, then outward toward the Atlantic Ocean by the whims of the tides.

The night before we were going to attempt the crossing, Francisco confided in us that he strongly believed we should come with the *Perolita* to the normal ship crossing at a place they called Ponta Negra—on the other side of the river.

We couldn't have disagreed more.

Ponta Negra, they told us, is the official crossing point where all the commercial boats—supertankers and oceangoing barges—cross the Para Bay. This is the commercial vessel's solution to getting around the Tocantins River mouth. The big ships don't mind traveling down the middle of the river. With their motors and their stability they can weather a big storm without the protection of shore. They can also easily motor wherever they need to go regardless of whether the tides are going in or heading out. They are not at all vulnerable to the same dangers facing little sea kayaks. These ships navigate the Amazon through the Para Bay—traveling downriver in the middle of the bay or on the left bank—until they are most of the way past the Tocantins confluence, and then line up at Ponta Negra. When they then cross to the river right bank, they end up down river of the Tocantins confluence, bypassing this huge river mouth and its menacing sandbars. They don't like to cross the Tocantins's mouth because shallow sandbars dot the route and, with their constantly shifting nature, are too unpredictable to allow safe passage for the big boats.

Ponta Negra also had the advantage of a twenty-four-hour watch crew checking weather and tide conditions and telling vessels when it is, or is not, safe to cross.

This is where the *Perolita* was crossing. It could take days of waiting before they got the green light for a safe crossing. When the horn blew alerting ships that it was time to cross, everyone would go together, en masse. There was the obvious problem that we didn't feel safe doing an open-water crossing sandwiched between gigantic supertankers. One rogue wave would be all it took to slam us into them, or worse, them into us.

Another major problem was that Ponta Negra was on the left bank. We were on the right bank. Crossing at Ponta Negra meant we'd have to cross from river right to river left, paddle downstream for about fifteen miles to the actual crossing station, then cross back again from river left to river right with all the boat traffic. If we crossed at Ponta Negra, we would land on the right bank downriver from the Tocantins confluence and wouldn't have to worry about crossing this huge river mouth. But we'd have plenty of other factors to worry about. For one, it would take us at least a day to cross the river, then probably another day to reach Ponta Negra.

We argued for hours, but eventually caved in and agreed to go to Ponta Negra with the *Perolita*. We knew it was a terrible idea, but we were probably just too exhausted to argue anymore. It became the plan. It took us one full day plus the morning of the next day to cross from the river right bank to Ponta Negra on the left bank. We chose the most protected route we could find, which involved island hopping and ducking into small side channels when we could. The Para Bay is shaped like a giant funnel, with its narrowest part—though even there it is still insanely wide—at its upstream end. After the Tocantins River comes in, the bay splays out, quadrupling in width. Crossing the river using a somewhat protected route was still possible upstream of the Tocantins confluence, so we took advantage of the protection.

One benefit of the side channels, with their snaking, sinewy courses, is that, often, when the tide was coming in on the main river, the small channels offered a refuge. We would enter a channel fully fighting the tide, get half a mile in, and find that the tide was now in our favor.

The tides are impossibly complicated on the Amazon River. Tidal events influence the river more than six hundred miles above its mouth. Incoming tides compete with the outgoing current, minimal as it is. As the tides start to go back out to sea, they collide with the next incoming tides, creating boundless confusion for kayakers trying to figure this out. Side channels would frequently form *U*-shapes to the main river with the effect that the tide would be coming in for half the small channel and going out for the other half. It was truly mind-boggling, and trying to deal with the tides became a new source of friction for our group. A typical morning went something like this:

"You miscalculated the tides, Darcy. We could have started paddling fifteen minutes earlier." Midge glowered at me as he said this, feeling certain he had something on me.

I wasn't doing much actual calculating. I woke up a few times each night to see what the tide was doing, wrote down my observations and then made my best guess as to when we should start paddling the next day. Midge, meanwhile, was endlessly trying to do the "maths" in his head. He lectured about the rate of flow of the river, times the cubic meters per second put against the knots of the incoming tide, all the while considering our distance from the sea and the topography the tides would travel through. It was a limitless bog of talking and calculating with absolutely zero real results. It epitomized our personality differences.

"Shut up, Midge," I countered. "The day you finally finish your calculations and wager a guess at the tides, then you can tell me that I'm wrong."

"Oh, I think someone is suffering from a credibility problem," Midge sneered, cutting at a nerve he knew would elicit a reaction.

Not being the most sharp-witted arguer, my final retort was normally "Fuck off, Midge."

The tide charts for the Amazon only go about as far upstream as Belém, just a few days' paddle from our ending point in the Atlantic Ocean. Most of the boat traffic is more concerned with navigating around sandbars than motoring against the tides. While river bottom maps are updated annually, the tide schedules upstream of Belém are all a matter of guesswork. Even the locals just watch the river, and when floating debris passes their house going upstream, the tide is coming in. When it passes their house going downstream, the tide is going out. It's that simple for them. It's only complicated if you are trying to build a preplanned schedule around the tides.

That afternoon, Francisco motored up to the crossing point to see what we were dealing with. We sat around and waited. He didn't return until late in the evening.

His report: impossible.

His opinion was that we'd never make it, and the crossing guards agreed. The route was wide-open, without protection, and extremely rough. He wasn't even sure he was going to attempt the crossing in the *Perolita*.

"You should," he said, "cross the Tocantins River."

A week ago, this suggestion combined with the events of the last forty-eight hours would have been cause for me to strangle Francisco and afterward to suffer a complete mental breakdown. But I was learning to cope. I was frustrated but felt oddly sanguine about the situation. So we'd lost two days and would lose another day or more crossing back over to the right bank. I felt strangely happy that we'd gotten to see the left side of the Para Bay. I accepted the situation. A lesson about the power of the mind.

The next day we crossed back to the right bank, taking a different route, but again island- and channel-hopping for maximum protection. We spent the night tied up to a family's dock. I convinced the father to sell me one of their two-foot-long, ten-inch-diameter shrimp traps as a souvenir for my parents—just what my mom and dad needed I'm sure. We would leave the *Perolita* early the next morning. Francisco's plan was to go back to Ponta Negra while we were crossing the Tocantins River. He would cross if he could, but no guarantees. We prepared not to see him again.

Crossing the Tocantins River mouth meant paddling 12.5 miles without the option of stopping. There was no land and no safety for the entire crossing. We could take no bathroom breaks, no rest breaks, no snack breaks.

There had been plenty of days in the last six weeks when we hadn't managed to paddle twelve miles in an entire day. Crossing the Tocantins, we had to make it. The other option was to float around in the middle of the river at the mercy of the tides. If the tides were incoming, we'd be pushed far up the Tocantins River. If they were outgoing, we'd be carried off toward the Atlantic in the middle of the bay. Either scenario was dangerous. We planned to start our crossing with an incoming tide, feeling that being pushed up the Tocantins was a safer option than being dragged out to sea.

We couldn't see the far shore when we started our crossing. On the map, we'd found five small side channels on the far bank of the Tocantins that would offer us sanctuary. Each side channel led toward the town of Abaetetuba where we planned to meet up with the *Perolita* in one to three days if we both succeeded in crossing. We marked each side channel in the GPS, starting with our preferred landing spot as plan A; then plan B, plan C, plan D, and plan E. We got out the compass and set our course. We tried to aim farther down the river than we wanted to land, knowing we'd be pushed hard up the river by the wind and the tides as we crossed.

We all set out that morning feeling confident we could make it, but the vast stretch of water was intimidating in the early morning fog. We saw only more water in front of us, our goal not even visible to us, when we set off. Questions of how long I could stay in my kayak paddling haunted my brain as I considered what would happen if we didn't make it to the other shore. This and other doubts crept into the back of my mind as we set out. I pushed them away only by paddling hard and turning all my focus on the jobs of keeping my boat angle in line with my compass needle and battling the relentless waves.

Crossing the Tocantins was harder than paddling down the Amazon. Going downriver, we were paddling into the waves head on, at a perpendicular angle. This made us feel much more stable. Crossing the Tocantins, we were paddling at a 45° angle to both the wind and the waves. Wind gusts routinely caught our paddles and threw us off balance. We had to lean hard into the breaking crests of the waves as we took them on sideways. At times, we couldn't find each other in the chaos, with each paddler bobbing alternately ten feet up, then down in the eternal waves.

It was tempting to turn our kayaks perpendicular to the waves, taking them head-on instead of sideways. This would have made our battle much easier, but it also would have meant we would be paddling indefinitely out to sea, no longer making progress toward the right bank of the Tocantins River, and eventually, the Amazon River. It took a lot of self-control—both mental and physical—to keep our kayaks sideways to the waves, and thus to keep making progress toward our goal.

The tops of the trees on the far shore came into view after a couple of hours, and were a welcome point of focus. For four more hours, we battled ten-foot waves and a fierce wind. The chaos of the conditions didn't allow any time for our minds to wander, every second demanded our full attention. My single-minded determination seemed to make the time pass by more quickly, and soon the shore was within reach. We started looking for our side channels.

Don and I feared we had overshot all the channels and were landing too far downriver, but we failed to appreciate the power of the wind and the tides. Midge thought we had been blown far up the Tocantins and would be landing at plan D or plan E. Don and I were certain he was wrong; what do computer programmers know about real life navigating? When we looked at the GPS, we saw we'd landed at the channel that was plan D; Midge had been right. We entered channel D ecstatic to have successfully made our crossing.

The crossing had been so rough that Don and I hadn't been able to open our spray skirts to get to our water bottles and we were dehydrated. Midge was wearing a hydration pack so he felt good, water-wise, but he was ready for food. We found a house with a dock and, with our broken Portuguese, tried to explain what we were doing and that we wanted to sit on their dock for a while. Sitting on shore wasn't an option now that we were firmly inside the Amazon's tidal zone. The river banks consisted primarily of mangroves, and the only dry places were docks and boardwalks that people had built, so we were at the mercy of the landowners now. The owner graciously agreed and a few minutes later his seven-year-old daughter brought out fresh mangoes for us. We gave her some popcorn in return and we all sat eating and contemplating the strangers we were each staring at.

We rested for less than an hour before one of us noticed that the tide in our side channel was in our favor and we forced our weary bodies back into motion. We thanked the family for their hospitality, said goodbye to the little girl, and got back into our kayaks. We started paddling with a delusional hope that we might make it all the way to Abaetetuba that night. We were able to stick to the small side channels the rest of the day, which gave our bodies a much-needed break from the wind, and our minds something to concentrate on as we got a close look at Brazilian life in the tidal zone.

Many Brazilian fishing and shrimping villages don't have much in terms of material wealth, but one thing they don't skimp on is sound systems and speakers. In one of these channels, the locals had six-foot-tall speakers and were blasting Alicia Keys's "This Girl Is on Fire" at excessive volume. Never mind that they didn't even have walls on their house. We could feel reverberations from the bass in the water under our kayaks. It was an interesting reminder of how connected our planet is. Despite feeling a world away from everything we were familiar with, and despite having just gone through something that few people could relate to, we were immediately re-grounded with the sounds of a familiar song and the sights of families going about their normal routines.

The sun began to set and we were still far from Abaetetuba. We needed to find a place to camp. In the Para Bay, tides rule everything, including the architecture. There is no longer a high-water mark caused by seasonal high or low water in the river. There is a high-tide mark that is clearly demonstrated by the tall docks and piers and houses on stilts. Every day, twice a day, the tide will reach the top of the piers. Every day, twice a day, it will drop fifteen feet.

We pulled over at a small, nice-looking village built on stilts with boardwalks connecting all the buildings. It was low tide and the dock was menacingly far above our heads. With failing energy, we pushed and pulled the heavy sea kayaks up the ladder. People came out to the dock to see what we were doing and eyed us with an uneasy suspicion.

These people were scared of us, and we were invading their dock.

We asked if we could camp on their dock and they didn't answer. After we asked a few more times, they said to ask another guy who would be back later. We sat on the dock for over an hour amassing an increasingly large crowd. The tone wasn't overly friendly and we talked little. I wanted nothing more than to cook a dehydrated meal. I was starving, but it didn't seem appropriate.

The man who might give us permission showed up. We had a long, circular conversation with him during which he continually asked us if we were assaltantes and we failed to convince him that we were not. We were about to give up when the conversation took a different turn. It took us a couple tries to figure out that he was trying to ask if we had a website or any other way of verifying what we were doing.

"Yes! We have a website," we said, pointing to the huge stickers on our kayaks that read: kayaktheamazon.com.

The man pulled a smartphone from his back pocket and typed in the web address. Looking over our website with varying grunts of amazement, his manner toward us turned friendlier. He finished and yelled something at the forty or so people amassed on the dock staring at us. They jumped up and carried our kayaks down a long series of boardwalks to an open-walled sitting room.

Presents, cake, and other party debris cluttered the room—the aftermath of a wedding they'd had the night before. The man told us we were welcome to camp there for the night, apologized for the interrogation, and explained he just had to look out for his community, saying, "There are lot of bad people on the river these days." He yelled something to two women who disappeared and came back with three plates of leftover wedding cake. I went through my embarrassed routine again explaining that I was a vegan. They looked disappointed, but seemed to understand.

"How about a fruit salad?" they asked.

"That would be great," I said, though I was wary of how they might wash the fruit. I figured I should just eat it anyway since I'd already been rude enough to say no to cake.

They came back with a huge cup of fruit salad. It was covered in cream. Damn. I politely re-explained that I couldn't even eat cream. I felt like a real jerk. Dejected, they handed me a bowl of acai.

"At least you can eat this. It's nothing but acai."

Even though I knew that the berries had been soaked in Amazon River water, I ate a few anyway. I decided that the need to give some concession to our hosts superseded the risk of gastrointestinal problems.

We all sat around for another hour or so asking each other questions. We asked about their lives on the river and they asked about our journey down the river. Eventually we all started to get ready for bed and one of the women brought me to her house to use the bathroom. Though unimpressive from the outside, the house was quite nice on the inside and overstuffed with trinkets, dolls, lacy pillows, and knickknacks. What in the world can they want with all this stuff I thought to myself? But then I remembered that I'd asked the same thing of many homes back in the U.S. The drive to amass stuff, it seems, is universal.

We tiptoed down the docks in the dark the next morning lugging our heavy kayaks as quietly as we could. We estimated that the tide would start going out around 3:00 A.M., and we wanted to be paddling by first light in order to make it to Abaetetuba before the tide started coming in.

When we reached the city a few hours later, we stashed our kayaks on the main dock in town and explored a little. We were starving and the boys found some crackers and fish. I could find no vegan food, so I drank a twenty-ounce beer. Calories are calories! We sat and watched life unfold in this city of 150,000 people. We had six hours to wait around before the tide was in our favor again. Boats constantly came and went and a steady stream of people filled the streets, staring at us for a few moments and then going about their business.

We called the *Perolita* but got no answer. We imagined that either the crossing had seemed too rough even for them or that they finally found a good excuse to abandon us and head home. Once the tide shifted again, we knew we had to start paddling, with or without the *Perolita*. Around 3:00 P.M., the tide was heading out to sea and we did the same. We paddled just a short distance past the city and found the *Perolita* on the outskirts Abaetetuba. They had made it, but the entire crew looked frazzled from the experience. Apparently, it had been rough going at Ponta Negra.

We wanted to keep paddling since it was still daylight and the tide was in our favor, so we didn't hear all the *Perolita*'s stories about their own adventure. As we left Abaetetuba and its relatively protected channel, we were forced back out into the bay where huge sandbars had become a problem. As the tide dropped, gigantic, miles-long sandbars emerged. The sandbars are what make navigation so tricky for the larger boats and why they stick to designated routes like the crossing at Ponta Negra. The sandbars added distance to our paddling as we went far out of our way to get around them. They also created some tricky, curling waves that came at us from the side, making it hard to stay upright.

Later that night, we paddled into yet another small channel. It was well after dark. We didn't normally paddle at night because the risks seemed too great, but this night we kept going. We had left the *Perolita* once again.

They were again taking a different route, and we hadn't reached our meetup point yet. The tide was still in our favor and we were in a small protected channel, so we decided to keep going rather than try to make camp in the mangroves—there were no villages here. We were rewarded with an amazing and completely unexpected bioluminescence show. The river was full of it, and the dark, moonless night made our paddle strokes and the movements of our kayaks through the water light up in an incredible glowing-green light show. I'd stick my hand in the water, disturbing the tiny, light-emitting microorganisms, and find the outline of my fingers glowing a florescent yellow-green color. We were mesmerized. Now we knew we were close to the ocean.

The bioluminescence renewed our hopes of making it to the Atlantic. We paddled in the dark a few hours before making it to where the *Perolita* was docked, our camp for the night. We started the next morning inside a tiny but heavily trafficked side channel. The channel was no wider than twenty-five feet and was lined on both shores with communities of houses connected by boardwalks. Kids sat on the docks dangling their legs over the edge watching boats pass by. The traffic in the winding passage was scary. Large boats that took up nearly the entire width of the waterway came careening around corners and we had to hug the shore tightly to avoid collisions. Our little channel spilled out into the Guamá River which forms the Bay of Guajará and we sat gaping at the scene. It was surreal. We were on the left side of a two-mile wide channel staring straight across at a waterfront of incongruously modern skyscrapers. We had reached Belém.

We were so close.

‿ᴑ

DECEMBER 18, 2013
DAY 144 OF THE EXPEDITION

We had gotten used to watching the scenery go by so slowly that it was often hard to tell if we were even moving. This was the case as we paddled past Belém. It was maddening to watch the same docked ship for an hour as we inched closer to it, a preposterously strong wind in our faces the entire time. Belém is an affluent city. Consequently, windsurfers and kite-boarders raced past us, harnessing the wind that we despised.

We had been fighting our way past the city's waterfront for hours when Midge broached an unthinkable prospect.

"What if we just stop at Ponta Taipu?" he asked.

Ponta Taipu was an old lighthouse *near* the mouth of the Amazon but still well inside the river. All the previous expeditions that Midge consid-ered to have legitimately completed a source-to-sea descent of the Amazon had gone past Ponta Taipu and out into the ocean. He had mocked those who stopped at the lighthouse, saying they'd come so close, but had failed to reach the Atlantic.

"Are you out of your mind?" I asked. "How could you paddle 144 days and then decide you want to quit ten miles short of your goal?"

"Well," he stammered, "if we quit at Ponta Taipu, we can make our December 22 flights home, get back in time for Christmas, and we won't have to change our tickets again."

Midge was losing it.

He doesn't give a shit about Christmas, that I knew.

A few months earlier, I witnessed Midge risk his life numerous times for this goal. I'd watched him suffer through months of hardship, months of mental torment waged by me, and months of ruthless fighting with Don. Why would he be considering stopping short now?

"I can only get business class, not first class, if we change our tickets again," he added.

This last statement, I think, was added half in jest, half in seriousness. Midge had booked a first-class ticket for his return to London as a special treat to himself after finishing his Amazon ordeal—and he was really looking forward to that flight—but was he really contemplating giving up his life's goal for this luxury? If the answer was yes, Midge had really gone off the deep end. I was speechless.

Don found his words more easily. "Midge, you can't do this. You've said it yourself many times that the expeditions that stopped at Ponta Taipu didn't actually make it all the way. You have to go to your ending point out in the ocean."

"I can't believe you are even considering this," I spit out.

We all paddled in silence for a while. Don and I were consumed with disbelief. Midge, I hoped, was reconsidering his suggestion.

After a while I spoke. "Midge, you know in your heart you need to go all the way to the ocean, past Ponta Taipu. I know we can't force you to go, but Don and I are going to the Atlantic, and I feel strongly that you should come with us."

"Midge," Don implored, "you are a logical guy. Think this through. You *have* to go all the way."

We battled the wind for another three silent hours that day. When we met up with the *Perolita*, Midge changed his ticket home one more time. He was going all the way.

Chapter 16

JUST OUT OF REACH

"Men [sic] go abroad to wonder at the heights of mountains, at the huge waves of the sea, at the long courses of the rivers, at the vast compass of the ocean, at the circular motions of the stars, and they pass by themselves without wondering."

—Saint Augustine

DECEMBER 21, 2013
DAY 147 OF THE EXPEDITION

STOP!" I screamed at the top of my lungs, hoping to end the mayhem that was unfolding in front of me.

Midge had just been redelivered to us by one of the regular ocean waves that came crashing into the protected bay where we bobbed around in our kayaks. He had ventured out of our relatively safe harbor to learn, empirically, how he felt about paddling in what now was the open ocean in the complete darkness of the moonless night. As the wave surfed him back into our bay—he was surfing accidently, but fortuitously—we heard him scream, "Ahhhhhhhhhh, I can't see in the dark!"

This was good information.

The wave, while scary, had brought Midge back to us, and now we knew we could scratch a night paddle off our list of possible solutions to our predicament. We were at Ponta Taipu, where an old solitary lighthouse stands to guide ships around this point of land. We had been warned that there was nowhere to camp here, that mudflats, mangroves, and open ocean were about all we'd find. We'd paddled around aimlessly before darkness fell trying to think of something that the few other Amazon expeditions who'd come this far had missed. We knew we were screwed, but we weren't yet ready to accept it.

During Midge's ride on that wave, something had snapped inside of him, and now we had a new and more immediate problem.

Midge couldn't stop paddling, and he couldn't stop yelling.

In between indiscernible yells, yelps, and what sounded like wailing, we interpreted a few actual statements. "I'm just too unstable with all this wind and these waves."

Then a few paddle strokes later, "It's the fucking wind and these fucking sea kayaks." Meanwhile, he frantically paddled around the bay without purpose.

He was effectively freaking out.

Midge had been almost unnaturally cheerful and cool-headed throughout most of the expedition. We had all had our moments of lost tempers, immature tantrums, and just flat-out dejection, but if I'm being honest, Midge had fewer of these moments than either Don or I did. At least fewer public breakdowns. Some weeks, Don or I would have almost daily outbursts of frustration, anger, or just plain insanity. My episodes were generally internalized, but I'd had plenty nonetheless. Midge, besides his lapse in Santarém, had kept it mostly together until now.

Midge's current breakdown had everything do with these facts: We were ten miles away from our ending point in the Atlantic Ocean. It was dark—pitch black—and we had nowhere to camp in the Amazon delta's tidal zone. Mangroves, mudflats, and salt water constituted our current habitat.

I had spent the waning minutes of daylight wallowing thigh-deep in sucking mud in my own moment of insanity earlier that evening. I was absorbed in a futile attempt to walk across a mudflat to find a camping spot when Don and Midge paddled past in their kayaks asking just what the hell I was doing. I was stuck, crotch-deep in the mud which, for unknown reasons, was starting to burn my skin. The more I struggled, the more entrenched I became. I ended up doing a slow body crawl across the muck while half on my kayak, which I pushed in front of me, half dragging myself through the mud. The ordeal had taken me half an hour to travel a distance of no more than a hundred feet and had used up precious calories that I did not have to spare.

I tried to wash the mud off in the salt water as the tide came in. We'd quickly eaten dinner on a small basalt rock before the ocean consumed it. It was high tide now and there was no solid ground that wasn't underwater. We were back in our kayaks, our eyes straining to see something in the dark. Contrary to all logic and reasoning, Midge and Don desperately wanted to finish this thing tonight so as not to prolong their suffering any more than necessary.

Back in the bay, Don implored, "Midge, just stop paddling, you are safe now."

"I'm not paddling!" Midge yelled as he paddled harder than we had seen him paddle in months. Don gave up and started keeping pace with Midge saying, "Okay, let's paddle, buddy. We'll paddle back toward the lighthouse and look for a place to camp."

The two of them took off paddling back in the direction we had come.

"Stop! Now!" I screamed again, this time straining my vocal cords to be heard over the strong wind and crashing waves. Finally, I had their attention. It scared them both to hear screaming come from my mouth—an unusual show of emotion for me—and they stopped paddling.

"Where exactly are you guys going?" I asked.

Don was clearly miffed about the entire situation. He had been mentally and emotionally over this Amazon trip since the first week, and now that the finish line was within his grasp, he desperately wanted to get there.

Besides the obvious dangers of paddling in a turbulent ocean in the dark, the Amazon delta also had a special set of difficulties. The delta is surprisingly shallow at low tide, exposing mudflats and sandbars that follow no pattern I could discern. The mudflats were dangerous for two reasons, the first being that they would break up the flow of the waves. While normally the waves would come at us head-on, allowing us to paddle straight into them, when mudflats were exposed, they caused the waves to break sideways to us, making it exceptionally hard to keep the unstable racing sea kayaks upright.

The second and more treacherous problem was that fishermen used the mudflats to set their fish traps. In the Amazon delta, a fish trap looks like an oversized outhouse built of sticks. The sticks are roughly fifteen feet tall, as thick as my forearm and, having normally been cut with a machete at a steep angle, have an incredibly sharp tip. When the tide was low, we only had to worry about crashing into the base of a fish trap, but when the tide was high, only the top few inches of the sticks were exposed and impaling the kayaks, or worse, ourselves, was a real concern. In the daylight, these two hazards could be largely mitigated by our ability to see them.

Despite the absolute darkness and all the dangers that it presented, Don wanted to go. Now. Since Midge's actions had just made it clear that he wouldn't be paddling the final leg in the dark, Don had apparently decided that going wherever Midge was going was better than not going anywhere at all. He impatiently explained to me, "Since there's nowhere to camp in this bay, and Midge can't see in the dark, we have to paddle back toward the lighthouse to look for a place to camp."

What immediately came to my mind was, have you both completely lost your minds? First of all Don, what kind of lunatic moment did you have sending Midge out of the bay to "test it out"? We know there are basically 300° of open ocean out there, twenty-five-mile-per-hour winds, giant waves, fish traps, and sandbars. Not to mention the fact that if we made a mistake, the ten-knot outgoing tide would carry us off into a dark Atlantic oblivion. Somehow you twisted this information in your mind to convince yourself that it was smart to paddle the final miles in complete darkness?

Then I imagined a smile spreading across Midge's face. I knew he would like nothing more than to hear me bitch Don out. I had tried (unsuccessfully) to be the queen of neutrality on this expedition. This had made Don and Midge disdain me with equal measure, each of them lying in wait for the time when I would attack one and vindicate the other. I turned my internal rant toward him: And, Midge, don't you smirk, I haven't even gotten to you yet. You wait until day 147 to mention you can't see in the dark (not that any of us could see much in the dark)? And if this is true, why did you go out of the bay in the first place? And while I'm at it, why couldn't you have been paddling this hard all along?

I suppressed all of this and out loud I said, "Just a couple hours ago, we paddled agonizingly slowly past the lighthouse in daylight and what did we see? Nothing but mudflats and mangrove swamps. What makes you think that now, in the dark, we will miraculously discover a camping spot we had overlooked before?"

Almost in unison they replied, "What else are we going to do?"

I didn't like our options any more than they did, but I knew what we had to do, and so did they. I just had to be the one to say it.

"We are going to sit in our kayaks and bob around in this bay until the tide goes down enough to expose that piece of basalt rock we had dinner on. Then we'll get on it and try to sleep."

Midge scrunched up his face. I could tell he was doing tide calculations in his head, and I interrupted him to say, "Yes, Midge, we'll be sitting in our kayaks until at least 1:00 A.M. It sucks, but we are out of options."

They knew I was right. We found the most sheltered part of the bay and grouped up. Midge found a tree that he could hang on to and Don and I bobbed around near him. Every twenty minutes or so I would hear a tired voice from the tree inquire, "Darcy, is our rock out yet?"

Each time I replied, "I doubt it, but I'll go look." Paddling up to the rock at least gave me something to do. I'd go check, come back and report. "Not yet."

Three hours later, during my rock check at 12:45 A.M. I found the rock was exposed just enough for the three of us to huddle on it and I called the boys over. Don set to work tying the kayaks to a nearby tree while we all tiptoed around each other on our sparse real estate.

Midge's nerves were frayed from his breakdown and the hours of being stuck in our kayaks in the dark unable to do anything but rock with the incessant rolling of the waves. Don was feeling chagrined that he had nearly killed Midge by sending him out on his test paddle. I was wondering why I was the only one who hadn't completely lost my mind, and then figured I probably had, too, but it was just easier to recognize in Don and Midge.

Yet as we did at least once every day, we pulled together as a team on that uncomfortable rock. We each helped one another unload gear from the boats, and then each politely took up as little space as we could in our ten-square-foot home for the night as we laid out our sleeping pads and sheets. Our simple good-night ritual grounded us firmly on the Amazon River, and we gelled once again.

"Night, Darcy."

"Night, Midge."

"Night, Don."

Noticing that my headlamp was illuminating a critter in the puddle an inch from my face, I added, "Sleep tight, don't let the water crabs bite." I was too tired to worry about the crab and was asleep in seconds.

Chapter 17

THE OCEAN

"You cannot swim for new horizons until you have courage to lose sight of the shore."

—William Faulkner

DECEMBER 22, 2013
DAY 148 OF THE EXPEDITION

We woke from our measly four and a half hours of sleep. The cacophony coming from above was both annoying and beautiful. A flock of brilliantly red-colored scarlet ibis and their dull counterparts, the tricolored herons, had congregated in the tree directly above our heads. Even with all my winters spent in Ecuador, I've never seen a bird as awe-inspiring as the scarlet ibis. They are bright red, like a ripe tomato, and they are big, about two feet tall when standing. They travel in flocks of thirty birds or more. Flying, they blot out the sky leaving a blur of red. Though I was annoyed to be woken up before the sun even rose, I couldn't help but smile as I looked up and found our tree filled with the birds. They were staring down at us, no doubt confused by our presence. They squawked nonstop, almost making a honking sound, which told us in no uncertain terms that they didn't like us on their turf.

Having passed the last four and a half hours sleeping intermittently with sharp pieces of rock jabbing into our sides and saltwater crabs sharing the puddles that our heads and feet now occupied, we rose unrested, but inspired nonetheless.

After traveling over 4,000 miles we were a mere ten miles from our ending point and were confident we would finish that day. The only problem was that the tide was now coming in. We had realized weeks ago that paddling against the tide was useless. At maximum effort against the tide, we averaged less than half a mile per hour. Even with the tide in our favor, the winds had become so strong that we rejoiced at a three-and-a-half-mile-per-hour pace. So, we sat and waited, as we had become so accustomed to doing.

We waited for five and a half hours with nothing to do but watch the waves roll in. After spending the last 148 days together, we had run out of things to talk about. Every now and then someone would speak, a two-minute conversation would ensue, and then we would fall back to our silent musings.

Bone-tired, marooned on a wave-washed rock ten miles from my objective, I revisited the idea of giving up on my adventuresome life. It was easier to swallow when it was a vague idea and I knew that the reality of it would be postponed for months, maybe forever if I didn't survive the expedition. Now I was hours away from becoming the first woman to kayak the Amazon. But I didn't feel like I was hours away from trying out a new lifestyle.

I had the naïve thought that after the Amazon I'd have seen it all. I'd have ticked off the pinnacle adventure and learned all that I needed to know about the world that I could absorb from a kayak. Yet, the farther down the river I traveled, the more I realized I didn't know. The people we'd met were fascinating and I'd only scratched the surface; I'd barely gotten to know a few of them. Traveling in this manner taught me that no matter how bad I thought my life might be going, however uncertain things might be, I had it pretty good. That I had the luxury to even contemplate (worry about) a retirement savings was something to be grateful for.

I'd spent a lot of time on this expedition pitying myself over losing my business. I also worried that my partner in all things—Don—wasn't all that interested in planning our next move. But the fact was, I had the time and ability to be in South America trying to kayak the world's largest river and that made me a lucky person. My plan to give it all up seemed crazy, especially since I'd realized that striving for social acceptance should not be that important to me.

Perhaps I should take it as a sign that two computer geeks (Midge and Guy—the guy who'd bought Small World Adventures) converged upon me in Ecuador to make this Amazon trip possible. They were both trying to escape the mundane stability that I thought I craved.

I wasn't sure if I'd just had a moment of brilliant clarity about my future, or if sleep and food deprivation had me on the verge of hallucinogenic revelations. I decided to put off making a final decision about my future a little while longer and, not trusting the state of my brain, I thought about something else. I turned my attention to the fact that all we could see for 300° was open ocean.

Once the tide shifted, the three of us got back into our kayaks and paddled silently, accompanied by the ever-present knowledge that a swim here would almost certainly mean being swept out into the Atlantic by the outgoing tide. I suppose it was good that the conditions were so rough. This meant we had to channel all our focus on paddling, and our minds couldn't drift to thinking about how we might feel when we finally finished this expedition.

We zigged left, then zagged right in wide, half-mile-arching turns to avoid the sandbars and the fish traps. We slowly plodded along, fighting fierce winds until all we could see was a tiny stretch of land off to our right. We hadn't seen another human being for the past forty-eight hours, a rare span of solitude on the highly populated Amazon River. The Atlantic Ocean stretched in front of us in a blue and vast oblivion.

Before the expedition began, we drew a line across the ocean on a map between the points of land on the north bank and the south bank that protrude farthest into the Atlantic. Then we chose a point that was close, but not too close to the right (south bank) where we thought we'd be paddling. Midge put the coordinates of this point into his GPS nearly five months ago. It had been our little beacon urging us on—keep going until you pass the dot. Unremarkable perhaps, but it somehow spurred us on through our low moments.

Without any type of celebration—the ocean was simply too rough—we reached our stopping point, crossed it, then paddled another hundred feet just for good measure. We were all nervous in the rough conditions and we didn't even pause to high five—an act that had caused Midge to swim a month earlier at the Rio Purús confluence. Midge turned and took off toward shore. Don took off after him and yelled over his shoulder, "I'm chasing Midge. You be careful!"

We could travel no farther down the river.

We had done it.

We paddled the entire Amazon River until the Atlantic Ocean consumed it.

I couldn't believe it.

I stayed out by myself a little longer to try to savor the experience. That moment of accomplishment seemed too fleeting and, after 148 days, I felt I deserved to enjoy it as long as I possibly could, even if it was only a few extra seconds. I, too, was feeling uncomfortably unstable in the rough ocean. After Don and Midge took off, I felt the watery desolation surround me.

When I turned my kayak toward shore, I was paddling parallel to both the tide and the wind, which intensified the battle to stay upright. I was having to do an upstream ferry against the outgoing tide on huge waves and it took every ounce of concentration to pull it off. I paddled hard to catch up with Don and Midge, but once we were together again, we decided to spread out to give each other space, each of us knowing there was little our teammates could do to help if things went wrong.

After twenty minutes of battling the sideways force of the tides and waves, we were within striking distance of the white-sand beach. Don and I surfed the waves that were crashing onto the beach and stepped out of our kayaks just in time to watch Midge tip over in the breaking waves. He was surfing a wave into shore, but his kayak turned sideways to the wave and it barrel-rolled him, face-planting him into the sand—a triumphant finish! The three of us gathered in the shallow surf and laughed because Midge was in about eight inches of water. He was bleeding and covered in sand, but he was not in danger of dying.

We had done it.

We stood—the three of us together—on the beach overlooking the Atlantic Ocean, a reality that seemed unlikely at so many points throughout the expedition. That we finished the expedition together is a testament to all of our patience, determination, and resilience.

We shared high fives and congratulations. We set up camp and then we spread out quietly.

One hundred and forty-eight days after leaving the source of the Amazon, we sat on a white-sand beach overlooking the Atlantic Ocean. After doing nothing but paddle downriver for months, it felt great to sit on the beach and watch the serenely beautiful horizon. The sun was setting in a spectacular blending of colors—golden hues of rose and purple that flitted off the clouds—and it held none of the fierceness of our final days battling out to the ocean. There was a sense of relief in both us and our environment. There were no people and no other land masses in sight. There couldn't have been a more fitting end to our journey.

I sat waiting for my feelings of elation, but they evaded me. Midge seemed to be silently crying. I found myself feeling jealous of him. He knew how he felt sitting on that beach. For him, ten years of training and dedication had culminated in achieving his life's biggest goal. He could move on now. He would go back to his job in London, sit in front of his computer where he was happiest, marry his girlfriend Rachel, have some kids, and get on with the life he really wanted—one of a successful computer programmer dining in fancy restaurants, drinking expensive Scotch in London, and taking ski vacations in the Alps.

I tried to be excited. We'd accomplished what so many people told us we couldn't, what I, at times, considered impossible. I proved again that Diminutive Darcy was capable of anything she set her mind to, even to becoming the Amazon Woman. So why wasn't I happier?

We'd each found the will to keep going despite our desires to quit, which were, at times, overwhelming. Midge, with his decade-long learning curve and tiny muscles, me, who had to muster an unprecedented amount of self-control and patience to stick with Midge through it all, and Don, who wanted to go home after seven days, but had somehow found the resolve to stick it out for the next 141. I wondered why we pushed ourselves like that?

Maybe life is about pushing limits and defying expectations of what we think is possible. It's about breaking down stereotypes of who can do what. Standing on that beach was the apex of success for me. But I had yet to find some happiness out of the completion of this expedition, and what good is success without happiness?

I had proven to the world that a skinny little vegan girl could kayak the entire Amazon; but did the world even care? Did I? I didn't feel any more special now that I was the first woman to kayak the Amazon.

I hoped that kayaking more than 4,000 miles down the world's largest river would get me something besides terrible sunburn and overdeveloped shoulder muscles, but so far I had nothing. Where was this overwhelming feeling of life-validating gratification that I had pinned all my future plans to? Where was the certainty that now, finally, I'm good enough, I've accomplished enough?

This was the postexpedition depression setting in. My head was screaming, "What am I going to do now?" Overwhelmed and hollow, I went to bed before the sun had finished setting.

Chapter 18

WHAT IT ALL MEANS

"My father . . .wanted me to come home—to come home, as he said, and settle down, and whenever he said that I thought of the sediment at the bottom of a stagnant pond."

—James Baldwin

DECEMBER 23, 2013
DAY 149 OF THE EXPEDITION

I started this expedition wondering just what was wrong with me. Wondering why had society rejected me so thoroughly? I had river acquaintances all over the world, but how many true friends did I have? This belonging everywhere yet nowhere was a real problem. Having no deep connections to any one place or group of people had left me truly untethered.

I came away from this expedition wondering if it was me who had rejected society rather than the other way around. Being disconnected had its benefits in terms of physical freedoms, but I was beginning to realize the emotional consequences of feeling alone. I also began to understand that you don't have to conform to societal norms in order to have a place in your community. This pressure to either conform or be outcast had been primarily in my mind, or at least the intense pressures I felt around this topic were.

There will always be people who don't understand my lifestyle, who will question me and who will feel uncomfortable by the choices I've made (myself included). But this doesn't mean I shouldn't keep doing what I love doing—albeit with the monumental modification of viewing the river as my passion and my happy place, rather than as my literal escape from a society that I don't yet know how to fit in to. But one thing was certain, I didn't need to abandon my adventuresome lifestyle to find what my life was lacking.

Throughout the expedition, and its multitudes of hardships, I rarely found myself thinking, I can't wait until I never have to do stuff like this again. Conversely, I was constantly amazed by what we saw and experienced. I had plenty of hard and frustrating times, but overwhelmingly, I felt privileged to be there, getting to witness every inch of the massive river. And instead of convincing myself to give up on my adventuresome life, I felt myself sinking deeper into it.

It is telling that self-help books are often top sellers. The self-help industry is said to be worth eleven billion dollars in the United States alone. Shouldn't we be asking ourselves how we got into this situation in the first place? Why do we need so much help? Why are we, collectively, so unhappy, so unfulfilled, and so in need of that undefinable and ungraspable fix?

Kayaking the Amazon emboldened me to continue doing what makes me happy. The alternative, it appears, is caving to pressures to conform—both internal and external—and then spending all my free time trying to figure out why I'm not happy.

I walked away from that white sand on the Atlantic with a resolve to follow my passions, but in a way that also allows me to connect to people, not just rivers. Of course, figuring out how to do this will be my newest challenge. I hope more people can be inspired do the same. It can be scary having no idea where these passions will lead you, but it will, undoubtedly, be an exciting adventure.

The problem is that many people allow their own minds to stop them from doing what they really want to be doing. The excuses for not doing something always come more easily than the reasons to push ahead and go for it:

"I can't take up kayaking, I'm a mom."

"I can't quit my job, I have a mortgage to pay."

"My parents would be so disappointed."

"I can't pursue my passion for art, it's not a real career."

"I can't go hike the Appalachian Trail, I have too many other responsibilities."

"I can't run for office. What if I lose?"

Perhaps this mind-set stems from a lifetime of subtle messages about what we can and cannot do. I know firsthand how powerful these can be. My hope is that people who read this book will push their doubts aside and do something, however big or small, that they've felt they couldn't or shouldn't do. You will never truly know until you try. There is a chance you will fail, but there is a chance you will succeed. Either way, you will learn something important, as the journey will be nothing like what you expect.

I watched the sun rise over the Atlantic Ocean the morning after completing the Amazon and I let go of any lingering desires to be more normal.

I tried to enjoy this newfound acceptance of my life and to reflect on what I had just done. But since reflection for me is analogous to having my fingernails ripped off one by one, I didn't succeed for very long. Plus, my fingernails had already suffered enough on the trip. Instead, I let my mind drift to what comes more naturally, and I started thinking about what the next adventure would be.

My thoughts were cut short because we had to go paddling one more time. The beach we slept on had no ties with the sorts of civilization we needed to start our homeward journey. Paddling the eighteen miles back up the river to the town of São Caetano de Odivelas was much easier than paddling down the river had been for the last couple of months. We caught the incoming tide, and now, with the wind at our backs, we made the distance in a seemingly effortless three hours.

Don hitchhiked into town on a motorcycle to buy us celebratory beers once we'd made land at São Caetano de Odivelas. When he returned, the motorcycle driver stayed and downed a few cold ones with us. He didn't believe us when we told him what we'd just accomplished, but he could tell we were happy and excited. We were, he decided, the kind of people he could enjoy a few brewskies with at ten o'clock in the morning.

Francisco showed up in a big dump truck to haul us back across the peninsula to the point where we'd left the *Perolita* three days earlier.

It started pouring rain as we pulled out of town. The downpour was impressive, even by Amazonian standards. I was cold, I was tired, and I was a little bit buzzed. I laughed to find myself sitting in an increasingly large and dirty puddle in the back of a dump truck in Brazil. Midge was entertaining us by attempting to crush beer cans against his head and shouting, "Darcy, you can't buy this feeling!"

Don was smiling and boisterous, thrilled, I'm sure, to be finished with the Amazon. It was not a glamourous situation by any criteria but I knew, with absolute certainty, that I was happy.

AFTERWORD

"There are many ways to salvation, and one of them is to follow a river."

—David Brower

I have spent two decades chasing various whitewater dreams and that hasn't changed since finishing the Amazon. These dreams started out innocently enough with my goal to become a good enough kayaker that I could work as a safety kayaker for the local raft company. Then I wanted to kayak the Grand Canyon on the Colorado River—a reasonable objective. But then my goals got a little more complicated: kayak all the famous multi-day high sierra runs in California, kayak the Amazon River from source to sea (once I got on board with Midge's plan), write my name in the book of legends on the Bashkaus River in Siberia, and kayak the Grand Canyon of the Stikine in Canada—one of the hardest big-water kayaking runs in North America.

Even after the Amazon, some part of my brain still believed that if I accomplished all these goals, I'd feel satisfied with my kayaking career. I'd feel that I had enough significant accomplishments under my belt that I'd be ready to move on to the next chapter of my life—whatever that was going to be. I had done away with any notions of caving in to the pressure to conform to American norms, but I still felt that I should eventually move on from an itinerant life of kayaking. This contentment with a past life and a readiness for the next stage was supposed to be the exact feeling I had when I got to the take-out of the Stikine River at Telegraph Creek.

Ever since I first started kayaking I had dreamt about driving over the Stikine River in northern British Columbia where the Cassiar Highway crosses it, hanging a hard left down to the beach and launching my kayak. It took me well over a decade of training to build up my skills to the point where I could even consider attempting this river. Then, a string of injuries and uncooperative water levels led me to believe I would never gaze up at the impossibly tight canyon walls from the bottom of the Stikine River. Year after year of training and prepping for the Class V+ big water with strength training, cardio, and breath-holding exercises ended in frustration after I broke my ribs, injured my neck, and the river never got low enough to attempt a descent. As Midge had obsessed about the Amazon, I obsessed about the Stikine.

In August 2016, it all came together. Don and I were fit from a monthlong paddling trip in Russia, during which we'd succeeded in paddling the notoriously hard and dangerous Bashkaus River. Partway through day one of this trip we scaled the almost sheer cliff above a massive set of rapids that claimed the lives of the leader and half the crew of the first expedition down the river. Midway up this cliff sits a plaque bearing the name and silhouette of the river running pioneer who had given his life for the Baskhaus River—Igor Bazilevski. Below the plaque is an alcove sheltered from the harsh Siberian weather that houses the Book of Legends. Here we clung to the side of the precipice just long enough to scribble our names into the Book of Legends, and to contemplate what this river had meant to the small group of river runners who had come before us.

We had another window of free time when we returned home from Russia, and the Stikine River was at a perfect level. Jet lag be damned, we drove the forty hours from Colorado to the bridge over the river and put in, just the two of us. It took me a few rapids to get used to the push and the power of the river, but before too long I was in a groove. I felt good. *I felt like I belonged there.* All of the old doubts were gone. The river was as big and hard as I expected, but I was prepared. The cliff walls were taller and much more intimidating than I'd imagined. The mountain goats were more agile than I thought possible. We didn't see another person on the river.

The trip was perfect. Paddling the Grand Canyon of the Stikine was one of the best experiences of my entire life; and yet that feeling of deep gratification, so deep that it would flood me with satisfaction to leave my sport behind, never came. If the Stikine didn't give me that feeling, I knew nothing ever could.

Now I do it for the chase. At forty-one years old, I've finally accepted that ultimate contentedness is never going to happen. Pursuing it feels good enough, though.

Haruki Murakami explains this feeling perfectly in his book *What I Talk About When I Talk About Running*. When asked why he continues to do running races well into middle age, he replies, "I hope that, over time, as one race follows another, in the end I'll reach a place I'm content with. Or maybe just catch a glimpse of it. (Yes, that's a more appropriate way of putting it.)"

Don and I bought back our adventure kayaking company, Small World Adventures, in April 2016. Don and me giving up being kayak guides in exchange for a more settled and more secure life hadn't worked out. We are all, I suppose, confined to specific destinies and mine seems to be chasing rivers.

AUTHOR'S NOTE

Both Don and Midge felt that I was unfairly harsh in my treatment of them in earlier drafts of this manuscript. This was not my aim, and I took their feedback seriously. The last thing I want to do is hurt either of them.

After they both told me how they felt about the book, I thought hard about revising it. I went back through my journal to make sure my treatment of them wasn't somehow clouded by hindsight. I ultimately decided to leave my account of events more or less as I originally wrote them. I softened the words and the criticisms at certain points throughout the book, but I left the overall tone as I felt it, remembered it, and then reread it in my journal. The main reason I didn't want to alter my account was because most of my anger and resentment came from internal factors, though I did tend to project it onto Don and Midge. While I most certainly was affected by what they did, there were certain things going on with me—my own flaws—that dictated how I reacted to them. I hope this comes out in the book as strongly as I meant it to.

I was in a panic the night before the final draft of this manuscript was due, and I reread every single page of my journal from the Amazon expedition trying to assure myself that I wasn't making this stuff up; that Don, Midge, and I all acted crazy, mean, and irrational at turns. I went into this project knowing that memory is imperfect and subjective and I tried to write my account based off both my memories at the time of writing, and what I wrote in my journal throughout the trip. Obviously, my journal writings are also biased because they reflect how I saw the expedition unfolding, and they do not take into account Midge's or Don's versions of events.

I believe I have produced the truest account of our journey that I could. I'm sure I still got a few things wrong and, according to the guys, probably have a skewed view of some of the happenings and incidents on the trip.

I'm grateful that I had the opportunity to become the first woman to kayak the Amazon River from source to sea, and that never would have happened without Midge's crazy idea or his planning and funding of the expedition. I have intense admiration and respect for Midge. He set his sights on a goal that truly would have been impossible for most people. But he worked incredibly hard, and pulled it off, which is nothing short of amazing. It also wouldn't have happened if Don had really decided to go home on day seven. The fact that Don stuck with it for the rest of the trip is an achievement I don't take lightly. Don and I are going on seventeen years together now and, while it hasn't always been easy, we have a rock-solid relationship. At times I worried the Amazon would break us, but in the end it made us stronger and gave us a deeper understanding and respect for each other. The fact that our relationship survived the Amazon gives me reason to believe it can survive anything.

BIBLIOGRAPHY

Adventure Stats: Keeping Track of Adventure History. "Amazon River." Updated September 1, 2016. http://www.adventurestats.com/tables /RiverAmazon.shtml

Amancio, Nelly Luna. "The Last Trees of the Amazon." *Mongabay*, November 12, 2018. https://news.mongabay.com/2018/11/the-last -trees-of-the-amazon/

Andean Air Mail & Peruvian Times. "Peru Aims to Tire out Drug Traffickers by Destroying Air Strips." *Peruvian Times*. January 8, 2014. https://www.peruviantimes.com/08/peru -aims-to-tire-out-drug-traffickers-by-destroying-airstrips/21135/

Bajak, Frank. "Police Meet Widows of Slain Indigenous Leaders," *Merced Sun-Star*, September 9, 2014. http://www.mercedsunstar .com/2014/09/09/3838891_police-meet-widows-of-slain-indigenous .html

Barksdale, Nate. "What Is the Longest River in the World?" *History*, Updated August 22, 2018. https://www.history.com/news /what-is-the-longest-river-in-the-world

Blacksmith Institute Online. "The Top 10 Worst Polluted Places." 2007. Accessed January 18, 2015. http://www.blacksmithinstitute.org/the -2007-top-ten-of-worst-polluted-places.html

Contos, James, Tripcevich, Nicholas. "Correct Placement of the Most Distant Source of the Amazon River in the Mantaro River Drainage." *Royal Geographical Society, AREA* 2014 46.1 27–39.

Degregori, Carlos Ivan. *How Difficult It Is to Be God: Shining Path's Politics of War in Peru, 1980–1999.* Madison: University of Wisconsin Press, 2012.

Degregori, Carlos Ivan. *Shining Path of Peru.* New York: Palgrave Macmillan 1994.

Engel, Zbyněk, Jansky, Bohumir, Kocum, Jan, and Ludek Sefrne. "The Amazon River Headstream Area in the Cordillera Chila, Peru: Hydrographical, Hydrological, and Glaciological Conditions," *Hydrological Sciences Journal* 56(1) February 2011. 138–151.

Guinness World Records. "Longest River." Accessed October 17, 2019. https://www.guinnessworldrecords.com/world-records/longest-river/

Moag, Jeff. "True Source," *Canoe & Kayak.* Accessed February 28, 2016. www.canoekayak.com/true-source-part-2

Roach, John. "Amazon Longer than Nile River, Scientists Say." *National Geographic,* June 18, 2007. https://www.nationalgeographic.com /science/2007/06/amazon-longer-than-nile-river/

Sayah, Selim M. "Cerro del Aguila 510 MW Hydro Plant: The New Peruvian Challenge," May 18, 2014. http://www.researchgate.net /publication/262379686_Cerro_del_guila_510_MW_hydro_plant _The_new_Peruvian_challenge

Stern, Steve J. *Shining and Other Paths: War and Society in Peru, 1980–1995.* Durham and London: Duke University Press, 1998.

United Nations Office on Drugs and Crime. "World Drug Report 2010." Accessed March 19, 2016. https://www.unodc.org/documents/wdr /WDR_2010/1.3_The_globa_cocaine_market.pdf

US Geological Survey. "Rivers of the World: World's Longest Rivers." Accessed October 17, 2019. https://www.usgs.gov/special-topic/water -science-school/science/rivers-world-worlds-longest-rivers?qt-science _center_objects=0#qt-science_center_objects

Varese, Stefano. *Salt of the Mountain: Campa Asháninka History and Resistance in the Peruvian Jungle.* Norman: University of Oklahoma Press, 1968.

Walsh, Brian. "The World's Most Polluted Places." Time online. 2007. Accessed January 18, 2015. http://content.time.com/time /specials/2007/article/0,28804,1661031_1661028_1661020,00.html

World Bank Study. "Justice for Forests. Improving Criminal Justice Efforts to Combat Illegal Logging," Washington, D.C. 2012. Accessed January 12,2015. http://siteresources.worldbank.org /EXTFINANCIALSECTOR/Resources/Illegal_Logging.pdf

ACKNOWLEDGMENTS

I owe my first debt of gratitude to David Midgley for coming up with this totally outrageous idea and then being determined enough to see it through. Midge, I never would have kayaked the Amazon without you and for all our ups and downs, it was a pleasure sharing this experience with you. Your brilliant mind, quick sense of humor, and singular focus that bordered on the insane are all qualities that helped our team succeed. I know we drove each other crazy at times, but I consider you a friend and I will always cherish our adventures together.

A special thanks to my amazing agent Suzy Evans. The speed and deftness with which you handled my project will never cease to amaze me. You had many reasons to give up on me, and I will be forever grateful that you did not. To my editor, Jessica Case, thank you for believing in this book and fine-tuning it into something worth reading! Your comments were always spot on and you helped finesse this book into a complete project.

I don't know what I would do without Don Beveridge. He has been gracious in putting up with me through crazy ideas like kayaking the entire Amazon and even crazier ideas like writing a book about it. It would have been impossible for me to get through this book, not to mention countless river adventures, without you. Your support in every facet of life means the world to me.

Michael Conniff, thank you for telling me in no uncertain terms not to self-publish and for guiding me through the writing and editing process. No doubt I would have been clueless without your guidance. Next I want to thank the people who were early believers in my book. When I was certain that no one would want to hear my story, your support, help, comments and encouragement was just what I needed to keep going: Eli Saslow, Grace Ross, Kimberly Beekman, Eugene Buchanan, Joe Kane, Sarah Rabkin, Patrick Hasburgh, and Peter Scott. Thanks also to Wendy Dale for her excellent writing class that opened my world up to the possibility of getting a publisher, and to Fran Lebowitz for kicking my query letter in the butt and helping me get the attention of a few literary agents! Thanks to Shawn Graham and Barbara Atwood for your time and your amazing edits, you both made my book infinitely better. Thank you, Bill Beveridge, for your early support and feedback. Thank you also for your last-minute edits to the book catching countless errors that I'd overlooked.

West Hansen and Lizet Alaniz generously gave up their time to fly to Peru to help us out with logistics during our first two weeks of the expedition. Your kindness, humor and enthusiasm were exactly what we needed to get started down the world's mightiest river.

Guillermo Castro Escudero selflessly gave us his time and pulled his strings to get us an escort with the Peruvian Navy. Thank you to the Peruvian Navy for putting up with our slow pace and for protecting us as we made our way down your country's amazing river. Thanks to Deborah McLauchlan for all your help organizing logistics for our trip, you truly were an immensely valuable member of the team. Thank you, Cesar Pena, for coming through the Red Zone one more time and thanks for being able to do at least 49 push-ups! Perolita crew—we had plenty of difficult times, but you did work extremely hard for the expedition and I am grateful for that. To everyone else who played a role in the success of our expedition—it truly does take a village—I have nothing but gratitude for your help and support.

To all of people in Peru and Brazil who showed us kindness and curiosity along the way, thank you. Your offers of help, your inquisitiveness and your kindheartedness helped us in untold ways. You helped prove to us that the Amazon River is made up of mostly good people.

Thanks to my parents and my sister for putting up with my adventures and shenanigans, for always supporting me, and always loving me. Most people aren't lucky enough to have a family like ours. Thanks to everyone who believes in underdogs. Speak your encouragement loudly and push your friends forward to achieve their goals.